The Politics of Plant Closings

STUDIES IN GOVERNMENT
AND PUBLIC POLICY

The Politics
of Plant Closings

John Portz

 University Press of Kansas

Published by the University Press of Kansas (Lawrence, Kansas
66045), which was organized by the Kansas Board of Regents and is
operated and funded by Emporia State University, Fort Hays State
University, Kansas State University, Pittsburg State University,
the University of Kansas, and Wichita State University

Library of Congress Cataloging-in-Publication Data

Portz, John, 1953–
    The politics of plant closings / John Portz.
        p.   cm. — (Studies in government and public policy)
    Includes bibliographical references.
    ISBN 0–7006–0472–3 — ISBN 0–7006–0473–1 (pbk.)
    1. Plant shutdowns — Political aspects — United States — Case
studies.   2. Municipal government — United States — Case studies.
    I. Title.   II. Series.
    HD5708.55.U6P67   1990
    338.6'042 — dc20   90–32817
                                                                CIP

British Library Cataloguing in Publication Data is available.

Printed in the United States of America

10 9 8 7 6 5 4 3 2 1

The paper used in this publication meets the minimum requirements of the
American National Standard for Permanence of Paper for Printed
Library Materials Z39.48–1984.

Contents

Tables, Figures, and Maps

Preface

On November 11, 1986, the *New York Times* carried the following headline: "General Motors to Shut 11 Plants; 29,000 Workers Will Be Affected." So began another round of layoffs and plant closings in the American automobile industry. Local policymakers in the affected areas—Norwood and Hamilton, Ohio; Willow Springs, Illinois; St. Louis, Missouri; Flint, Pontiac, and Detroit, Michigan—faced very difficult questions: Should they initiate actions to avert the closing? If so, what type of action should they take? Furthermore, would such actions be supported by workers at the plants, officials at General Motors, and the general community? Alternatively, assuming the plants actually closed, how should local officials assist workers and others during the transition period? What would be the best policies to help workers and the general community recover from the closing, while also respecting the rights of the company?

Such questions are not unique to these General Motors communities; many local officials have faced similar challenges. Indeed, industrial plant closings were a sign of the times in the 1970s and 1980s, as the American economy shifted from manufacturing and basic production to service activities.[1] Recessions and the restructuring of American industries resulted in mass layoffs and plant closings across the United States, not only in the automobile industry but also in the steel, tire, and other manufacturing industries. Recognizing this trend, a senior analyst at the Conference Board noted that "director of plant closings" had become a new managerial career.[2]

The academic and popular presses typically focus on the economic and social fallout of closings, in particular the loss of jobs, decline in incomes, increase in crime, and similar consequences.[3] At the national level, for example, job losses are often the center of attention. One study of plant closings notes that from the mid-1970s to 1984, plant closings in large manufacturing firms eliminated over 900,000 jobs each year; in the recession years of 1980–

82 this rate of job loss doubled.[4] Using a different data base, another study identifies the closing between 1977 and 1982 of over 650 manufacturing establishments that once employed 500 or more workers.[5] A federal government study concludes that nearly 10 million workers lost their jobs between 1983 and 1988 owing to plant closings and layoffs.[6]

At the local level, reports of plant closings often add broader social and economic costs to the list of consequences. The closing of a major plant has a ripple effect throughout the local economy. As blue-collar jobs are lost in auto communities in Michigan, steel-mill towns in Pennsylvania, and other "company towns," the entire community feels the economic pinch. According to one study, the closing of a major auto plant in a community of 200,000 could result in a 20 percent drop in overall employment, 10 percent drop in population, 50 percent decline in new house sales, 35 percent decline in government tax revenues, and 200 percent increase in the local unemployment rate.[7] In addition, such losses are often accompanied by an increased incidence of crime, mental health problems, divorce, and other family troubles.[8]

These are all important consequences of plant closings, but in this book I pursue a different line of interest. What the studies cited above miss is the political dynamic—the "clash of politics"—in communities facing significant economic dislocation. The threatened or actual closing of a major industrial facility is often accompanied by a variety of actions and responses from local parties: workers at the plant mobilize to prevent the closing; the business firm plans a closing strategy to maximize its position; different community groups stake out a position on both the closing and possible transition paths for economic adjustment; local government officials attempt to meet the different demands and goals of community members as well as their own agenda.

There is a compelling political side to plant closings: local policymakers must come up with acceptable and viable responses within the constraints of the local political economy. This is a challenge faced by an increasing number of American communities in a rapidly changing economy; Norwood, Willow Springs, and the other General Motors communities are not alone. How policymakers in these and other communities meet this challenge is the question that guides this study.

My analysis of the politics of plant closings is shaped by the words and thoughts of scholars and government practitioners as well as case studies I conducted in three American communities. These case studies—in Louisville, Kentucky; Waterloo, Iowa; and Pittsburgh, Pennsylvania—constitute the core of this book. Each case study is based on a review of existing studies of the particular plant closing; on interviews with key individuals in government, labor, business, and academe; and on analysis of local economic reports, minutes from government meetings, financial statements, planning studies, newspaper clippings, and other relevant material.

In conducting the case studies and in pulling together the final product, I have acquired numerous debts to those who supported, inspired, and cajoled me through the many days of research and writing. Although the words and conclusions that appear in the following pages are my responsibility, they would not be there without the assistance of many friends and colleagues.

In Louisville, Waterloo, and Pittsburgh's Mon Valley, I would like to express my appreciation to the many interviewees who offered their time and valuable insights. These individuals, who are listed at the end of the book, provided a range of perspectives on the experiences of their communities and are the source of brief quotations in the chapters. In particular, special thanks are due to Carroll Teague of the Brown & Williamson Corporation, Don Wade of the Black Hawk County Economic Development Committee, and Bob Erickson of the Tri-State Conference on Steel. These individuals proved to be especially helpful as I attempted to understand the plant-closing experiences in their respective communitites. In addition, much of the field research for this study was conducted on a shoestring budget that benefited from lodging and similar support provided by individuals in each community. In this regard, special thanks go to Paul and Lucille Shrock in Louisville, Russ Woodrick and Dennis Grady in Waterloo, and Jon and Janet Nordenberg, Lynne and Tom Crenney, and Bob Erickson in Pittsburgh.

The academic critiques came from several quarters. In Madison, Wisconsin, where the first drafts of this book were written, I am indebted to Peter Eisinger, Leon Lindberg, Graham Wilson, Bill Gormley, and Ken Bickers for their numerous comments and suggestions. Peter Eisinger, in particular, served as adviser, reviewer, and supporter through this period. In Boston, where this book took its final form, I would like to thank Chris Bosso, Garry Prowe, and Jessica Whitmore-First for their assistance; Chris provided numerous editorial suggestions as well as an invaluable sounding board as I completed the final revisions; Garry and Jessica assisted with the final preparation of the manuscript.

Finally, I would like to acknowledge my parents. While others provide support for the moment, parents provide a foundation that spans the ups and downs of graduate school as well as the early years of a professional career. There is an eternal optimism that seems to reside with parents. As my mother was fond of saying, "It all works out in the end." Although I sometimes thought the end would be a half-completed manuscript, her wisdom left its mark. Thus, it is to her, and my father, that I express my final appreciation.

1

Plant Closings, Local Governments, and Policy Responses

Politics is about forming alliances, mobilizing resources, and pursuing goals and interests. A study of plant closings offers an excellent opportunity to observe and analyze politics as it unfolds; few experiences capture better than a plant closing the diversity of resources, interests, and goals of different members of a community. As is apparent in the case studies that follow, workers, government officials, business leaders, and other members of the community can interact in the political arena to yield quite different political experiences.

Among candidates for political action, workers at the plant are typically the most interested — their jobs are at stake and they stand to bear the most immediate costs. Yet how workers will respond to a plant closing is far from clear. Certainly in some communities the primary labor response is to mobilize in opposition to the closing. Rallies, picket lines, demonstrations, union meetings, and other forms of collective action are common. In many cases the labor contract outlines the forum for labor's opposition to the closing. The contract may require advance notification of the closing and stipulate labor-management negotiations to address key problems at the plant. Alternatively, workers may turn to organizations or forums outside the formal structure of labor-management relations. In a number of cases, such as the closing of U.S. Steel's Duquesne mill near Pittsburgh (Chapter 5), workers are joined by a community coalition of academics, clergy, and other supporters. Local, state, and even national government leaders can also be approached as possible allies of labor.

In other instances labor may be much more ambivalent or divided on how to respond to the closing. Some workers may accept the closing as inevitable and beyond their control, while others view severance provisions as acceptable compensation for the loss of jobs. In the latter case, supplemental unemployment benefits, early retirement, relocation options, retraining assis-

1

tance, and other provisions negotiated with the business firm may represent an attractive package to many workers. As in the Brown & Williamson tobacco plant closing in Louisville (Chapter 3), such a labor-management accord may represent the primary response within the community. The politics in this type of response — structured around receiving the best severance package for workers — contrasts sharply with the political dynamic in cases where labor mobilizes to oppose the plant closing.

But many, if not most, plant closings are dictated or dominated by the business firm that makes the closing decision and establishes the initial terms of debate. The firm's control of private investment affords it a very powerful position. Yet political challenges are likely. Labor leaders, government officials, and other community leaders may try to convince or pressure the firm into changing its decision. Citing economic costs to workers and the community, local leaders often suggest alternatives to the closing.

The role played by the business firm is likely to vary, depending on the firm's characteristics and purposes. For example, whether the plant is owned locally or by a multinational corporation can be significant. A multinational corporation is less subject to local pressures and in most cases less concerned about an individual plant in a distant community. Also, whether the relevant industry is in a period of expansion or contraction, and whether the company plans to remain competitive in the industry, can influence a business's response strategy. Perhaps most obviously, whether the business firm is financially strong or experiencing operating deficits can be critical.

Thus, a multinational corporation that plans to close a plant because of excess industry capacity will have a very different position than will a local firm seeking to revive its primary production facility. The corporation concerned with excess capacity is unlikely to have any interest in keeping the plant open; the locally owned business attempting to avoid bankruptcy may view keeping the plant open as its primary goal. Both of these scenarios are captured in the case studies that follow — U.S. Steel in Pittsburgh and Brown & Williamson in Louisville were convinced that excess capacity existed in their respective industries; Rath Packing Company in Waterloo (Chapter 4) was fighting for its own survival. These different circumstances have quite different implications for the political dynamic in each community.

The politics of plant closings is also shaped by government policymakers. At the national, state, and local levels are numerous examples of public policymakers intervening in a plant closing, either reactively or proactively, to shape the outcome of the adjustment process. In some instances the policy focus is to avert the plant closing by providing financial assistance, infrastructure improvements, or some other form of support. In Waterloo, for example, government officials provided loans to Rath Packing Company to help avert a shutdown. In other cases, however, the policy goal is to minimize negative consequences after the closing occurs, through reemployment centers, retraining programs, and other forms of government assistance.

Government officials do not merely respond to lobbying by business, labor, and other community groups; officials vary in terms of goals as well as access to policy tools and resources. For example, the desire to be reelected may prompt one official to oppose a plant closing, while in another community the motive of building business support may lead an official to support such a closing. Variations in policy capabilities are also important. Financial resources and the ability to use them vary among urban communities, as does the ability of local policymakers to tap state and national government policy resources.

To summarize, the political dynamic in a plant closing is likely to include government officials, representatives of the business firm, labor leaders, and others in the community. This is a complicated and often contentious setting. As is often the case, this is a game of winners and losers. The politics of plant closings becomes a politics of priorities: "Who will have to sacrifice, how will that be determined, and who will benefit from the sacrifices?"[1] Helping the community answer these questions is the challenge for local policymakers, who must recognize and accommodate the goals and interests of workers, business leaders, and others while simultaneously serving their own particular concerns. Whether local policymakers are in a position to meet such a challenge is a question that merits closer attention.

LOCAL GOVERNMENTS AND POLICYMAKING: THE DEPENDENT CITY

In the American federal system local governments do not stand alone. Public policymaking is a collective endeavor that often includes national, state, and local governments. Thus the formulation and implementation of responses to plant closings might involve congressional representatives, federal bureaucrats, state legislators, county officials, mayors, and city councillors.

Still, local governments occupy a particularly important place in a study of responses and economic adjustment to plant closings. After all, counties, cities, and towns are the political units most immediately affected by the closure of the plant. Intergovernmental efforts may be possible, but the pressures for action and the economic consequences of a closing fall in the immediate domain of local policymakers. They usually are the first to meet with business and labor representatives to assess the situation and begin formulating an appropriate government response.

Yet local governments may be the weakest unit of political authority to address the challenges. They operate in an environment of legal, fiscal, politi-

cal, and economic constraints and thus have only limited capacity to formulate and implement public policies in a number of significant areas, including economic adjustment. It is no wonder that "dependent city," "city limits,"
and similar phrases are commonplace in recent studies of urban policymaking.[2]

These themes of urban dependence and policy weakness are manifested
in two major ways. First, legally, the very existence of local governments is
dependent on the interests and actions of policymakers at the state level.
State governments determine, either through constitutions, statutes, or char-
ters, the basic limits of local government structures, powers, and responsibilities. Counties, cities, and towns, as legal creations of state government,
are constrained in the policy options they can adopt. For example, cities typically must depend on state-enabling legislation to create independent authorities that promote urban economic development. State policymakers are thus
able to shape the degree and form of local government intervention in the
private economy. State policymakers can also restrict the taxing authority of
local governments by retaining final authority to determine which taxes can
be applied at the local level and, in many cases, how those taxes are levied.
Although legal dependency is not absolute — "home rule" clauses in state
statutes and constitutions allow local flexibility in a number of areas — the
shape of local political institutions and the actions they may take are constrained significantly by state actors.[3]

Second, economically, a city's financial health depends heavily on other
levels of government as well as on decisions made by private actors. States
typically provide approximately 20 percent of city government general revenues, while the federal government provides an additional 6 percent. This
assistance, whether in the form of project-specific grants, categorical aid, or
unrestricted revenue sharing, provides critical support for specific economic
projects as well as general city operations. Not surprisingly, local policymakers are quick to develop the skills of intergovernmental lobbying and
grantsmanship.

Economic dependence also extends to a reliance on decisions made by private economic actors. The single most important measure of this dependence
is the city's reliance on property taxes. On average, 21 percent of city government general revenues comes from local property taxes.[4] A sharp decline in
the property base of a community, as when an industrial plant closes, represents a major blow to the fiscal health of local governments. When capital
investments are withdrawn from a steel mill, auto plant, meatpacking plant,
or other major facility, the impact on the financial health of the community
can be devastating. This mismatch of capital mobility and governmental
boundaries leaves local policymakers at a decided disadvantage. As Bryan
Jones and Lynn Bachelor note, "The leverage of industrialists comes from
the simple fact of the mobility of capital; the constraints on public officials
come from the geographic confines of the modern statutory city."[5] Local

governments are also subject to economic decisions made in private capital markets. Local governments turn to borrowing in capital markets to meet operating costs as well as to finance long-term projects. A city's bond rating, as determined by private bond agencies, is an area of constant concern for local officials.

Thus, we are left with this general proposition: local government officials have limited policy capabilities and options. Local governments may still have a range of choices and options within this environment of legal and economic constraints, but the dominant theme is that of urban dependence.

We are also left with the basic question as to whether or not this theme of urban dependence holds true in local responses to plant closings. That is, are urban policymakers substantially constrained in their ability to respond to plant closings? Or are they able to overcome constraints as they pursue different policies? With these questions in mind, three case studies of very different responses to plant closings will be presented in the following chapters.

RESPONDING TO PLANT CLOSINGS: A TYPOLOGY

The case studies described in later chapters are indicative of three general types of responses to plant closings, presented here as ideal types derived from both a review of actual plant closing experiences and theoretical writings. Although many responses of local government demonstrate elements of two or more of these ideal types, the typology nevertheless provides a useful orientation to the range of policy possibilities.[6]

Table 1.1 encapsulates the typology. Two dimensions serve to differentiate the responses according to the involvement of public and private sector actors. The first dimension—major participants in decision making—specifies the actors directly responsible for key decisions in the adjustment process to an actual or threatened plant closing. With respect to "offset" and "bystander" responses, private-sector actors, such as the labor union and the business firm, are primarily responsible for adjustment decision-making, while in the "player" response category, government officials join private-sector parties in the decision-making arena.

The second dimension—source of adjustment resources—identifies the provider of key economic resources used to address the adjustment problem. Financial capital and labor-retraining funds are two examples of important adjustment resources. Here, private-sector actors are the primary source in a bystander response, while in offset and player responses a combination of private and public sector parties provide adjustment resources.

Table 1.1 Adjustment Responses to Plant Closings

	Bystander	Offset	Player
Major Participants in Decision Making	Private Sector	Private Sector	Public/Private Sectors
Source of Adjustment Resources	Private Sector	Public/Private Sectors	Public/Private Sectors

A "Bystander" Role for Local Governments

In many plant closings local governments are little more than bystanders to the adjustment process; they observe rather than participate. In cases where the closing is subject to debate, local officials may be present at community or labor-management meetings, but they do not take part in negotiations and discussions. If a plant closes, local policymakers play little role in the transition. They assume a neutral stance, declining to grant advantage or favor to any party concerned with the closing. While the community experiences economic dislocations, purposive public policy has little role in shaping such consequences. Whether this bystander role is assumed by choice — as when local officials are philosophically opposed to government intervention in the marketplace — or from a paucity of policy capabilities — as with a lack of financial resources to aid the firm — the common denominator is an arm's-length distance during the adjustment process.

Thus, in a bystander response the adjustment process is shaped primarily by the decisions, strategies, and actions of labor, management, and other private-sector groups. For example, labor-management negotiations often occupy center stage. Negotiations may be over wage and benefit reductions to keep the plant open, or they may focus on severance benefits for laid-off workers. Alternatively, community-based organizations may enter the fray to prevent the plant from closing or, having failed that, to ensure its reuse. In these responses local policymakers are standing on the outside looking in.

The political component in these experiences is confined primarily to private arenas, such as the collective-bargaining table and community rallies, and in these arenas the power and resources of private parties determine adjustment outcomes. The business firm, for example, can rely on its legal control of private economic resources, including the plant itself and the investment it represents, while labor unions rely on their ability to mobilize the work force.

In this type of response private market forces typically play the major role in allocating the costs and benefits of economic change. Implicit in this acceptance of a private adjustment process is the recognition that winners and losers are inevitable in a market system. In a changing economy plant closings and job losses are the accepted counterpart to business openings and job creation. As Richard McKenzie notes in a study of plant closings, "The history of progress is a history of the destruction of jobs and businesses."[7] This process, which Joseph Schumpeter referred to as "creative destruction," allocates costs and benefits among members of the community without government intervention.[8] As a recent federal task force concludes, plant closings are an "inevitable consequence of a dynamic world economy."[9]

However, the story does not end here. National and state governments and, to a lesser degree, local governments, play a significant role by providing the framework within which this private adjustment process takes place. For example, public laws and judicial institutions support a legal system that specifies and protects rights and responsibilities of property ownership. Legal rights of private ownership, as in the ownership of an industrial facility, establish basic parameters within which private actions take place. These rights, which are so fundamental in a plant closing, are supported and enforced by government. As another example, the federal government provides the legal framework for union-management negotiations. Under the auspices of the National Labor Relations Board, relevant laws, and court rulings, government has established the basic boundaries for labor-management negotiations.[10]

By establishing a framework for the private settlement of differences, government provides what Robert Solo refers to as a "housekeeping" function. In this role the purpose of government is to "maintain the institutional underpinnings of individualized choice and to render services to private interests."[11] The housekeeping role is to facilitate, rather than hinder or challenge, a private adjustment process. The setting that is established provides boundaries and rules that private participants must abide by, as with labor-management law, but the participants determine the ultimate outcomes; government provides a framework for private action rather than an avenue for public intervention. For local governments, involvement in this "housekeeping" function is minimal.[12] City and county officials play little role in the legal system that protects private property, nor are they usually involved in the legal framework for labor-management negotiations.

The closing of the Brown & Williamson tobacco plant in Louisville, detailed in Chapter 3, illustrates the bystander role. In this closing, announced in 1979, the legal framework that supported the process of labor-management negotiations represented an important governmental function but not one in which local officials participated. The clash of interests took place over the collective-bargaining table. The final settlement between the company and the union became the primary mechanism for the distribution of costs and benefits from the closing.

Although such a bystander role for local governments is not uncommon, it is relatively rare for local officials to maintain this position throughout the adjustment process of the plant closing, particularly if the industrial plant is a major employer in the community. Pressures for government intervention often come from workers at the plant, different officials within government, or other parties. In response, policy strategies are considered either to avert the closing or to minimize negative consequences for the community. Thus, despite legal, fiscal, and economic constraints, local officials often pursue a more interventionist role. This takes us to a second type of local policy response.

An "Offset" Local Response

In an offset response local officials assume a more active role in the adjustment process. Rather than defer to private-sector actors, as in the bystander role, local officials intervene to influence the adjustment outcome. While private-sector parties still retain primary decision-making responsiblities in the adjustment process, local policymakers join the discussions and establish a public purpose. Typically this public purpose takes the form of "jobs for the community," "health of the local economy," or some similar statement. To help achieve this goal, local governments provide key economic resources, such as a financial assistance package to a business firm or a retraining center for workers.[13]

In an offset response local policymakers face at least two critical steps. First, a problem must be identified that is amenable to government intervention. This is not a simple task, nor is it noncontroversial; competition and conflict often arise as different parties put forth their definitions of the situation. The business firm, for example, may view the closing as an inevitable consequence of changing markets, while the labor union often finds primary fault with corporate decision-making. Government officials, who may have their own definition of the problem, must sort through these contending explanations.

Assuming a clear definition can be established, a second key step is to identify and organize public policy resources that can ameliorate the problem — also not a simple task. Policy resources, such as a financial loan to an ailing business firm, must be secured and designed to offset the problem. Not only must local officials build community support for this effort, but they must also face legal and economic constraints outlined earlier. To help meet this challenge, local governments often turn to state and federal governments.

Local offset responses can take two quite different forms, the shape of which depends on goals or purposes. If the goal is to keep the plant open, the focus is on resolving problems that pose a hindrance to the plant's operations. The critical problem might be obsolete equipment, unsuccessful marketing plans, or inadequate transportation access, for example. The primary role for policymakers is either to provide resources to the private-sector parties able to address the problem, such as a loan given to a firm to modernize its facility, or to undertake specific improvements in the public infrastructure, such as a new highway interchange constructed near the plant.

Assume, however, that the plant closes. In this case an offset response takes a different form, by necessarily focusing on the needs of unemployed workers and finding new occupants for the now-vacant building. As one writer notes, "Jobs are the name of the game. Securing jobs for displaced workers in different businesses and industries is essential."[14] The newly unemployed typically require job search assistance, income support, and retraining, and policymakers try to offset these problems through programs designed for the targeted group. To assist in reuse of the facility, local officials can add the vacant plant to their marketing list of industrial property available for prospective tenants.

Unlike bystander responses, in both variants of an offset response government policymakers not only provide a critical resource or service but also encourage other participants, particularly labor and the business firm, to make necessary adjustments and changes. In such a tripartite response, government, labor, and management combine to provide a capital infusion, tax reduction, cut in labor costs, change in management practices, or other actions. This consensus-building process is designed to reach a compromise that maximizes worker and community welfare while preserving the firm's right to control its economic resources.

The case of the Rath Packing Company in Waterloo—detailed in Chapter 4—represents an offset response. In 1978 the company was on the verge of closing its meatpacking plant. The ensuing policy response involved an offset strategy in which city, county, and federal governments provided financial assistance to Rath to increase production and modernize its operations. In addition, Rath management agreed to a variety of corporate changes, while workers accepted wage and benefit deferrals as well as an employee stock-ownership plan. Local policymakers played a central role in arranging this government-labor-management rescue package.

Although such a response constitutes a major step beyond the bystander role, there remain important boundaries or limits to public intervention. In particular, an offset role is primarily reactive. As one group of researchers notes, "It is assumed that the [closing] decision is the province of management and that the communities are constrained to adopt reactive roles."[15] Robert Solo observes in his study of American public policy that "the political authority as offsetter does not plan and organize. It stands by and waits for trouble. And when trouble comes, or seems in prospect, the political authority compensates and adjusts; fiddling with the machinery, compensating for slack, or reducing the heat."[16] In essence the rationale for an offset government role "is never with reference to what [government] can do, but to what the market cannot do."[17] Reacting to market failures is at the heart of an offset strategy.

In addition, although government provides important resources and assistance to private parties, the burden of success or failure in a market economy remains with labor, management, and others in the community. Policymakers are unlikely to pursue actions that intrude upon management decision-making or otherwise involve government officials in an ongoing role of reshaping the market. Political authorities play an important role in offsetting identified problems, but they "remain outside the nexus of economic activity."[18] To cross that boundary, to assume a directive or ongoing part in the adjustment process, is beyond the character of an offset response.

A Local "Player" Role

There are times when officials cross the line and use policy tools and resources to reshape and redirect the adjustment process, when they assume a player role by asserting a public voice in the decision-making process. Policymakers assume an active part not only in defining the problem but, most important, in implementing a solution. In essence government policy is meant to do more than just create an equal playing field; government officials are to be players on that field.

The form of a player role can vary. In one version local officials rely on the authoritative sanctions of government to restructure the adjustment process. For example, plant-closing laws, lawsuits against a recalcitrant business, and eminent domain proceedings have been used to require or stipulate that adjustment to the plant closing proceed in a certain way. Statutes require advance notification of a plant closing from the business firm, legal representatives seek financial compensation for damages done to the community, and eminent domain proceedings can be used to assume control of a private industrial plant. The goal is to direct the adjustment process to ensure that public benefits are realized.[19]

A second variant of a player role relies on the active and ongoing participation of local officials in the adjustment process. Rather than use government sanctions to require certain actions, government officials become actively involved in key decision-making. For example, government officials might play a part in identifying a new product line at the firm, finding a new chief executive officer, determining new marketing strategies, establishing wage levels, or participating in other aspects of the adjustment process. To ensure an ongoing role in the adjustment process, government officials might sit on the board of directors of the business firm, establish a monitoring team to oversee financial decisions made by the firm, or institute some other mechanism of involvement.

In either variant of a player role, policymakers assume an equal, if not directive, part in the adjustment process. This is truly a test of local government capabilities. Local officials are called upon to anticipate problems, formulate solutions, and implement, usually in conjunction with private market actors, a remedial strategy. Government must be able to "initiate, plan, organize, and manage complex activities in pursuit of goals selected through the process of political choice."[20] To succeed, political, fiscal, administrative, and legal skills are critical.

The political nature of a player response can vary, depending on the relationship between local officials and private actors. At opposite ends of an ideological spectrum are what I term *corporate* and *populist* variants of a player role. The corporate variant is characterized by close cooperation between the business firm and government.[21] For example, if keeping the plant open is the goal, local officials work closely with management to address specific problems at the firm. Government officials might help redesign business plans, find outside financial assistance, hire new managers, or restructure the operations at the production facility. While examples of this type of player role exist, they are relatively rare. American business corporations, particularly those voluntarily closing a plant, are reluctant to seek or accept this degree of government involvement in corporate affairs (see Chapter 7).

In a populist variant of a player role, local policymakers are allied with labor and community groups rather than the business firm.[22] In fact, the player actions of this government-labor-community coalition are usually opposed by the business firm. In a typical populist scenario, government officials seek legal action to prevent a plant closing and then work closely with existing owners, new owners, or a worker-community coalition that buys the plant. The premise of this populist response is, as one proponent argues, to "add new players, create new roles, and demand new results from the economic development process. Economic life can no longer be shaped solely by corporate actors."[23] While examples of a populist player role exist, they are partial and fragmented. Existing local governments often lack either the will or the resources to assume a player role that must contend with a hostile business firm.[24]

The efforts in 1985 of a labor-community-local government coalition to prevent the demolition of a steel mill in the Monongahela River valley south of Pittsburgh exemplifies the populist player response, further explored in Chapter 5. The culmination of this effort was the formation of the Steel Valley Authority by nine area municipalities. The Steel Valley Authority, which still exists today, has governmental powers that include the exercise of eminent domain, the right to issue bonds, and the right to sue in court. Although the Steel Valley Authority was unsuccessful in its first effort to prevent a plant closing, it nevertheless provided important insights into the possibilities as well as hurdles for a populist player response. It represents an important example of efforts to overcome economic, fiscal, legal, and ideological constraints that handicap local governments.

Regardless of the variant of a "player" response, whether corporate or populist, the critical element is a policy role whereby local officials attempt to restructure the adjustment process. No longer content with simply deferring to private decisions (as in the bystander role), or providing compensatory resources (as in the offset role), policymakers in a player response provide key adjustment resources and find themselves in the midst of decision making that guides economic change.

2

Explaining Policy Responses: An Analytic Framework

Typologies are useful, but they have limits. The three-part typology presented in Chapter 1 outlines quite different local government roles, but it leaves unanswered a number of important questions. For example, why do policymakers in one community adopt a bystander response while those in another engage in an offset or player response? What policy skills or resources are most critical in each type of response? What factors account for the success or failure of different policy responses? To answer these questions we must look beyond typologies. As government officials, workers, business leaders, community activists, and others vie for advantage during a plant closing, we need a set of analytic tools to explain the course of events. If we are to learn from past policy experiences, we must understand how the results came about.

A variety of explanatory frameworks might be used for this purpose. Advocates of pluralist analysis, for example, see urban politics as an arena of competing groups, where no one group long dominates the political game. Advocates of elite analysis, on the other hand, identify a small group or set of individuals with key resources as controlling or dominating the urban political process.[1] Proponents of a class perspective emphasize the economic divisions in society and the way in which capitalism fundamentally structures urban politics.[2] More recently, a political economy approach that draws elements from a class perspective has focused on the economic nature of the community and the manner in which economic processes shape politics and coalition building. From a political economy perspective, the ability of government officials to initiate and implement different public policies is constrained by the nature of the local economy.[3]

Each perspective has its merits, but the explanatory framework used in this study builds primarily upon that of political economy. This framework has two key elements. First, three levels of analysis — economic accumulation, institutional system, and political alliance formation and mobilization — are presented as a way to consider the relative importance and interrelatedness of different elements in the urban experience. This orientation is premised upon the argument that there is a "nested" relationship among explanatory variables whereby certain ones, such as the economic organization of a society, shape or otherwise limit the range of expression of other variables, such as the structure of government institutions. This approach, elaborated below, is based on the concepts of structure and agency that are so central in a study of the political economy.

While levels of analysis offer a general context for analyzing the policy process, the second element — problem definition — provides a more focused tool to study the agency side of the political equation. In particular, problem definitions specify what different individuals and groups see as the causes of and solutions for a particular policy problem; such definitions reflect the perceptions and interpretations that actors bring to the policy process. To a significant degree policymaking is guided — some would say driven — by the frames of reference and interpretation created by key participants. In the case of plant closings, how a closing is defined often establishes the terms of debate for a policy response.

LEVELS OF ANALYSIS, PROBLEM DEFINITION, AND THE URBAN POLITICAL ECONOMY

To explain policy responses, we must contend with the relationship between political action and structural constraints. This is not an easy task. Policymaking can be a very complicated process in which individuals and groups seek to realize their goals within an environment structured by organizations, patterns of behavior, and other influences. Most students of politics agree that not all elements or components in this process are of equal importance, but there is much less consensus over which elements are most important. Furthermore, how to differentiate the more important from the less important is equally controversial.

Adopting a levels-of-analysis perspective is one response to this challenge. The core tenet in this perspective is that not all variables in a political setting interact on an equal plane; some shape or limit the expression of others. As one social theorist notes, "Human agents, individuals, groups, organizations and nations, are subject to material, social, structural and cultural constraints on their actions."[4] Thus, political happenings cannot be attributed simply to the observable actions of individuals and groups. Rather, those happenings are shaped by an array of phenomena in the larger environment that may not be as readily observable. As one writer argues, "A state of affairs is not explained by an agent and its actions but by the set of relations in which the agent is embedded."[5] This "set of relations" involves constant and

enduring features of the political environment that influence politics irrespec-
tive of the particular goals and strategies of individual actors. Thus, our attention turns to structural features in the human environment. These structures or relations create an "enduring set of penalties and rewards that mold
action independent of the motivation or purposes of the actors. . . . Simply
stated, what is attempted and achieved is affected by how it must be done."[6]

For example, a highly structured organization with a detailed set of rules
and procedures makes certain kinds of individual action more likely than
others. Thus, organizational rules and procedures operate at a higher level
of analysis and shape the possibilities of individual action. To take a more
abstract example, some writers argue that a capitalist economic system af-
fects the nature of government institutions by making some forms of government, such as representative legislatures, more likely, and some public policies, such as government production of basic commodities, less likely. From
this perspective, capitalism entails principles of economic organization that
constrain the form and actions of governments; capitalism operates at a
higher level of analysis than political institutions.

Ira Katznelson, in a study of urban politics, states the issue succinctly:

> Analyses of games or contests, political or otherwise, must do more
> than describe the players and their adversary play. They must also say
> something about the boundaries of the contest, which define its limits
> prior to the playing of the game itself. Such boundaries are an integral
> part of the rules of the game: they determine who may participate, what
> identities participants may assume, what they may legitimately do, and
> so on. Such rules preclude certain outcomes and make others improbable.[7]

However, rarely is this interaction between "boundaries" and the "play of
politics" seen as deterministic. How one variable structures or limits another
is a matter of degree rather than rigid determination. Thus, at a lower level
of analysis certain outcomes are more likely than others given the presence
of structural features, but there remains a range of possibilities that might
occur. Which outcomes actually occur will depend on strategies and actions
taken by relevant political actors as well as the constraints of the larger
environment.

Furthermore, there is the potential for political action to actually alter the
form or nature of the broader structural environment. As Robert Alford
notes in his study of urban politics, "Structural factors establish the framework within which situations for action arise, although the outcomes of
those actions may in turn alter the structure."[8] Such a process defies simple
claims of unidirectional causation; the political arena is a dynamic between
structural constraints and human agency.

The explanatory challenge, then, is to analyze the nature of and interaction between the play of politics and the relatively enduring and constant features of the political environment within which it is nested. As Clarence Stone argues, the key intellectual challenge in political analysis is "how best to talk about political choice and structural context."[9] John Mollenkopf raises the same issue:

> The nub of the problem is that structural explanations suppress the issue of action and therefore tend toward the ahistorical, abstract and static. Reliance on individualism, however, continues an opposite weakness. Concentrating on individual actions tends to produce voluntarist, pluralist conceptions of how social systems operate. . . . The real problem is to construct theories which operate at *both* levels simultaneously and which isolate the key interactions among these levels.[10]

In response to his own challenge, Mollenkopf offers a framework to consider these levels of analysis. As a first step, he argues that "cities concentrate and contain two kinds of relationships: those of production and economic accumulation and those of social interaction and community formation." According to Mollenkopf, production and economic accumulation refer to how a society "creates, expands, and distributes its means of well-being." In capitalist societies market relationships, driven primarily by the profit criterion, characterize the central means of economic accumulation. In particular, market relationships are based on the control of private property as well as competition among economic actors. Both fundamentally inform human relationships.

However, urban communities are also home to relationships based on social interaction and community formation. As Mollenkopf argues, social interaction and community formation highlight the "bonds people build with one another which enable them to trust and rely on each other."[11] Reciprocity, mutual support, and informal helping patterns are part of community relationships based on ethnicity, kinship, place of residence, or other common characteristics. Unlike competitive economic relationships, these bonds are premised on mutual or shared characteristics that support cooperative interactions.

While accumulation and community can be interrelated in a number of ways, Mollenkopf argues that it is the "asymmetric and ultimately antagonistic interdependence" between the two that serves as the basis of an urban system. In a brief review of American urban history, Mollenkopf notes that economic accumulation has played the dominant role in "shaping and constraining the choices made by urban actors." Although efforts to create a stronger sense of community have occupied a subordinate role, they nevertheless have played an important part at certain times in the evolution of urban society. As Mollenkopf concludes from his historical survey, "Most

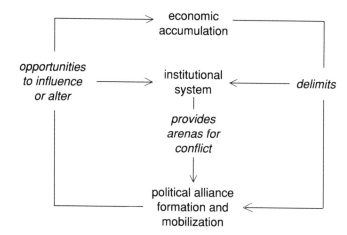

Figure 2.1   Three Levels of Analysis

evident is a cycle of growth and conflict in which the accumulation process leads to the formation of communities which it ultimately finds to be an impediment to further expansion."[12]

Building upon this dynamic between economic accumulation and community formation, Mollenkopf presents four levels of analysis as tools to analyze urban development. Adapting Mollenkopf's framework to the present study, I propose three levels of analysis as a way of specifying the "nested" nature of economic accumulation and community relationships (see Figure 2.1). These three levels capture the complicated interactions of economic, social, and political variables in an urban community. Applied to the responses to plant closings outlined in the previous chapter, these levels provide a framework to help explain the adoption of different public policies in different communities.[13]

Economic Accumulation

At the most general level of analysis is the process of economic accumulation itself. As noted previously, economic accumulation refers to the way a society produces and reproduces its means of economic sustenance. In American capitalism private markets play the central role in organizing work and establishing economic relationships between individuals and institutions. The capitalist tenets of private ownership of productive assets and private economic gain broadly define the nature of American society. Thus, institutions and social interactions are molded and constrained by the private work-place and the private pursuit of economic gain. For example, the owners of an industrial plant relate to others through the medium of economic return on production from their plant, while the world of workers is structured by the wage and employment relationship. The protection and support of this market system is a basic feature in a capitalist society.

Furthermore, private market values not only define the material forms of economic interaction but also inform the nature and possibilities of general discourse. Ideas and proposals that question the tenets of a private market system are typically deemed illegitimate, if not dangerous and subversive. For example, government ownership and operation of a basic production facility, such as an automobile plant, rarely is raised, let alone actively considered, by government policymakers. While the boundaries set by capitalism do not rule out any consideration of such a strategy, they do make discussions of this nature a rarity in the United States.

In an economy dominated by capitalist accumulation and free market ideals, political authority is structured to support interactions based on market values. Supporting a private enterprise economy, whether through legal protections of private property or other policies, is an important role of American governments. As many writers have noted, governments rely on the success of private accumulation for both general economic prosperity as well as tax revenues necessary to support government programs and services. Both are critical to the survival of government. As Charles Lindblom concludes, the control of investment and economic resources by private businesses bestows upon the business sector a "privileged position" in the American political economy. The failure of businesses to successfully perform their tasks can lead to a general economic decline in the community and, as a result, a decline in popular support for incumbent politicians.[14] Thus, in public policymaking the basic legitimacy of capitalist accumulation is rarely challenged; private property and the private control of investment are seen as prerequisites to a healthy economy. As Martin Shefter argues in his study of New York City, urban officials must meet several "imperatives" of local politics, one of which is maintaining the health of the local economy.[15] Making a similar point, Norman and Susan Fainstein contend that one of the "constant elements" in the urban policy environment is government support for private accumulation.[16] In short, as these authors emphasize, capitalist accumulation constitutes an important structural feature that fundamentally shapes the urban policy process.

However, as argued earlier, molding the policy process does not mean determining specific policy outcomes. Quite different public policies might be considered and implemented within the general context of a capitalist system, ranging from laissez-faire to business assistance packages. Furthermore, this range of possibilities can become even broader if existing economic circumstances raise questions concerning the viability of capitalism. In particular, during economic hard times, when the benefits of capitalism are few and far between, capitalist accumulation may become the subject of debate as policies are considered to address economic problems. A more interventionist government role, such as the player role introduced in Chapter 1, may be the result.

The closing of an industrial plant introduces important elements at the level of economic accumulation. The decision to close a plant raises the issue of private control of investment resources and also poses a threat to the health of the local economy. The nature of the resulting policy response is likely to depend on the condition of the local economy and the importance of the plant to that economy. For example, in a local economy already suffering from adverse economic conditions, the closing of a plant that employs a significant part of the local workforce and is a major part of the local tax base may well lead to an active and interventionist policy response. Alternatively, if the plant is a relatively small part of a healthy local economy, the call for for government action is much less imperative. In both scenarios economic accumulation shapes the policy response, but in quite different ways. Whether these expectations hold true is a question we will return to in the case studies.

Institutional System

A second level of analysis involves the institutional system in the urban political economy. As Mollenkopf argues, institutions in both the public and private sectors "create the social capacity to act." Business enterprises, labor unions, government agencies, community organizations, and other institutions "assemble and transform streams of resources" to meet the goals of their members.[17] Although institutions are circumscribed by the prevailing process of economic accumulation, they retain an important degree of flexibility to accommodate a range of purposes. In so doing, institutions play an important part in shaping the range and character of individual actions.

The institutional system involves quite different organizations in both the private and public sector. In the private sector, business firms, labor unions, and interest associations are key institutions with quite different goals, resources, rules, norms, and operating procedures. These different characteristics circumscribe the role the institution or organization plays in the policy process. Business firms, for example, are typically organized along hierarchical lines that maximize top-down control of decision making. While the policy role of the business firm usually reflects this control, variations are likely depending on ownership structure, number and nature of product lines, resource availabilities, and other characteristics of the particular firm.

From an institutional perspective, the key resource of an organization is particularly important in establishing the very nature of that organization and the way the organization relates to its surrounding environment. For example, labor unions and business corporations have quite different resource bases that shape the way each operates. While labor unions are organized around membership support as their critical resource, business corporations rely on the control of financial investments as their central resource. These different resources support different organizational dynamics and lead to quite different roles in the policy process. Labor unions rely on the mobilization and actions of their membership to influence policymakers, while business corporations use control over financial investments as their source of leverage.[18]

Relationships among private-sector organizations are also central in molding the urban political economy. Focusing once again on business firms and labor unions, the collective-bargaining contract between the firm and union represents an important set of rules and procedures. The labor contract specifies in considerable detail the nature of the relationship between workers and management. The contract covers wages and basic conditions of employment and establishes the procedures through which labor and management interact. In the case of a plant closing, the labor contract can play a central role in shaping labor-management discussions and the overall adjustment process, thus becoming a major part of the closing response.

Institutional structures are also important in the public realm. The policy tools, legal arrangements, and historical experiences of governments shape the course of urban policymaking. As Douglas Ashford argues in an essay on policymaking, "The state is governed more by its previous decisions, its internal organizational and institutional constraints, and its own agenda, however we suspect these may be formed, than by external forces."[19] Striking a similar note, Martin Shefter concludes in his study of fiscal crises in New York City that local policy responses are dependent in part on a local "regime's institutional and organizational capacity to enact and implement decisions made at the top."[20] Thus, the local policy process is heavily influenced by the nature of political institutions. For example, the availability of economic policy tools — grant and loan programs, tax incentives, bonding authority, land use regulations, and so on — varies among local governments and sets important parameters on policymaking. A political body's organizational basis may also influence the policy process. A municipal council-manager system has a diffuse political base, while a popularly elected mayor has a separate, discrete base of governmental power, and each has different implications for the nature of government actions as well as for the strategies of individuals and groups attempting to influence public policy. In addition, the division of authority and responsibilities among city and county governments can also be an important ingredient in shaping local government capabilities.

The system of American federalism also establishes an important setting for local governments. As discussed in Chapter 1, state and national governments impose numerous restrictions and limitations on the form and actions of local governments. State governments, in particular, play a major role. From restrictions on revenue-raising abilities to authorization for the creation of new agencies for economic development, state governments can determine to a great extent the nature of local political institutions.

Finally, established relationships between public and private organizations can also play a considerable role in guiding the urban policy process. Public-private partnerships that link government and private economic organizations are becoming increasingly common.[21] In Pittsburgh, for example, the Allegheny Conference on Community Development provides an important forum for discussions among local government, business, and university leaders. These partnerships establish certain routines and channels that shape interactions among members. Extending this theme, a number of writers have identified "urban growth machines" as important institutional arrangements that combine government, finance, and business in support of land-based economic growth.[22] While the "growth machine" does not operate without strains, it does constitute an influential policy forum with established patterns of interaction among government and private-sector organizations.

Political Alliance Formation and Mobilization

"Nested" within economic accumulation and the institutional system is a third level of analysis that Mollenkopf refers to as political alliance formation and mobilization. This level of analysis highlights the political dynamic among different groups and individuals as they use various resources and strategies to realize their respective goals. Political actors in the public and private sector have quite different goals; the resources they control, which are largely dependent on institutional position, vary; and the strategies they employ to realize their goals also differ. In this setting, entrepreneurial efforts, brokering, and negotiating are common. The result is what Alford and Friedland refer to as politics — "a strategic alliance creating the possibilities of action to reinforce or change institutional arrangements."[23]

Alliance formation and mobilization take place in both the private and public sectors. For example, in the private sector, business leaders may turn to low-key lobbying efforts as the preferred strategy to build alliances, while labor leaders might emphasize a voter education campaign as the best means of mobilization. Although the strategies available to each are certainly shaped by the nature of their respective institutions, the possibilities for mobilization and coalition-building remain relatively broad.

Social movements and community-based organizations rely even more extensively on mobilization and coalition building. Lacking the staff, resources, bureaucratic structure, and permanency of labor unions and business firms, social movements and community organizations often turn to various forms of pressure politics as well as public demonstrations to achieve their goals. Mobilization is critical for these groups.[24] As one community activist in Minnesota remarked during a plant-closing fight, "Don't count too much on the politicians for help unless you've got an awful lot of people behind you so they know they have to do something."[25]

Alliance formation and mobilization are also important in the public sector. Government officials, whether elected or appointed, adopt different coalition-building strategies to achieve their goals. Although the institutional environment sets the stage, political leadership guides the action. The political organization is, as one student of bureaucratic politics notes, "simultaneously a bundle of constraints and resources."[26] The challenge for political leaders is to mobilize and utilize those resources to their advantage.

How, or even whether, political leaders achieve the mobilization of resources depends on a variety of factors, including the individuals involved as well as the environment in which they operate. Personal likes and dislikes, career goals, and interpersonal rivalries can affect their mobilization efforts. A rivalry among political leaders can undermine an otherwise successful alliance-building campaign. Furthermore, different environments and circumstances entail different mobilization strategies. While private, informal discussions may be appropriate for securing a supportive city council vote, another situation may call for a public lobbying effort joined by labor or business supporters. Deciding which strategy is most appropriate is one of the tests of political leadership.

The challenge to political leadership is analagous to the challenge faced by the business entrepreneur. The political entrepreneur "gathers and risks political capital or support in order to reshape politics and create new sources of power by establishing new programs or products."[27] The entrepreneur employs innovative strategies to mobilize existing or newly created resources to reach particular goals. Although the institutional environment creates boundaries within which coalition-building takes place, there is, as Bryan Jones and Lynn Bachelor argue, slack or "loose coupling" in this environment that allows for "creative, albeit constrained, leadership."[28]

Combining Levels of Analysis

Considered together, the three levels of analysis offer a framework to assess the relative importance of different variables. Thus, the setting for the policy process in the United States is established by capitalist economic accumulation and the current status of the economy. Within this setting institutional structures serve to further define the nature of policymaking, while mobilization and alliance-building efforts constitute the political dynamic of competing individuals and groups.

Although these levels of analysis are related in a nested manner (see Figure

2.1), it is also possible that actions at a lower level can alter or "break open the shell of constraint" imposed by higher levels.[29] For example, political mobilization can be used to alter existing institutional arrangements or, in a less likely case, the prevailing system of economic accumulation. In fact, such changes often point to critical periods during which important or fundamental alterations occur in the political economy. The creation of a new redevelopment authority through mobilization and coalition-building efforts, for example, represents a substantial institutional change in the community. The analysis of the Steel Valley Authority in Chapter 5 is a case in point.

Political explanations, then, require consideration of all three levels and the interactions among them. Even though one level may prove particularly critical, and thus serve as the initial focus, the interaction of all three remains central. As Mollenkopf argues, "No single level can displace the others as an exclusive mode of explanation. Nor can the overall phenomenon of urban life be understood without conceding that each level makes a contribution."[30]

Problem Definitions

As different individuals and groups participate in the policy process and seek to mobilize support, one of the most critical steps is establishment of a supportive problem definition. Problem definitions point to what different individuals and groups see as the main issues facing a community. In essence, problem definitions establish the terms of a policy debate and provide the bases for political action.

Problem definitions can have at least three key dimensions. First, a definition typically involves a standard of judgement.[31] Before a condition can become a problem, there must be a standard for measurement or comparison. Without such a standard, there is no point of comparison to judge a particular condition as unsatisfactory. For example, in economic affairs efficiency is a common standard used to judge the status of a particular condition; thus, an old industrial facility is targeted for closure because of economic inefficiencies attributed to the plant, which can no longer successfully compete in the market. In contrast, others might argue that the plant be evaluated according to a standard of community welfare. Judged by this measure, it might be appropriate to keep the plant open because of the critical role the plant plays in the community's economic base. In the realm of policymaking, other standards are also common. For example, equality of opportunity is a common standard of judgment in the policy process. Affirmative action programs in hiring new personnel exemplify a policy guided by equality of opportunity. Based on this standard, equal access to key resources is the central concern. This multiplicity of available standards sets the stage for competing problem definitions and alternative mobilization efforts.

Along a second key dimension, problem definitions often include an explanation of causation of the events that resulted in the problem. Implicit, if not explicit, within this "factual" account is an attribution of responsibility. That is, an explanation of causation identifies who or what is responsible for the problem as well as the sequence of relevant events. As Joseph Gusfield notes in his study of drinking, driving, and public policy, "causal responsibility [is an] assertion about the sequence that factually accounts for the existence of the problem."[32] To return to an earlier example, if an industrial plant is deemed economically inefficient, the problem definition will also state how that came about as well as attribute responsibility for this problem to specific parties or circumstances, such as poor business-management decisions or high labor costs. As with competing standards, there are also likely to be competing explanations of causation.

The third and final dimension typically found in a problem definition is an outline for a course of remedial action and an assignment to one or more parties of the responsibility to mobilize requisite resources — in essence a plan for the solution. In this regard, government policymakers are often given responsibility to use public resources to address the problem. However, public policymakers are not the only candidates. For example, it might be argued that market forces of supply and demand should provide an appropriate and acceptable course of action, as a response to the dislocations of economic change.

As is clear from this outline of key dimensions, competing definitions of a particular policy problem are common; problems, such as plant closings, are not self-defining. As David Dery notes in a study of problem definition, "Problems are not objective entities in their own right, 'out there,' to be detected as such, but are rather the product of imposing certain frames of reference on reality."[33] Similarly, Roger Cobb and Charles Elder argue that "policy problems are not simply 'givens,' nor are they simply matters of the 'facts' of the situation. They are matters of interpretation and social definition."[34]

Determining which frame of reference or interpretation survives is often a contentious affair in which different actors in the political economy attempt to establish, as Gusfield says, "ownership" of the problem definition. "The structure of public problems is an arena of conflict in which a set of groups and institutions, often including governmental agencies, compete and struggle over ownership and disownership, the acceptance of causal theories, and the fixation of responsibility."[35] Further, as Cobb and Elder note, "Control over how the issues of conflict are defined means control over the choice of battlefields upon which a conflict will take place."[36] Business corporations, labor unions, and political leaders maneuver to establish their definition of a problem as the favored one to shape the policy process.

Problem definitions can be established in different ways and with quite different contents. In many plant closings the business firm establishes the definition. The firm uses the market and/or its own balance sheet as the standard of judgment and argues that changing market conditions and obsolete facilities are the reasons for the closing. In this case the definition of the problem is within the domain of private economic decision-making; public critique is unnecessary. The appropriate remedial response is for all parties to follow price signals and market supply and demand to adjust to a changing economy. A self-equilibrating market is the remedial strategy. In contrast, another problem definition might involve a standard of community justice. As Staughton Lynd argues in his study of plant closings in Youngstown, Ohio, there is a "community property right" that should be considered in plant closings.[37] In this definition the cause of the closing might be defined in terms of poor management decisions, with responsibility for a remedial strategy falling upon government officials working with labor and community groups. Market forces are not irrelevant, but they should not be the sole criteria to drive the policy process.

Which problem definition is accepted depends on its compatibility with the larger economic and institutional environment as well as the ability of individuals and groups to present their interpretation as most persuasive. For example, a definition that declares government assistance to ailing businesses to be inappropriate would be most acceptable in a community with a robust economy and flexible job market. In such an environment, private market forces offer an acceptable solution. However, in a community experiencing high unemployment and a sharp economic downturn, this same definition might be contested. A battle over redefinition could ensue as individuals and groups in the community seek government assistance for faltering businesses. Winning acceptance in this setting requires political skills and effective mobilization. Problem definitions, then, can be a reflection of prevailing environmental conditions as well as a catalyst for change. In either case, they are an important context for political action.

In the three case studies that follow, problem definition provides a useful vantage point for understanding the policy process. As Robert Alford notes in his study of Wisconsin communities, "The course of conflicts may be partially understood by reference to the ability of groups to establish their definition of the situation as the appropriate one."[38] While in some instances, as in Louisville (Chapter 3), there is little debate over the problem definition, in other cases, as in Pittsburgh (Chapter 5), problem definition becomes a central point of contention. However, regardless of the degree of controversy, how the plant closing is defined offers a useful window on the process of political mobilization and alliance building.

Levels of analysis along with problem definition constitute our tools for exploring the politics of plant closings. Levels of analysis help us understand how public policy is molded by political alliances formed within an economic and institutional setting. The problem definitions that business leaders, labor leaders, government officials, and others bring to the policy process help us focus on the goals and strategies of mobilization and alliance-building that drive the political dynamic. Capturing this complex set of interactions is the challenge as we look at plant closings in Louisville, Waterloo, and Pittsburgh.

3

A "Bystander" Response: Louisville, Kentucky, and the Brown & Williamson Corporation

The 1960s were good years for the Brown & Williamson Corporation. Backed by sales of KOOL cigarettes, the company increased its share of the domestic cigarette market from 10 to 17 percent, becoming a major actor in the tobacco industry. While continuing production in its plants in Louisville, Kentucky, and Petersburg, Virginia, the company began planning for a new manufacturing plant. By the early 1970s a site was selected in Georgia for construction of a new state-of-the-art production facility. Brown & Williamson was poised for expansion. Market growth, however, soon came to an end. By the late 1970s, optimism was replaced with the realization that the company had overbuilt. A drop in market share after 1974 resulted in excess capacity. Tough choices were ahead. With a tradition of corporate privacy, Brown & Williamson avoided public debate as it assessed its options. In January 1979 the decision was announced: the Louisville plant would close. The closing of this fifty-year-old plant never became a major item on the public agenda. Brown & Williamson made the decision, and as one labor leader commented, "I don't think Jesus Christ could have come down here and changed that company's mind." Although labor unions negotiated an attractive closing package for workers leaving the plant, public policymakers were not part of this process; the business firm dominated the adjustment process. Local government officials were bystanders.

THE SETTING

The Political and Economic Terrain

Known as the City at the Falls, Louisville developed in the nineteenth century as a key port on the Ohio River. By 1860 Louisville had a thriving mercantile

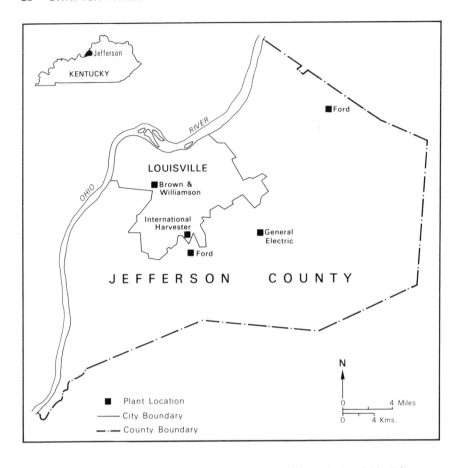

economy and was America's tenth-largest city. Although the Ohio River no longer plays such a pivotal role in the economic life of the city, Louisville remains a major metropolitan area and the largest urban area in Kentucky. The river location at the boundary between "North" and "South" has left Louisville with a mix of cultural, economic, and political influences.[1]

In recent years demographic shifts have been particularly significant in Louisville. Similar to many other older metropolitan areas, Louisville has been the victim of suburban migration. The city of Louisville, which reached its population peak in 1960 with 390,700 residents, declined to 312,000 by 1978.[2] In contrast, Jefferson County, which includes Louisville as well as surrounding communities, grew rapidly. Whereas the non-Louisville area accounted for only 7 percent of the county's population in 1940, by 1978 the same area contained 57 percent of the county's 719,000 residents. This shift in population lead to a decline in the downtown retail-business core. Focusing political resources on the problems of the metropolitan area became a major challenge for the citizens of Louisville and Jefferson County.

The political landscape of the Louisville area was, and continues to be, dominated by the city of Louisville and Jefferson County. In 1978 Louisville was governed by a new mayor, William Stansbury, who was in the first year of his four-year term, and a twelve-member board of aldermen, elected at-large for two-year terms. In this mayor-council system the mayor had considerable independent authority over the executive functions of the city as well as item veto power over appropriations actions taken by the board of aldermen. As will be noted later, 1978–79 was a rather disharmonious time for the incumbent mayor and a majority on the board.

Political affairs in Jefferson County were conducted primarily by the fiscal court, although several other county officials (e.g., sheriff, attorney) were independently elected and thus had an important degree of autonomy. The fiscal court, which was restructured by the state legislature in 1978 to remove previous judicial functions, consisted of a popularly elected county judge/executive and three commissioners elected at-large but designated as representatives of districts. Although the county judge/executive had more staff support and executive authority than the commissioners, all four voted as a single body on major policy issues. As in Louisville the working relationship in 1978 between County Judge/Executive Mitch McConnell and the three commissioners was less than harmonious.

While county and city officials shared several policy functions, such as development of the port area through the Louisville-Jefferson County Riverport Authority, they tended to operate in separate spheres and in some cases actually competed for fiscal and economic resources. Political fragmentation was perhaps more apparent when city and county officials competed with financial incentives and other forms of assistance to draw the same business firm to a site within their respective boundaries.

In economic terms Louisville and Jefferson County represented important manufacturing centers. The largest employer in the county, General Electric Corporation, employed over 20,000 workers in the early 1970s. The GE facility represented a small community in its own right. The second-largest employer, Ford Motor Company, operated two major plants in the county. Other major employers included International Harvester and Brown & Williamson. Another major manufacturing facility, the American Tobacco cigarette plant, closed in 1970.

Although manufacturing was a central component of the local economic base, important changes were taking place. While manufacturing jobs in 1940 represented 40 percent of nonagricultural employment in the county, by 1978 the comparable measure had declined to 33 percent.[3] Services, trades, and other types of nonmanufacturing employment were becoming increasingly important. Louisville was slowly moving into a postindustrial economy. The announcement to close the Brown & Williamson factory highlighted this shift as well as the changing nature of the American tobacco industry.

The American Tobacco Industry

Located in an important tobacco-growing region, the Louisville economy for many years had relied on the tobacco industry for a significant number of jobs. Brown & Williamson, which had been in Louisville since 1929, as well as operations by American Tobacco, Philip Morris, and Lorillard, became Louisville's connection to this high-wage industry.

In the years prior to 1979 the American tobacco industry was dominated by the "Big Six"—R. J. Reynolds, Philip Morris, Brown & Williamson, American Brands, Lorillard, and Liggett & Myers.[4] By 1975 these six companies controlled 99.8 percent of U.S. tobacco sales. R. J. Reynolds was the clear leader, with 32.5 percent of the market, followed by Philip Morris, with 23.8 percent. Brown & Williamson, which had only 7.8 percent of the U.S. market in 1940, was third, with 17.0 percent.[5]

In the last twenty-five years cigarette companies, including Brown & Williamson, have pursued a number of different strategies to protect their markets and increase sales.[6] One set of strategies is based on industrywide cooperation to refute the challenges of the antismoking movement. Since the late 1950s cigarette companies have faced mounting attacks because of the detrimental health effects of smoking. In response the companies banded together to support lobbying and public information campaigns. In contrast, a second set of strategies involve intense competition among companies over market share. Product innovation, market segmentation, and cost efficiencies have proven critical. Advertising, for example, is central to building brand loyalty. To cite the most prominent case, the "Marlboro Man" campaign helped move that brand from number nine in 1960 to the number-one seller in 1976. In addition, such product innovations as filter and low-tar cigarettes have been central to maintaining or increasing sales.

And finally, a third set of strategies is based on diversification and overseas expansion. Diversification began in the 1960s as cigarette companies entered such markets as packaging, food and beverages, and consumer products. By 1971 nontobacco sales represented 53 percent of sales at Liggett & Meyers, 32 percent at American Brands, and 25 percent at R. J. Reynolds.[7] In addition, sales of cigarettes overseas became increasingly important, particularly for Philip Morris and R. J. Reynolds.

Two important consequences of these strategies, particularly diversification and the search for cost efficiencies, were a stagnant labor market in cigarette manufacturing and a decline in the number of major production facilities. Between 1958 and 1982, despite an increase in total consumption of cigarettes, the production work force in cigarette manufacturing increased only marginally, from 31,000 to 32,200. During this same time period the number of cigarette manufacturing establishments employing 20 or more workers declined from 16 to 13.[8] The casualties included the 1970 closing of a Liggett & Meyers plant in Richmond, Virginia, idling over 800 workers, the shutdown of the American Brands plant in Louisville, ending about 1,000 tobacco jobs, and the closing of the Louisville plant by Brown & Williamson.

Brown & Williamson Corporation

Brown & Williamson (B & W) began in the late nineteenth century as a small North Carolina partnership specializing in snuff and rolled tobacco. In 1927 the fortunes of the company took a positive turn when it was purchased by the British-American Tobacco Company of England. British-American Tobacco, created in 1902 by several American and British tobacco companies, was looking for a point of entry into American markets; B & W provided that opportunity. To establish a position in the U.S. cigarette market, a new factory was constructed in Louisville, and the B & W offices were moved there in 1929.

Brown & Williamson became a mainstay of the Louisville economy and a growing contender in the tobacco industry. In the 1930s B & W maintained a workforce of 3,000 at its Louisville plant and constructed another plant in Petersburg, Virginia.[10] Capacity or near-capacity production was the norm as B & W introduced KOOL cigarettes, one of the first menthol brands, and Viceroy, one of the earliest filter-tip brands. Redeemable coupons on Raleigh cigarettes also proved to be a successful marketing technique. Although its market share dipped in the 1940s, B & W sales rose in the 1950s, and by 1960 it had a solid 10 percent of the American market.

In the 1960s and 1970s B & W followed other tobacco companies by diversifying into nontobacco product lines as well as seeking greater cost efficiencies in production. Diversification included a controlling interest in Kohl supermarkets and retail stores, the purchase of Gimbel Brothers and Saks Fifth Avenue, and ownership of Vital Food Products. By 1974 nontobacco annual sales exceeded $1 billion. While tobacco remained the dominant product line, diversification was reflected in a corporate reorganization around the new name Brown & Williamson Industries.

Diversification was part of a larger trend by B & W's corporate parent, the British-American Tobacco Company (BAT). Acquisitions in British paper companies, German department stores, and Brazilian supermarkets were added to those in the United States. By 1973 BAT's nontobacco assets exceeded those in tobacco. Still, BAT remained Britain's third-largest corporation and the world's largest tobacco company, producing 20 percent of all cigarettes sold in the West and the Third World.

Table 3.1 Domestic Market Share of Brown & Williamson (percentage of total)

Year	Market Share	Year	Market Share
1960	10.4	1974	17.5
1965	13.3	1975	17.0
1970	16.9	1976	16.5
1971	16.8	1977	15.8
1972	17.3	1978	15.3
1973	17.6	1979	14.5

Source: James Overton, "Diversification and International Expansion: The Future of the American Tobacco Manufacturing Industry with Corporate Profiles of the 'Big Six,'" in *The Tobacco Industry in Transition*, ed. William Finger (Lexington, Mass.: D. C. Heath and Company, 1981), p. 161.

For B & W the 1960s and early 1970s were years of expansion in tobacco production. Market share and sales were continually growing (see Table 3.1). To accommodate this growth, B&W expanded the Louisville plant. In 1965 a $17.5-million project added 1,000 jobs and increased output by 80 percent.[11] In addition, B & W began preparations in the early 1970s for construction of a new cigarette-manufacturing plant. Planning for a new facility began with site visits in several southern communities and culminated with the decision to build in Macon, Georgia.

The Macon site was presented by the company as an addition to, rather than replacement of, existing production capacity. As the president of B & W said in 1973, "Because this would be a completely new facility, the job security of our present 12,000 employees will not be affected. We will continue to operate our existing plants on a normal basis to meet required production."[12] By 1981 the company hoped to employ 2,500 in the new plant. Construction of the facility began in 1974 and was completed in 1976. The $150-million plant was a state-of-the-art, single-story facility with the newest cigarette-making machines. Limited production began in 1976, and by 1979 approximately 900 workers were employed at the plant.

CLOSING THE LOUISVILLE PLANT

The Closing Decision

Although the early 1970s were good years for Brown & Williamson, by 1974 the company's fortunes began to turn; B & W's market share took a steady slide downward (see Table 3.1). New brands, such as FACT, were unsuccessful in raising sales.[13] A temporary halt in construction at Macon was followed by an internal reassessment. With the hope of a turnaround in sales, construction was resumed; however, a turnaround didn't happen. Despite the continued success of KOOL, overall unit sales of B & W cigarettes declined from 103 billion in 1974 to 88 billion by 1979.[14]

Brown & Williamson faced an important decision. As one corporate official wrote, "By 1978 . . . it became clear that we had overbuilt. The company's sales had not improved, and total U.S. tobacco sales were leveling off. Realizing that a production cutback was inevitable, we weighed our options."[15] Central to this assessment was a comparison of manufacturing facilities. Both the Louisville and Petersburg plants were 45-year-old multistory facilities, whereas Macon represented a modern, single-floor plant.

Although prospects for the Louisville plant appeared bleak, the company declined to negotiate or publicly discuss its review with labor leaders or government policymakers. However, rumors of a closing reached such a high level in November 1978 that the company made a public announcement concerning its general review. Citing a decline in sales, technological improvements, and its current operating capacity, the company issued a memo to employees:

> We have been studying and analyzing a variety of possible alternatives regarding how best to balance capacity with demand. Among these various alternatives, we have looked at a possibility that would include the eventual phasing out of the Louisville manufacturing operation. No conclusions have been reached on this or any of the other alternatives we are considering.[16]

However, as one worker commented to a reporter from a local newspaper, "The memo really leaves no doubt. It's in the planning stages. We think it's just a matter of time."[17]

The "time" was not far off. On January 18, 1979, the decision was announced — the Louisville plant would close. As the headlines of the *Louisville Courier-Journal* appeared on the following day, "3,000 at Brown & Williamson learn they're losing their jobs." Citing its internal studies, the company noted that a "number of alternatives regarding the best way to balance manufacturing capability with developing market requirements" had been considered. The decision to close the Louisville plant was made by the company as the "most efficient use of [its] manufacturing resources."[18] In simple market terms, demand no longer matched supply. Since demand was not rising, supply (production capacity) would have to be reduced.

To further reduce supply, B & W also announced that the 3,000-employee workforce at the Petersburg plant would be cut by one-third. As the announcement made clear, the Macon plant would be the major B & W production facility in the future. However, and particularly important to understanding the Louisville experience, B & W announced that it would keep its corporate headquarters, with approximately 2,000 employees, in Louisville. Although the production facility would close, Brown & Williamson Industries was not leaving Louisville.

While the decision to close the plant was presented by the company as an accomplished fact, the actual closing process was subject to discussion and would not be an overnight affair. Brown & Williamson anticipated a three-year phase-out of production at the plant, and the company vowed to help workers and the community adjust to the closing. To help plan for the closing, the company hired two industrial relations experts from the academic community. With their assistance the company emphasized the importance of a gradual reduction of the workforce and a joint labor-management effort to complete a successful transition.[19]

Negotiations and the Settlement Agreement

Thus, labor-management negotiations over the effects of the closing dominated the closing experience. In a closed-door union meeting, the Bakery, Confectionery & Tobacco Workers International Union (B C & T), which represented approximately 2,000 workers at the plant, informed its members of impending negotiations over closing benefits and the need to maintain production continuity.[20] On January 29, one week after the closing decision was made public, company and labor representatives met in Washington, D.C. (B C & T's headquarters) to begin negotiations.

For the next three months in Louisville and other cities in the region, negotiations continued over the effects of the closing. During this time negotiations with the B C & T proceeded separately from those with other unions, the largest of which was the International Association of Machinists. In early April negotiations concluded, with all parties meeting in Lexington to announce the tentative settlement. On April 7 the agreement was accepted by the local B C & T membership in a standing vote.

In the resulting document, referred to as the "Settlement Agreement," the company and unions reached a quid pro quo: B & W agreed to provide a variety of financial and reemployment benefits for workers in exchange for union cooperation in maintaining orderly production at the plant during the closing process. As the agreement stated, the union waived any "rights now or in the future to bargain over the plans of the Company to restructure its manufacturing operations or the effect of such plans on the employees."[21] According to the agreement, layoffs would occur in increments determined by the company, with the final closing not anticipated until 1983.

Benefits available to laid-off workers covered a variety of areas. Financial benefits included severance pay, starting at twenty-six weeks pay for one to six years of service and increasing on a scale determined by the number of years worked; deferred early retirement for those qualifying by years of service and age but not yet fifty-five years old; supplemental early retirement for those age fifty-five or over and qualifying by years of service; and profit sharing during the year of severance. In addition, life and medical insurance would be continued for up to six months. As one further step, the company joined with the union to successfully lobby state officials into revising unemployment compensation rules to allow employees receiving severance benefits to also receive unemployment benefits. Nonfinancial benefits included a range of employment and reemployment services. For those wishing to stay with the company, relocation opportunities to the Macon plant and the Winston-Salem branch were provided for a limited number (325 to 375 production jobs at the Macon plant would be set aside for Louisville and Petersburg workers). The company would provide comprehensive financial assistance to help employees transfer to Macon.

For those leaving B & W an outplacement program included employee counseling and job search assistance. For those wishing to take the high school graduate equivalency test, B & W contracted with state officials and the local school board to provide classroom education on company premises. In addition, the company financed an outside skill-retraining program for a specified group of workers. Job search efforts were also assisted by a mailing to industries throughout the state indicating the availability of skilled and semiskilled former B & W employees.

Although union officials noted several weaknesses in the Settlement Agreement, most accepted it as one of the best plant-closing packages in the industry. As the president of the B C & T local commented, "I think the company went the last mile on it."[22] An international union representative called the agreement the "best plant closing agreement I've ever seen — probably the best ever reached in the country."[23]

A Bystander Government Role

Throughout this adjustment process local officials played little part. While concern was expressed, policymakers generally viewed the closing decision as outside the bounds of public policy. As one staff person in the city's economic development office recalled, the closing was "essentially a business decision over which the community had little control." In similar fashion an assistant to the county judge/executive described the closing as an "internal business management decision" that was not open to government influence. Continuing this theme, the former president of the board of aldermen noted that "city government assistance was not sought or given."

The only public record indicating possible city involvement was a resolution passed by the board of aldermen on November 11, 1978. Citing public accounts of the possible closing of B & W as well as of Sears, Roebuck & Company, the aldermen urged both companies to reconsider and called upon the mayor's office to work with the companies to develop alternatives to closing. The resolution passed unanimously by a voice vote, without discussion. However, in subsequent meetings, including those held after the January announcement by B & W, there was no recorded discussion of B & W or the

Sears closing. While the mayor's office may have had contacts with B & W officials, there was no record of concerted efforts from that office to alter the closing process.

In brief, throughout the closing process public officials remained on the sidelines. Policymakers did not attempt a mediating role, nor did they mount an effort to reverse the company's decision to close the plant. When government appeared, it was primarily in the form of federal labor-management law that provided basic boundaries for the negotiating process; it was a "housekeeping" function supported by the federal government. These boundaries established the legitimacy and basic contours of collective-bargaining contracts and negotiations, but they did not specify substantive outcomes. Collective-bargaining results would be dependent on the economic resources and strategies of the engaged parties. Although policymakers lauded the Settlement Agreement, they had no hand in specifying its content. Thus, the Settlement Agreement between B & W and the unions was the product of private negotiations and private power.

THE BROWN & WILLIAMSON CLOSING: PRIVATE POWER AND POLICYMAKING

Although private negotiations and private power appeared to dominate the B & W plant closing, a closer look at the underlying dynamic is needed. Brown & Williamson's control of the closing process was not preordained. As the next two chapters show, other plant closings have resulted in quite different adjustment experiences. In Louisville as well, other threatened plant closings had elicited a more active public policy response.[24] Why B & W's control went largely uncontested remains unclear. To take a closer look, we return to the levels of analysis presented in Chapter 2.

The Louisville Economy

The economic accumulation process in Louisville set the basic boundaries within which the adjustment experience would take place. Basic tenets of capitalism, particularly the private control of investment, as well as the health of the local economy, constituted the stage for political action. In general, economic conditions in Louisville in 1979 were relatively robust. Unemployment in Jefferson County was only 5.1 percent in 1978 and 4.7 percent the previous year. In addition, the labor force and the number of employed in the county had been steadily increasing. From 1976 to 1979 the total labor force in Jefferson County increased by 24,000 workers while the number actually employed increased by a comparable figure.[25]

Yet this relatively optimistic economic portrait masked two quite different trends. As noted in the introduction to this chapter, Louisville in 1978–79 was entering a transition period from a basic manufacturing economy to a more diversified service-oriented base. Since the mid-1970s, employment in Jefferson County had been slowly shifting from manufacturing to services, trades, and professional activities. Between 1974 and 1978, manufacturing employment declined from 107,100 to 97,600, while employment in the service and finance sectors increased from 66,100 to 82,100, and in wholesale and retail trades, it rose from 70,500 to 79,700.[26]

The closing of the B & W plant was indicative of the declining side of the economy; however, B & W was not alone. Employment at General Electric, the largest employer in Jefferson County (and largest private employer in Kentucky), peaked in 1973 at 23,000. By 1980 employment was down to 15,000 as appliance lines were moved elsewhere, demand slackened, and automation took its toll. Ford Motor Company, the second-largest employer in the county, operated two plants in which employment peaked in 1978 at close to 10,000. International Harvester, the third-largest employer, had a payroll of approximately 6,500 in 1965 but just over 4,000 by 1978. The announced closing by Brown & Williamson, the fourth-largest employer in the county, joined in the downward trend. Employment at the B & W plant peaked at 5,000 in the early 1970s, but by the 1979 announcement, production employment had dropped to 3,000.

As noted, the nonmanufacturing side of the economic ledger presented a different picture—one of growth and expansion. As the Louisville mayor said in a 1979 public forum, "We're losing some jobs, but we're gaining more. In fact, over the past decade Louisville has averaged a gain of about 6,500 jobs a year."[27] And as the mayor's economic develoment aide concluded at the same forum, "Louisville is changing from a manufacturing base to a white-collar and service-industry base. That base is downtown, and it's growing."[28] In the downtown area in 1979, major projects under way included the $90-million Riverfront Square hotel and office development and the $10-million Seelbach Hotel renovation. Medical, office, parking, and government projects were also in progress. Ground breaking was planned for a $90-million Galleria office and retail project as well as a new $24-million cultural complex.[29] As the president of the major downtown development organization observed, "More and more, Louisvillians are beginning to recognize that Louisville is Downtown Louisville—the area establishes the character of the city and sets the pace for the city, region and state."[30]

These two sides of the Louisville economy offered different points of orientation for public policymakers. On the one hand, a decline in manufacturing pointed to a loss of jobs and government tax revenues. At the time of the B & W closing announcement, the Louisville Area Chamber of Commerce estimated the plant payroll at $48.8 million annually and local taxes paid by workers at $1.1 million.[31] While tax losses from a closing would not bankrupt the city, the losses would nevertheless be significant. In response, an active policy role targeted to the declining manufacturing sector might be expected. Public policies could be designed to focus on retention and attraction of industrial and other manufacturing operations.

Alternatively, public policymakers could turn their attention to downtown development as the arena for economic growth. Downtown office and retail development offered white-collar and service employment as compensation for manufacturing losses. To support this area of growth, the city had already been engaged in a number of public-private partnerships. The city played an important role in providing infrastructure improvements, land-use packaging, and financial assistance for a number of downtown projects.[32] As stated in a planning document for the downtown, "The role of City Government in its attempt to stimulate investment and reinvestment should be that of cultivating sound conditions for private investment."[33]

Although neither of these policy paths — industrial retention/attraction or downtown development — was predetermined, the prevailing policy focus was on downtown and service employment as the growth side of the local economy. In support of this economic path was a collaboration of private and public leaders, with economic rewards of jobs and downtown construction being realized. While an active, interventionist policy response to stop the decline in manufacturing was still possible, it was less likely. It would require a significant challenge to the existing pattern of change in the private economy.

In this regard, the Brown & Williamson closing actually captured both sides of this dynamic economy. That is, although B & W was closing its manufacturing facility, it was also planning to keep its corporate headquarters in Louisville. At the time of the closing announcement, employment at the headquarters and related research offices was close to 2,000. By keeping this part of its operations in Louisville, B & W would maintain its contribution to the growing professional and service base of the economy. As one former city official recalled, a "good deal of the B & W money stayed in Louisville." In fact, three years after the closing announcement, B & W purchased for its corporate headquarters one of the twenty-six-story office towers in the new downtown Galleria complex (see "Update" in this chapter.) While these plans were probably not known to public officials in 1979, the company's stated intention to keep its headquarters in Louisville constituted valuable compensation for the loss of manufacturing jobs. In this context a strong policy initiative to convince the company to alter its closing decision could actually put "at risk" this compensation. That is, in response to an aggressive or combative stance by local policymakers, the company might move its headquarters as well as close the manufacturing facility.

In summary, when viewed at the level of economic accumulation, there was no clear incentive for policymakers to attempt a more active government role with regard to the B & W closing. The loss of the B & W plant was significant, but compensation existed in the form of service jobs and a growing economy. Louisville was in the midst of a fundamental shift in the local economic base, and although such transitions are often difficult, Louisville policymakers appeared to accept the costs as a consequence of economic change. Support for the downtown and service-sector development followed the economic logic. The capitalist dynamic was structuring the range of likely policy actions.

Institutional System

Not only did the pattern of economic change point to a limited role for policymakers in the B & W closing, but the nature of existing institutional arrangements in both the private and public sectors also reinforced a bystander role. In the private sector, for example, the collective-bargaining contract set in place a set of rules and procedures (elaborated below) that structured a labor-management response to the closing rather than leaving the response open to general discussion. Correspondingly, in the public sector, the limited nature of available policy tools and other institutional capabilities handicapped a public response.

On the private sector side, the collective-bargaining contract between B & W management and the Bakery, Confectionery and Tobacco Workers International Union not only set wages and working conditions for production workers but also established benefits and procedures in the event of a plant closing.[34] The B C & T contract required eighteen-months' notice prior to a plant closing and six-months' notice prior to a shift closing. In addition to notice requirements the 1977 contract included a number of other benefits and options for those laid off: supplemental unemployment benefits, lump sum conversion, special option for voluntary resignation, and relocation possibilities.[35] As noted in the union newspaper, these provisions would provide workers with the "means to withstand the economic shock that would be imposed upon them in the event of layoffs or reduced work weeks."[36] This delineation of procedures and benefits provided the basis for subsequent labor-management negotiations over the exact composition of the Settlement Agreement.

Although the labor contract proved to be an important framework for negotiating benefits once the plant closing was announced, it was not a platform for labor's critique of the decision to close. The focus of the contract was on worker benefits rather than maintaining existing jobs or adding a labor role in corporate decision-making. Thus, when the announcement to close was made, the dominant response of the tobacco workers' union was within the established pattern; it sought the best benefit package for the soon-to-be former B & W workers. Certainly labor leaders would have preferred to keep the plant open, but since the company seemed determined to close it, the labor contract provided the logical framework for discussion. As a company representative commented, "The unions did not challenge the proposed closing of the plant; instead, they were concerned (along with management) with the effects of closure on their members."[37]

The private nature of the response to the closing in Louisville was also reinforced by the institutional structure of Brown & Williamson. Although the company was an important employer in the community, B & W was known as a very private company; it did not pursue a high-profile public image. Furthermore, B & W was not a "local" firm, even though it had been in Louisville since the late 1920s. B & W was part of a much larger multinational corporation—B.A.T. Industries of England—that included department stores and other operations in the United States as well as overseas tobacco and numerous other operations. Thus, decision making within B & W followed very complex lines of a corporate organization that spanned city, state, and national boundaries. These lines of corporate authority constituted an organizational environment that protected the private character of the company.

The institutional environment in the public sector also played an important role in shaping the policy response. One of the most noted features of the local political terrain was the fragmentation of governmental authority. In 1979 Jefferson County contained eighty-seven separate governments and over one hundred special districts and independent agencies. Efforts to consolidate this array of political authorities and functions dated back to at least 1956.[38] The result of fragmentation was, according to one research report, a "maze of jurisdictions" resulting in "duplication" and "inefficiencies."[39]

For example, the city of Louisville and Jefferson County operated their own economic development programs and, while occasionally cooperating, actually competed in several cases for prospective businesses. Because of this "divided authority," Louisville faced the future, as one commentator remarked, "without a strong governmental power center that can deal on somewhat equal terms with other governments and with private power centers."[40] This fragmentation placed county government on the sidelines of the B & W plant closing. According to county officials, since the B & W plant was located in the city, city government would be the "first line" of action. Although the B & W plant was important economically to both the city and the county, the city reaped the tax benefits from occupational license fees.[41] County officials would assist in policy actions if asked, but primary responsibility rested with city government.

Louisville's city government was substantial in size—with over 4,900 employees and an $89-million budget—however, the institutional framework requisite for an active policy role was less substantial. This weakness was evident in at least two areas. First, the city government operated from a limited base of historical experience. Although the mayor was independently elected, occupied a full-time position, and had an office of professional assistants, the mayor was statutorily prohibited from serving consecutive terms of office. As a result education in the policy process was typically limited and fragmented. Following each mayoral election a new group of administrators moved into city hall. The new administration often discounted actions of previous mayors and administrators as inappropriate models. As one former city official noted, every four years there was a "hostile take-over" that resulted in a significant "lack of institutional memory." Policymaking did not benefit from a learning process.

Second, even if there had been greater continuity in government administrations, the limited nature of existing policy tools posed another roadblock to an active government role. Policy tools available to Louisville government officials included land and tax incentives, industrial revenue bonds (IRBs), government business consultants, and small business loans. Certainly these policy tools were not insignificant. For example, industrial revenue bonds, which were authorized by the city but did not carry municipal liability, were used to assist business firms with various costs of expansion, including site acquisition, building construction, and machinery purchases. From late 1977 to June 1979 the city issued seven IRBs for a total of $19.5 million. In addition, these resources could be combined with state and federal support. For example, a $2-million federal Urban Development Action Grant (UDAG) and $12-million federal loan guaranteed by the Economic Development Administration (EDA) were being used for hotel restoration and creation of a business-loan program.[42] As another policy tool, the city's office of economic development, first formed in 1974, had a staff of ten in 1979 involved in minority business promotion, commercial rehabilitation projects, neighborhood revitalization, as well as industrial and business conservation. Economic development staff monitored the issuance of IRBs and business development loans and from March 1978 to March 1979 made 145 calls on Louisville businesses to provide information and assistance in solving problems.[43]

However, the utility of these tools in addressing problems at a 3,000-employee plant was open to question. Not only would the financial needs of a large plant be considerable, but policymakers had very little experience in trying to use these tools in the context of plant closings. As one member of the city staff noted, they were "not geared up to deal with closings." The focus was on business attraction and loans to small businesses; "business retention was not a major item on the menu at that time."

Thus, on both the public and private side, the institutional system in Louisville did not point to an active government role as a likely possibility in the B & W plant-closing situation. Such a setting is not immutable, but it does indicate the terrain upon which any mobilization efforts would need to be mounted. It is to such efforts (or the lack thereof) that we now turn.

Political Alliance Formation and Mobilization

The nature of economic accumulation and the patterns established by institutions may shape politics and policy, but they are not deterministic. To be certain, in the B & W plant closing neither of these pointed in the direction of an interventionist government role, yet the possibility of mobilization and alliance formation to create such a role should not be ignored. While such an effort would be difficult given the prevailing environment, it would not be impossible. Individuals or groups in the private or public sector could lobby, bargain, and mobilize in an effort to alter existing patterns. That such an effort did not take place in Louisville deserves consideration.

In the private sector the labor union represented the most likely candidate to appeal to government policymakers to prevent or otherwise alter the closing process. After all, it was the jobs of union members that were being lost. Although several labor leaders recalled sending letters to government officials asking for assistance to keep the plant open, by their own admission they were not persistent. There was an acceptance by many in the leadership and general workforce that the closing was going to happen regardless of what they did; the appropriate strategy was to negotiate for the best possible closing benefits within the structure of the collective-bargaining agreement. As an academic observer recalled, there was a sense of "resignation without explanation" among the B & W workforce.

The lack of mobilization to alter this pattern can be attributed to at least two additional factors. First, the union was not losing its representation of production workers at Brown & Williamson; the new Macon plant would remain a union plant. Despite Georgia's "right-to-work" law and the potential cost appeal of operating a nonunion plant, B & W chose to recognize the union when a sufficient number of authorization cards at its Macon plant had been signed. For the former Tobacco Workers International Union (TWIU), this was critical. Since the late 1960s, union membership had shown little overall growth. In 1968 the union had 30,644 members and in 1978, 30,739.[44] This relatively small membership made support for union causes increasingly difficult. In response the TWIU merged with the Bakery and Confectionery Workers in 1978. While this consolidation of membership lists was important, maintaining the number of tobacco workers in the union remained a primary task. Thus, although the Louisville closing was regrettable, B & W's recognition of the Macon local meant the union would still represent workers at the company.

Second, a more general factor that contributed to the lack of mobilization was the absence in Louisville of a critique of capitalism. Unlike Pittsburgh in the early 1980s (as described in Chapter 5), Louisville lacked past or present examples of social and political challenges to corporate power, which is not to say that Louisville was politically inactive. Controversies involving school busing in the mid-1970s and a public employees' strike in 1978 provided numerous examples of political activity. Yet when it came to a more fundamental challenge of the economic system, Louisville had no clear precedents. As one academic observer concluded, there was "no legitimate leftist presence in the city" to pose alternative ideas to the established pattern of doing business.

Furthermore, even if history offered examples of leftist critiques, cooperation among existing labor and social groups was limited. As another academic observer noted, local groups in Louisville tended to "fight battles within their own organized containers." Autoworkers, tobacco workers, and others in the labor community were not unified in a manner that would support strong opposition to corporate decision-making. Thus, even if a challenge to the B & W closing could be organized, gathering general support from local groups was doubtful.

The lack of mobilization among workers was matched by a similar situation in the public sector. Among government officials, the likely candidate for assertive policy action was the mayor of Louisville, William Stansbury. However, not only did the mayor operate from an institutional base with limited resources, but his political energies in 1978–79 were absorbed in an ongoing controversy with the twelve-member board of aldermen. Beginning in mid-1978 a series of accusations had been made against the mayor concerning campaign contributions, the hiring of assistants, honesty in reporting government travels, and other issues. At one point calls for the mayor's resignation were heard from several aldermen, the county Democratic Executive Committee (Stansbury was a Democrat), and the *Louisville Courier-Journal*. In late 1978 and continuing into 1979, at the same time the B & W closing was taking shape, the Select Committee on Inquiry was established by the board of aldermen to investigate the mayor. The mayor's refusal to cooperate with the investigation only fueled the controversy.

Amid this political battle, city government in 1978 and 1979 was poorly positioned to support a united policy initiative. While the mayor received periodic support from the board of aldermen, the general relationship was not conducive to policy innovation. Said one alderman, the board was "never included in the administration; [the] only thing we knew was what we read in the newspaper." Echoing this sentiment, the *Louisville Courier-Journal* described a "hide-and-seek" style of civic leadership:

Louisville needs a mayor who can think and plan and lead, not someone trapped in a bunker who sallies forth merely to squabble with the aldermen over patronage. If as seems sadly clear, Mr. Stansbury isn't ready to resign, the aldermen should get cracking on the business of impeaching him.[45]

While the mayor continued in office through his term, a lack of political unity and leadership remained common themes. By 1981 the president of the board of aldermen referred to Stansbury as a "caretaker mayor."[46] In assessing the mayor's tenure, the *Courier-Journal* concluded that "Stansbury personifies dullness in office. . . . In the end, his supporters say he did well, his critics say he did little — and all agree there were few innovations."[47]

This portrait of an embattled city government must be kept in context. Government still functioned and policy actions were taken. In particular, as mentioned earlier, this was a time of considerable progress in downtown development. The mayor, in fact, was noted in several accounts as having a good relationship with downtown developers. Such a public-private partnership is not surprising given the nature of the Louisville economy. However, in areas where there was less public-private consensus, such as responding to the decline in manufacturing, sharp divisions within city government diminished the likelihood of coalition building and alliance formation. Political battles, more than policy initiatives, seemed to dominate.

On the county government side the story was similar; political disagreements and partisan battles were commonplace between the incumbent judge/executive, Republican Mitch McConnell, and the three Democratic county commissioners. Although such disagreements did not preclude joint action, active leadership by the judge/executive, who was the only one of the four in a full-time position, was problematic. In addition, it was assumed by most that McConnell's main agenda was running for the U.S. Senate. In this regard his style was not an interventionist one; he was not likely to disrupt established interests in the community. Building an electoral coalition was not done by alienating area businesses, such as Brown & Williamson. And since Brown & Williamson was not asking for government assistance and was keeping its headquarters in Louisville, there was little demand for policy intervention.

In an apt summary of political leadership in both the county and the city, one academic observer remarked that "if it [the plant closing] is a non-issue, don't make an issue of it." There were no private-sector pressures — from labor, business, or general community groups — for a government response; it was not a major public issue. In this instance, Louisville politics operated in a manner akin to what Harvey Boulay describes in his study of Massachusetts cities as "risk avoidance."[48] Since there were no clear solutions to the closing and it had not yet been raised to the level of a political issue, there were more risks than benefits to challenging the existing adjustment process. Thus, government officials were an unlikely source to seek a change in the existing institutional arrangements.

The lack of mobilization and action on the part of government and labor leaders fitted well with the interest and actions of Brown & Williamson. In fact, it was B & W's goal to minimize political mobilization and alliance building. The company was not interested in mobilizing different groups in the community, nor was it interested in government action. From B & W's perspective the process of closing the plant was best kept as a private affair. This preference was clear in the problem definition that B & W established for the closing.

Problem Definition

Through its problem definition, Brown & Williamson assumed "ownership" of the closing. It established a standard of judgment to measure the problem, determined causal responsibility for the problem, and presented the strategy for remedial action. Each element of the problem definition reinforced the dominant role of the private sector as well as the lack of need for political action and mobilization.

The standard of judgment used by B & W was located squarely in the private sector. As the company noted at the time of the closing announcement, its primary concern was "to balance manufacturing capability with developing market requirements." In a private market economy, business success is judged by sales and corporate growth; those were the critical standards to define the problem. Based on such standards, B & W recognized that it had run aground. Its sales and market share had been slipping since 1974.

Causal responsibility for this problem was also placed in the private sector. Causation was attributed to changing market conditions that required a corporate response; the company could not be blamed for trying to expand in a competitive industry. The decision to build in Macon was a logical effort to expand markets by constructing an efficient facility to meet consumer demand. The subsequent slump in sales, and resulting overcapacity, forced the company to make hard choices about future use of its facilities. In the weighing of assets and liabilities, the Louisville plant came out on the bottom. The age of the facility and its outmoded production system made it the logical choice for closure; for the company to remain competitive, the plant would have to close. As one company official noted, "Long-term survival is the bottom line; that's the reality of a capitalistic system."[49] This was not a decision open to public discussion.

Having made the decision to close the plant, Brown & Williamson declared that the next "major concern as a company was to do the best we could for our people."[50] Outside mobilization was unneccessary; B & W assumed responsibility for remedial action to mitigate the effects of the closing. Workers would not be summarily dismissed and left to fend for themselves in the labor market. B & W would work with the company's labor unions to help determine the closing's consequences on the workforce and the community. The collective-bargaining relationship would suffice for guiding the adjustment process.

This problem definition left little space for political mobilization and government policymakers. Government was not cited as a cause of the closing, thus it had no obvious role in a solution. Government was not identified as the party responsible for assisting workers, thus it lacked status in the adjustment process. Brown & Williamson "owned" the problem definition; the company established both content and boundaries for the closing process.

This interpretation of the plant closing fit nicely with the prevailing economic and institutional environment. The emphasis on private responsibility for the adjustment process was compatible with the private dynamic that was leading the area's growth in service employment and downtown development. By most accounts the private market economy was working reasonably well, so the company's response to market cues represented a reasonable way to view the closing. At the institutional level, reliance on the collective-bargaining relationship to address adjustment issues reinforced the sense of private-sector responsibility. The fragmented and weak nature of existing public institutions was not of concern as long as the problem definition relied on the labor-management relationship.

Corporate Power in Louisville

Thus, Brown & Williamson was left in a position of considerable power. Unchallenged by labor and government leaders, the company's problem definition pointed to the private market economy as the key arena for the resolution of differences over the closing. And in this arena, B & W occupied a "privileged position" in the local economy. As Charles Lindblom and others argue, business control over the allocation of economic resources, whether through investment or disinvestment, provides a platform from which the corporation can guide the political economy. Clearly Brown & Williamson stood on that platform. The company's decision to close its manufacturing plant was a key disinvestment decision, while retaining corporate headquarters in Louisville represented continuation of an important investment in the community. In short, policymakers were captives of private economic decisions. The company did not have to lobby or pressure policymakers; its decisions became the premises for the policy process.

In the end, then, the "privileged position" of Brown & Williamson embodies the essential element in an explanation of this bystander response. This position was based on the role of the corporation in the economic accumulation process as well as the contractual labor-management relationship that dominated the institutional environment. While other factors, such as weak governmental institutions, contribute to our understanding, this was an adjustment process largely defined and dictated by the business firm.

CONSERVATIVE POLITICS AND PUBLIC POLICY

Conservative Politics and Louisville

The policy response in Louisville, with its emphasis on a privately negotiated adjustment process, captures the basic nature of conservative politics. In this form of politics the market serves as the descriptive and prescriptive image of political and economic society. As Alford and Friedland argue, "Conservative ideology holds that people make their own choices to participate in political and economic markets."[51] Participation motivated by self-interest provides the driving force in markets, while competition ensures that no single individual or group dominates the market. Conservative politics extends these exchange principals of self-interest and competition to political society. As Milton and Rose Friedman argue, "Voluntary exchange is a necessary condition for both prosperity and freedom."[52]

In its emphasis on markets, self-interest, and competition, conservative politics holds that the private sector is the primary arena for social interaction and resolution of differences. "A conservative society . . . perceives the private sector as the source of jobs, incomes, individual status, and achievement."[53] Managers, workers, and other privately defined actors are the key participants in conservative politics. According to Sam Bass Warner, "Under the American tradition, the first purpose of the citizen is the private search for wealth; the goal of a city is to be a community of private money makers."[54]

Although the private sector is on center stage, government does have a role in conservative politics. A primary concern of government is preservation of the basic rules of society that protect individuals from transgressions by others. This role encompasses a broad range of responsibilities that include protecting private property and administering a system of justice. In addition to this legal role, government provides the economic infrastructure not provided by private actors pursuing their self-interest. This provision of public goods and services is a legitimate responsibility of government. In addition, government has the responsibility to protect its citizens from foreign invasion.

While these government roles are important, they are limited in scope. In conservative politics government best serves its citizens by allowing private parties to pursue their self-interests. While certain infringements upon private actions are necessary to carry out prescribed public roles, such infringements should be kept to a minimum. As Todd Swanstrom notes in his analysis of conservative growth politics, "The public sector, at best, is a sideshow."[55] Limited government is the theme.

Conservative politics dominated the Brown & Williamson plant closing. Corporate self-interest was the driving force behind B & W's decision to close its manufacturing plant. Faced with competitive market pressures, the company concluded that closing the Louisville facility was the appropriate response. Self-interest was also driving the labor union as it negotiated the Settlement Agreement with the company. To preserve the international union while securing benefits for Louisville workers, the union sought a negotiated settlement. For both the corporation and labor union, the pursuit of self-interest was a private-sector phenomenon.

Government policymakers played their role, but it was a limited one. The federal government's housekeeping role consisted of general property laws that protected the right of the corporation to close the plant and federal labor-management laws that provided a legal structure for collective-bargaining negotiations. This legal role was important but did not involve government officials in the closing decision or negotiations over the effects of closing. Meanwhile, local officials remained bystanders to the adjustment process.

Privatism and Public Policy

In the world of conservative politics public policy facilitates a "tradition of privatism," in which private actions become the major forces shaping society. The essence of privatism lies "in its concentration upon the individual and the individual's search for wealth."[56] While government actions are not to be ignored, their primary purpose is to support this private "search for wealth."

From this perspective, then, analyzing the strategies and actions of private parties becomes as important for understanding local economic adjustment as does analyzing the actions of government policymakers. Several writers emphasize this theme. Mark Nadel, for example, argues that public policy is best understood, not by focusing on the actions of public organizations, but by considering the effects of both public and private actions. As Nadel states, a "public policy is any policy whose fundamental impact is a binding allocation of values for a significant segment of society." In this context, a policy may originate from either governmental or nongovernmental actors as long as it is "authoritative, binding and intentional."[57] Thus, the actions of a business corporation, such as polluting the air or, in this study, closing a plant, can have a binding impact on members of society and thus constitute a "public policy." Whether such actions are implicitly or explicitly sanctioned, Nadel argues that they represent a delegation of authority by government to private groups.

Philip Selznick offers a different argument but a similar conclusion. In Selznick's analysis the "tradition of privatism" is rooted in the nature of the law.[58] In the United States the legal order is drawn principally from the theory of contracts. Contract theory is based on a system of rules and authority designed around reciprocal obligations and the elimination of noncontractual arbitrary actions. Such a legal system offers a defined arena in which claims are argued and obligations enforced. Once this arena is established, the determination of outcomes and to a large degree the future shape of the arena are dependent primarily on the actions of private parties.

As an example of legal privatism, Selznick cites labor-management law. Selznick argues that labor-management law provides a legal system in which labor and management establish obligations that receive the sanction of government authority. As the U.S. Supreme Court noted in a 1960 case, "A collective bargaining agreement is an effort to erect a system of industrial self-government."[59] In this system of self-government private power shapes the outcome. Public policy provides general boundaries, but it also becomes a "resource labor and industry would appropriate and adapt to their own needs."[60] In such cases public purpose is subordinated to the private interests of labor and management.

Although Selznick and Nadel offer different arguments, their conclusions are similar regarding the importance of private actions. This theme of privatism complements the discussion by Bachrach and Baratz, Crenson, and others on decisions and nondecisions.[61] However, rather than argue that government policymakers are involved in nondecision making, as those authors do, privatism points directly to private decision-making as central to understanding policy experiences. Thus, a study of public policy in a conservative political setting must consider the private-sector dynamic as well as the boundaries and setting established by government policy.[62]

In the Louisville adjustment experience, privatism was apparent in the central role played by labor-management negotiations, Brown & Williamson holding the dominant position. By establishing the problem definition, the company established basic terms of discourse. Negotiations would take place, and the company would make concessions, but the terms of debate were clearly within boundaries acceptable to the firm. Brown & Williamson was the major beneficiary of privatism in the policy process.

The Limits of Privatism

In the tradition of privatism the quality of economic life experienced by most people is shaped by the interplay of private parties; that quality can vary. In the case of the B & W closing, privatism yielded a process and result that was acclaimed by many in the community. One representative of the B C & T International noted a "terrific sense of cooperation" between labor and management; "if there is a model way to close a plant... I think what happened at B & W certainly could act as a model."[63] In a similar vein, a company spokesman commented, "What could have resulted in sabotage, wildcat strikes or slowdowns became an orderly procedure, with loyal, however saddened, employees continuing to work regularly and diligently."[64]

However, there can also be a less positive side to privatism. In a number of plant closings that follow a bystander pattern, there is little discussion between labor and management, and workers receive few benefits when released from their jobs (see Chapter 7 for examples). As one observer of the tobacco industry commented, the Brown & Williamson experience was the exception rather that the rule.[65] If government officials decline to intervene when a business firm refuses to discuss either the closing decision or effects of the closing, workers and the community may be left without resources to begin the transition to new jobs and sources of growth. In such instances the interplay of private actors results in a less-than-desirable outcome.

In more general terms privatism diminishes possibilities for the resolution of problems that are not defined according to private interests. Policy proposals that are defended as a public purpose are disadvantaged in a conservative society that relies on self-interest and competition among private parties. Broader conceptions of community welfare and individual equality receive secondary status. As Selznick argues in his study of legal privatism, "Public policy serves as a resource and to some extent as a spur; it is something less, however, than an effective exercise of public will."[66] Expressions of public interest are subordinated to those of private actors.

Going one step further, the public interest may actually be redefined to accommodate the particular interests of private parties. In labor-management law, for example, efforts to alter the existing framework or broaden the scope of the law can be held captive to private interests. As Selznick concludes, "The law of employment, in remaining very much a 'private' law, has been little inspired by larger ideals of democracy and freedom."[67] In general, privatism threatens to "weaken the political community."

Providing a more central role for the "public will" calls for a more active government; a bystander role is insufficient if the goal is a public voice in the political economy. How local policymakers might step beyond a bystander role is the subject of the next case study in which a plant closing in Waterloo, Iowa, and the offset response of government officials are considered. However, before turning to Waterloo, the following update completes the Louisville story.

UPDATE

Brown & Williamson Industries

The closing of the Louisville production plant proceeded along the basic outline of the Settlement Agreement between the company and the labor unions. Layoffs in the workforce occurred gradually, and a variety of reemployment, education, and counseling services were offered to workers. Approximately 370 workers took advantage of transfer options and moved to the new Macon, Georgia, facility. In July 1982 production ended at the Louisville plant, leaving only 200 maintenance workers at the facility. Brown & Williamson attempted to sell the plant but was unsuccessful. In April 1986 the five-story, seven-building complex was demolished and converted into an open area adjacent to the company's remaining research building.[68]

In the years following the closing announcement, Brown & Williamson continued down the path of corporate restructuring. In January 1980 the parent of B & W, B.A.T. Industries in Great Britain, reorganized its U.S. operations into three divisions—tobacco, retail, and paper—under the corporate structure of Batus, Inc. In 1982 Batus became a holding company with Brown & Williamson the subsidary for the tobacco division. Tobacco sales by B & W rose slowly from a 1982 level of $2.13 billion to a 1986 level of $2.3 billion. Although B & W continued as the third-largest American tobacco manufacturer, its domestic market share slipped to 11.7 percent in 1986.[69]

The Louisville plant closing was not the last for the company. As part of its restructuring, B & W announced in December 1983 that the Petersburg, Virginia, plant would close. This plant, which employed approximately 5,000 workers in the mid-1970s, was similar in age to the Louisville facility. As in the Louisville closing, the company negotiated a Settlement Agreement with the unions that included severance pay, insurance continuation, early retirement benefits, counseling, educational benefits, and reemployment assistance. The company also provided over $100,000 to support a community task force that would consider redevelopment plans for the area. In addition, B & W donated warehouse facilities for the establishment of a small business incubator. As in the Louisville experience, the company received praise for its corporate responsibility in the closing process.[70] With the Petersburg plant closed, all tobacco production now takes place at the Macon, Georgia, plant.

Although Brown & Williamson was consolidating production operations in Georgia, the company kept its 1979 pledge to retain its corporate headquarters in Louisville. In fact, as noted earlier, B & W became one of the stars of downtown development. In November 1982 B & W paid over $33 million for one of the new twenty-six-story Galleria office-retail towers in downtown Louisville. In late 1983 the company moved its headquarters to the Galleria from older buildings adjacent to the now-idled production facility. This move added approximately 750 clerical and professional workers to the downtown area.[71]

Louisville, Kentucky

While Brown & Williamson was restructuring in an effort to remain competitive, Louisville and Jefferson County faced their own economic transition. The downward trend in manufacturing employment continued throughout the early 1980s. Between 1980 and 1984, manufacturing employment in Jefferson County dropped by 17 percent. While service sectors provided partial compensation, overall employment in the county declined during this period. By 1984 Jefferson County faced an unemployment rate of 8.3 percent.

This was a difficult transition period for Louisville. Closings of manufacturing plants continued to take their toll. International Harvester, for example, phased out its Louisville operations in the early 1980s. Once employing 6,500 workers, by 1983 most of Harvester's operations were closed, and workers were on layoff. Other closings in the early 1980s included an American Standard fittings plant with 430 employees and a Joseph Seagram's whiskey plant employing 550. In 1985 another cigarette manufacturing plant — Lorillard — closed. This company's move to North Carolina cost Louisville approximately 900 jobs.[72] The optimism of many public officials in 1979 was put to the test in the early 1980s.

One city official noted that regarding the policy response to these closings, contacts were often made with companies, but many of the closings were for various reasons beyond the control of local policymakers. In the International Harvester case, for example, the city agreed to seek $5 million in federal funds to assist a local group to purchase the plant, but the deal never materialized. Depending on one's perspective, blame was placed on the local labor unions or on Harvester's corporate headquarters. Failing to prevent plant closings, the primary policy response was to mitigate negative consequences of closings and identify reuse possibilities for closed facilities.

However, during the 1980s, Louisville and Jefferson County undertook a number of important steps to develop and improve economic policy capabilities. For example, in 1983 the state legislature authorized the creation of an enterprise zone in Louisville and Jefferson County. Covering 45.7 square miles, the zone provided a variety of financial (e.g., tax exemptions, building permit waivers) and nonfinancial (e.g., expedited review process, special assistance) incentives for business and industrial development. The use of industrial revenue bonds to assist new and existing businesses also blossomed. By June 1986 the city had issued over $185-million worth of such bonds.

As another step to build policy capabilities, the city and county ended their long-standing "battle" over the allocation of occupational license fee receipts (an important source of revenue for both governments). With state legislative approval, a Cooperative Compact was enacted in July 1986 that effectively froze for the next twelve years the existing proportion of occupational tax receipts received by the city and county. The effect was to end city-county competition for work sites (which provided the basis for occupational taxes) and stop city proposals to annex most of the unincorporated portions of the county.[73]

By ending competition for work sites, the Cooperative Compact also facilitated a formal consolidation of city and county economic development offices. In 1986 the Office of Economic Development was established with joint city and county funding to pursue a broad range of economic development activities in both Louisville and Jefferson County. By mid-1987 the office operated with approximately thirty-five staff members to provide business and economic development assistance. Business loans were combined with a business-retention program that included information assistance, site visitations, and regular "breakfast meetings" with members of the business community.

By 1987 Louisville and Jefferson County had made important strides in replacing the weak and fragmented economic development offices of 1979 with a more formidable array of policy tools and capabilities. The city was prepared for a more active role in economic development.

4

An "Offset" Response: Waterloo, Iowa, and the Rath Packing Company

In May 1978 the Rath Packing Company, the second-largest employer in Waterloo, Iowa, appeared on the brink of closing. Noting a quarterly loss of $2.1 million, the company sent a letter to its 2,500 employees asking for cooperation to overcome mounting financial difficulties. As the letter concluded, "Management and the Board of Directors are exploring all options, reviewing all operations, and pledge to you that it is determined to do all in its power to continue operations."[1] A second letter followed, specifying wage and benefit concessions needed to keep the company afloat. In its letter to employees the company displayed a spirit of optimism:

> We have made progress. We are projecting better times. We are producing a product respected across the country. For the future of the company and the security of all, I hope you will look at this proposal favorably.[2]

However, even with concessions from labor, long-term viability of the plant was uncertain. As the president of Rath was quoted in the local newspaper, "I must tell you that this is no permanent solution."[3]

Although starting as a labor-management issue, the problems at Rath quickly moved to the public agenda. News reports were carried over local media, and public officials entered the discussions. Unlike Louisville this was not to be a private affair. The editors of the *Waterloo Courier* commented, "This firm's long-time precarious financial condition has deteriorated to a crisis stage."[4] The editors concluded with a call for public support to address the problems at Rath.

Indeed, the stage was set for a policy response quite different from the Louisville experience. Rather than an adjustment process dominated by private decision-making, as in Louisville, public officials in Waterloo would play a key role in responding to the threatened plant closing. The entrepreneurial role of local government leaders would be instrumental in fashioning an assistance package to save Rath. This policy response, what I have called off-set, highlights a consensus-building process in which labor, management, and government play a part.

THE SETTING

The Political and Economic Terrain

The response to the possible closing of Rath was led by political leaders from the city of Waterloo and Black Hawk County. Waterloo, with a population of 75,000 in 1978, and Black Hawk County, with a population of 135,000, were the two major political jurisdictions in the area. While officials from nearby communities, such as Cedar Falls, expressed concern over the situation at Rath, the key political actors came from Waterloo and county government.

In Waterloo, nonpartisan politics was the formal rule. The mayor and the seven-member council met weekly to oversee the affairs of the city. The incumbent mayor, Leo Rooff, was a self-professed conservative who had been in office since 1974. In early 1978, plant closings and economic development concerns were not major agenda items for city officials. The local economy was relatively strong, and the focus of city government was on the basic concerns of transportation, public safety, and housing.

In Black Hawk County, partisan politics played a larger role. In fact, 1978 was an election year for two of the five members of the county board of supervisors. One of the supervisors on the ballot, Democrat Lynn Cutler, would play an instrumental role in the policy response to Rath. Since Black Hawk County did not have a county executive, the county board relied heavily on a consensus-building process. The primary concerns of county officials were similar to those in Waterloo—transportation and public welfare.

As for the local economy, Waterloo was located in the heart of America's breadbasket. In 1978 this agricultural base supported two major manufacturing industries in the area—farm implements, represented by Deere & Company, and meatpacking, represented by Rath. Deere & Company, with facilities at several sites in Waterloo and elsewhere in the county, was the largest employer in the area. With approximately 16,000 Deere workers, Waterloo was labeled by many a John Deere town. Rath Packing Company, the second-largest employer in the area, provided manufacturing employment as well as a market for local hog farmers. Rath's financial troubles in 1978 reflected not only conditions at the company but also difficult times in the meatpacking industry.

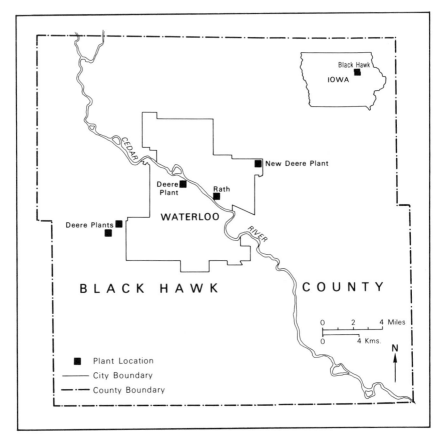

The American Meatpacking Industry

In the meatpacking industry Rath was not alone in its financial plight. The 1960s and 1970s were difficult years for many packers in this high-volume-low-margin industry.[5] Competitive pressures came from several sources. Consumer demand was one area of concern. For those packers, such as Rath, that operated primarily in the pork subsector, declining consumer demand was a significant problem. Since 1960 a decline in per capita consumption of pork products had accentuated competitive pressures in the industry. Even in beef products, per capita consumption was starting to decline after showing steady increases since 1960.[6]

Competitive pressures also came from new firms in the industry, particularly from the Iowa Beef Processors (IBP). Opening its first plant in Denison, Iowa, in 1961, within twenty years IBP surpassed Armour Food Company as the industry sales leader. During those years, IBP set new standards for the industry through low-cost boxed beef production, wage levels below the prevailing labor contracts of older packers, and new single-level plants that optimized an assembly line method. By the late 1970s IBP dominated the beef subsector and was poised to expand its role in pork products.[7]

In response to this competitive environment, a variety of strategies were pursued by different companies. As in the tobacco industry, diversification was one response. Wilson Foods, for example, expanded its line of sporting goods, and Armour invested in pharmaceuticals. In addition, many of the major packers became part of larger conglomerate operations. High-volume sales by meatpackers appealed to many conglomerate managers interested in showing a strong cash flow. Wilson, for example, was acquired by LTV, and Armour was purchased by Greyhound.

Another set of strategies involved specialization. For a number of firms this meant abandoning either the pork or beef subsector. In most cases this involved an older full-line meatpacker, such as Rath, reducing or terminating its beef operations as the least-cost response to IBP's command of beef markets. Another specialization strategy sought cost reductions by reducing or eliminating slaughtering operations. While historically many packers were involved in both slaughtering and meat processing, the higher value-added nature of processing led a number of packers to purchase slaughtered meat from outside suppliers while concentrating their own resources on processing operations.[8] Rath also moved in this direction.

This trend toward specialization, conglomerate acquisition, and increased competition resulted in a wave of plant closings. The older multi-level facilities, such as Rath's plant in Waterloo, were being replaced by single-story plants built to optimize an assembly line method of production. The number of meatpacking plants with 20 or more employees declined from 1,510 in 1967 to 1,280 in 1982.[9] Using a different data base, the major union in the industry reported a decline in the number of plants from 1,365 in 1969 to 960 ten years later.[10] It is in this context that we turn to Rath Packing Company.

Rath Packing Company

Founded in 1891 by E. F. and John Rath, the Rath Packing Company started in Waterloo as a $25,000 venture by the Rath family and seven other local businessmen.[11] By the mid-1920s Rath employed 1,900 workers and maintained one of the largest hog kill and processing operations in Iowa. Even during the Depression years Rath continued to thrive. In 1936 the company employed 3,000; by 1939 employment rose to 4,600. By 1940 the original buildings had been razed as the company modernized its operations. In the increasingly competitive industry, Rath established a regional and semi-national market for its "Black Hawk" label.[12]

In the 1950s Rath initiated a variety of expansion strategies as employment continued to rise. While the plant in Waterloo remained the primary facility, processing and distribution operations were established at plants in Texas, California, and Indiana. To meet rising demand, construction began on a new plant in nearby Columbus Junction, Iowa. By 1958 Rath employment hit 8,000, with 6,200 of those employees at the Waterloo operations. Rath was the ninth-largest meatpacker in the nation.[13]

However, the late 1950s were not good years for Rath. In 1957 earnings slipped to 0.5 cents on the sales dollar, compared to the record 1.37 cents in the previous year. While earnings volatility was not unusual in the industry, Rath's ledger sheet continued to show poor results in succeeding years. Other changes were afoot. In 1962 corporate restructuring removed the Rath family from an operating role in the company, and a major labor strike further eroded the company's position in 1964. To meet its financial needs, the company established in 1965 a new $20-million line of credit.[14] Following a $3.1 million loss in 1965, the company abandoned its remaining beef operations as a segment of the industry in which it was no longer competitive.

The financial plight of the company reached a critical stage in what some officials termed the dark days of 1967. Pressure by existing creditors led Rath to turn to a "factor" finance company, James Talcott Inc., to secure funds. Rath borrowed $14 million from Talcott at 6 percent above the prime interest rate.[15] Since continuation of this line of credit depended on inventories and accounts receivable, Rath management put increasing emphasis on short-term production goals rather than long-term capital needs.

In subsequent years Rath experienced several positive marks on the year-end balance sheet, but after 1971 the slide continued. In 1974, in an effort to broaden its base, Rath acquired Stark, Wetzel Inc., an Indiana meat processor; however, this addition provided little relief. In 1975 Rath losses totaled $5.9 million, and in 1976 the red ink hit $6.8 million.[16] These losses came despite agreements with the labor union to defer pension benefit contributions in both years.

When Talcott informed Rath that its line of credit might be reduced, the company sought other financial sources. In March 1976 Rath obtained a $6-million loan from a group of Waterloo financial institutions and a Pittsburgh bank. This loan was 90 percent guaranteed by the federal Economic Development Administration (EDA) and secured by mortgages on property and equipment at the Waterloo and Columbus Junction plants.[17] For local civic leaders Rath was important to the community. Said one bank president, "You don't want to see 2,000 workers lose their jobs. That would have been a disaster."[18]

However, Rath continued on a path toward "disaster." By 1978 the company could claim profits in only eight of the previous eighteen years and showed losses of approximately $18 million in the previous four years. As an indication of this decline, the debt-to-equity ratio for Rath had gone from 1.48 in 1973 to 7.83 in 1977. For the meatpacking industry as a whole the comparable figures were 0.91 and 0.78.[19] Furthermore, stockholders had not seen a dividend check since 1961. The 1976 loan provided a brief reprieve, but it was short-lived. In the first three months of 1978 the company recorded a loss of $2.1 million. Rath Packing Company had indeed reached a critical point.

SAVING RATH: AN OFFSET POLICY RESPONSE

By 1978 the precarious condition of Rath Packing Company was public knowledge. The letters sent in May from Rath management to the company's employees served as catalysts for public attention. As the editors of the *Waterloo Courier* noted, "Survival is now at stake and the partnership approach to this crisis is crucial."[20]

Mobilizing for Action

A "partnership approach" did indeed become central to the community response. While the union and management focused on company requests for labor cost reductions, public officials used an existing organization – the Black Hawk County Economic Development Committee (EDC) – to establish an alternative forum for discussion. Organized in 1972 to discuss local economic issues, the EDC was composed of area representatives from business, government, and labor. Although only an advisory body and a relatively minor organization, over the next year the EDC would play a central part in the community response.

Positioning the EDC to perform this role was Lynn Cutler, a Black Hawk County supervisor and chairperson of the EDC. At a May 12 meeting the Rath situation was discussed, and Cutler moved for formation of a Rath Study Subcommittee. This subcommittee – composed of twenty-one representatives from social services, the employment service, the chamber of commerce, congressional staffs, local government, and Rath management and labor – became the initital "economic action team" to formulate a response to the problems at Rath.

On May 23 and June 2 the subcommittee met to address the "crisis." As Cutler noted in a later congressional hearing, "We wanted to have disaster plans ready and also to assess the potential avenues of help."[21] One working group of the committee considered strategies in the event of Rath's closing, such as retraining and job search assistance, while another group focused on policies to keep the plant open. Of the two approaches, however, the emphasis was on keeping the plant open. As a subcommittee report stated, "The study committee approached the problem from the viewpoint that Rath Packing Company, with financial assistance, will continue in business."[22]

The subcommittee adopted both short- and long-term strategies. For the short-term, a deferral of payments on the 1976 EDA-guaranteed loan was critical. After negotiations with EDA and private lenders, this goal was accomplished. For the long-term, major capital improvements would be needed. To identify needs, Rath management presented a list of requisite capital and operating improvements with a price tag of $10.2 million. Discussion centered on identifying funding sources. As Cutler commented after one meeting, "What we did today was the first step to find out what local, state and federal resources are available toward that solution [of capital improvements]."[23]

A report by the EDC, released on June 6, presented the findings of the subcommittee.[24] Not only were capital and operating improvements outlined, but the consequences of a Rath closing were emphasized. As the second-largest employer in the county, Rath provided a $32-million payroll to 1,800 workers. The loss of this payroll would ripple through the economy, affecting other businesses as well as local governments.

Consensus was building around a common goal: find outside capital and reduce existing costs. In June, Lynn Cutler led a delegation to Washington D.C., seeking federal support and financial assistance. Contacts with elected officials were followed by discussions with representatives from the EDA and the Department of Housing and Urban Development (HUD). The favorable, if guarded, response was reflected in headlines in the *Waterloo Courier*— "White House commitment to Rath seen" and "Cautious hope for Rath, but it's only a beginning." While federal officials were supportive, they agreed that a study of the situation was needed. A technical assessment of Rath was a prerequisite to financial assistance.

Feasibility Study

The Development Planning and Research Associates of Manhattan, Kansas, with the assistance of Globe Engineering Company of Chicago, Illinois, conducted a feasibility study of Rath. Funded by a $60,000-EDA-technical-assistance grant, the study was initiated in July with a report due in late August. The study design focused not only on physical problems with the aging Rath plant but also on current management, marketing, and labor practices. On September 8 a summary of the report was released.[25] The full report, over 100 pages in length, contained confidential information on Rath and was presented to the EDC in November. Both documents outlined key problems at Rath and presented a series of alternative responses. Eight different steps were identified for inclusion in a response:[26]

1. Obtain short-term financing.
2. Restructure marketing and sales programs.
3. Restructure and reduce management staff.
4. Improve financial reporting and information systems.

5. Make plant modifications and necessary repairs.
6. Review labor practices and costs.
7. Obtain long-term financing.
8. Build and staff new facilities.

In each of these areas the study outlined possible changes. In marketing, for example, the study recommended that Rath adandon national efforts while focusing on regional markets and that the company adopt less expensive advertising strategies with a reduced number of products. In the area of labor practices, the study identified such policies as plantwide seniority and incentive pay as disruptive and costly for the firm's operations. At the management level the study recommended a restructuring of staff lines to eliminate "excessive centralization, insufficient delegation of authority, and an inadequate information system."[27]

In the short-term (next three years), implementation of these recommendations could, according to the study, improve Rath's financial position. Changes in plant and equipment, market and sales procedures, and management and labor practices could yield annual savings of $7–14 million in each of the next three years. "At the end of FY 1981, Rath would have only $2 million of debt, employ 1,700 people in the Waterloo facility, and have a net worth of nearly $30 million."[28] In the long-term, however, Rath's prognosis was quite different. Short-term changes could not overcome liabilities of the existing facility. As the report concluded:

In the longer-term, the Rath-Waterloo plant cannot be renovated to produce meat at economically competitive levels. In general, its age, construction characteristics and general layout, and its maintenance and operating costs are all critical and will likely lead to a plant closure in three to five years at best.[29]

The point was made—the seven-story facility was outmoded in an industry moving to single-story plants with new operating practices.

The study outlined three options that combined short-term assistance with construction of a new plant. Each option was dependent on the level of government support (see Table 4.1). Further, each option presented a different package for public and private participation. The high government-spending option called for construction of a slaughter-process plant with federal loans. While this option retained the largest number of employees, the report recognized that federal support at this funding level was unlikely. The moderate government-spending option involved a process-only plant with a lower level of government support, while the third option, low government spending, also called for a new process-only plant, but funding would come primarily through wage and benefit reductions accepted as part of an employee owner-

Table 4.1 Options for Rath

	High Government Spending	Moderate Government Spending	Low Government Spending
Operating Basis	Rath management	Rath management	employee ownership
New Plant Costs	$45.2 million	$26.2 million	$26.2 million
Employees Retained	1,050	500	?
Short-Term Government Funds	$6.5 million	$6.5 million	$6.5 million
Long-Term Government Funds	$45.2 million	$26.2 million	0
Total Government Funds	$51.7 million	$32.2 million	$6.5 million

ship plan. All three options called for short-term government funding to increase immediate production and make essential plant and equipment modifications. Futhermore, whichever option was followed, the study emphasized that success depended on a combined effort by labor, management, and government.

The release of the feasibility study was heralded as the blueprint for a community response. The *Waterloo Courier* carried a front-page article detailing the key recommendations of the study. The article — entitled "Timetable suggests new Rath plant in '81" — highlighted not only long-term options but also the need for $6.4 million in government support to make Rath viable in the short-term. The stage was set; a financial offset package was in the making.

An Offset Government Role

City, county and federal governments would play a part in this offset strategy. Based on the feasibility study, $6.5 million was the short-term financial target. However, arranging such a loan was not a simple task. As a first attempt Rath sought $3 million in loans from area lenders to be backed by a 90 percent EDA guarantee. Although this was a similar strategy to the 1976 loan, legal issues derailed the loan package; according to state law private lenders could not take a second position on a mortgage as collatoral for the loan. Without financial assistance, Rath laid off 360 workers in September and temporarily closed its Columbus Junction facility. Said Lynn Cutler, "We're back to the drawing board. I want people to understand we're not giving up."[30]

A second effort involved direct government financial assistance. As government officials concluded, "The usual sources of short term financing are unavailable due to the financial condition of the company."[31] At the urging of EDA officials the Black Hawk County EDC met on September 29 and initiated procedures to apply for an EDA Title IX grant. However, according to federal requirements the EDC had to be an incorporated organization to receive a grant. What followed was a whirlwind of political maneuvering. Within one week the EDC incorporated, elected Lynn Cutler president, and sent Cutler to Washington with a $3-million grant application. A special "crisis" team at EDA approved the application on October 11, Cutler returned to Washington to accept the check, and a $2.98-million loan was made to Rath on October 16.[32] In just over two weeks the EDC had incorporated, applied for, received, and disbursed federal funds to assist Rath.

The ninety-day loan at 6-percent interest was to help the company increase production during the upcoming holiday season. As the EDA application noted, "The company's financier had placed limitations on the amount of borrowing Rath may receive from them. This limit does not allow for the company to increase production for the profitable holiday season."[33] In January 1979 Rath was given the first of a series of thirty-day extensions on the loan.

At the same time that the county EDC was seeking funds, the city of Waterloo began the application process for an Urban Development Action Grant from the Department of Housing and Urban Development. On October 2 the city council approved a $4.6 million application that was then forwarded to HUD. The application provided a list of machinery purchases and plant modifications designed to help Rath through the next three years. However, unlike the EDA grant, officials at HUD required assurances of private-sector participation before the grant would be awarded. Said one HUD official, "The primary thing we'll be looking at is what the private sector is willing to do. We won't make grants if the situation is helpless."[34] Initial efforts focused on seeking an outside party to purchase Rath and thereby provide financial support. When the most likely prospect declined, attention turn to both workers and management to provide private leverage.

For their part, workers would purchase 1.8 million shares of Rath stock (constituting 60 percent of the stock) and defer for three years cost of living adjustments as well as various benefits and wage increases. In turn, Rath management agreed to make a variety of changes in advertising, marketing, inventory purchases, and other plant improvements.[35] Putting this package together, particularly the employee stock purchase plan, was a difficult and time-consuming process. Although tentative approval was given by HUD officials in July 1979, the award was not made until October 1980.[36] From the $4.6-million grant, the city loaned Rath $4.56 million for ten years at an interest rate that varied between 3 and 6 percent over the course of the loan. The city's Community Development Board and the county's EDC would be responsible for monitoring the loan.

Throughout 1979 and into 1980, community efforts continued in an effort to keep Rath open. In mid-1979 the EDC completed a long-range plan for Rath that incorporated the feasibility study recommendations into a timetable for monitoring Rath's progress. On the financial side the EDA loan was renewed every thirty days and extended into a three-year loan in July 1980. Throughout this period compromise and collective effort constituted the theme. As the mayor of Waterloo commented after the initial approval of the city's grant application, "Approval of the grant is a culmination of the cooperative efforts of many people and organizations."[37]

Although Rath's troubles were far from over, the company did show signs of improvement. In August 1979 Rath reported its first quarterly profit in years; for the fiscal year ending September 27, 1980, Rath recorded earnings of over $2 million.[38] Other changes were also taking place. Reflecting the new corporate identity, Rath's ownership and management structures were altered with the assistance of outside consultants from Cornell Univeristy. A three-tier management system was instituted to increase employee participation in the operation of the firm. In addition, when the employee stock ownership plan was put into place, the union selected ten directors for the expanded sixteen-member board of directors. An offset strategy that included government, labor, and management was in place to address the problems at Rath.

POLICYMAKING IN WATERLOO:
POLITICAL ENTREPRENEURS AND PLANT CLOSINGS

Clearly the policy response that unfolded in Waterloo was quite different from the Louisville experience; these were very different political experiences involving equally different policy responses. In accounting for these differences the most obvious contrast is in the stated positions of each company. In Louisville, Brown & Williamson was determined to close the plant and was not interested in public assistance; in Waterloo, Rath was trying to avert a closing and was seeking support from labor or any other receptive party. Although these differences are central in an explanation of each experience, they do not tell the entire story. A closer look is needed at the economic and institutional setting as well as the politicial dynamic. For that we turn to the levels of analysis.

The Waterloo Economy

As in Louisville the nature of the local economy set the stage for the policy response. Also as in Louisville the Waterloo economy was relatively strong. In 1978 unemployment in Black Hawk County was 4.8 percent, only slightly above the 4.4 percent level of the previous year. In addition, the labor force was slowly expanding, from a 1976 average of 48,200 workers to 52,600 in January 1978.[39] Although manufacturing employment had leveled off, increases in service and trade sectors provided compensation. As in Louisville an argument could be made that the overall economy was strong.

The strength of the local economy was closely identified with the major employer in the county — Deere & Company. Headquartered in Moline, Illinois, Deere & Company was one of the largest farm implement manufacturers in the United States. In 1979 Deere employed approximately 16,000 workers at its Waterloo facilities, infusing a $400-million payroll into the local economy. By 1979 one in every four workers in Black Hawk County was employed by Deere.

The contrast between the economic fortunes of Deere and Rath was quite vivid. In 1978 and 1979, as the Rath situation was reaching its crisis point, Deere was building and expanding. In the previous twenty years Deere had built several new facilities in Waterloo. In 1956 a Product Engineering Center was constructed, and in 1975 a new engine-works plant opened. Between 1975 and 1978 investment in Waterloo continued as part of Deere's $550-million local capital investment plan. As part of this plan, not only were existing operations expanded and upgraded, but Deere also began construction of a new tractor assembly plant that would be a state-of-the-art facility by the time of its scheduled opening in 1981.[40]

Local policymakers could look with pride upon this growth. Deere & Company had record earnings that translated into growth and prosperity for the Waterloo economy. In January 1978 the mayor of Waterloo cited expansion at Deere facilities as a key component in the health of the local economy. As one Deere official noted at a local banquet, "Waterloo has our largest factory, and since I see nothing but a bright future for Deere & Company, I can see nothing but a bright future for Waterloo."[41]

From a policy perspective the experience of Deere reinforced an abiding faith in the potential of the free market and the appropriateness of a hands-off policy approach. The growth at Deere had come through private investment with minimal government assistance; the company shunned government aid programs. Even in later years, when the company was laying off workers, an official commented that "Deere is strong enough to weather the storm without government assistance."

While Deere offered an example from the growth side of the economy, Rath exemplified the potential for decline. Beginning with the letters mailed to Rath employees in May 1978, the likely consequences of a Rath closing received considerable public attention because of its importance to the local economic base. Government reports and grant applications laid out the economic costs to the community. Consequences were measured in terms of losses to the private economy as well as losses in tax revenues to local governments. As for the private economy, employment at Rath represented approximately 4 percent of county employment. According to calculations by the Waterloo Chamber of Commerce, the loss of approximately 1,900 jobs at Rath could ultimately affect 10,500 jobs in the community.[42] Depending on multiplier effects and time lags, estimates of county unemployment after a Rath closing ranged from 8 to 15 percent.[43] In addition to job losses, $32 million in annual payroll would be lost to the community as well as $40 million in Rath livestock purchases from local farmers and ranchers.[44]

The effect on local governments would also be significant. In local property taxes Rath paid $545,000 to the city of Waterloo, a figure representing 5.7 percent of city property taxes and 3.5 percent of own-source city general revenues. In addition, Rath's annual sewerage fee of $180,000 was the largest single fee in support of the city's waste treatment system.[45] The closing of Rath would also put a major burden on government social and training services. With an average age of fifty-two, Rath employees would probably face a difficult transition to new employment or early retirement.

Viewed from this perspective the closing of Rath was a source of significant concern for local policymakers. The condition of the private economy as well as continuity of government revenues were at risk if Rath closed. The EDA grant application emphasized this point:

> The "do nothing" alternative is not a cost-effective strategy. This alternative will result in the immediate loss of jobs and will likely result in the Company's closure within a short time. The "do-nothing" alternative results in higher social costs to the community and in high costs for unemployment assistance and retraining programs.[46]

The implication was clear, policymakers needed to organize an assistance package to help Rath. As the mayor emphasized, the consequences of losing Rath were simply too great; the "good of the community" was the determining factor.

Thus, as in Louisville, the local economy provided two rather different points of orientation. On the one hand, Rath was caught in a downward spiral with the likelihood of significant negative consequences for the community. Whether Rath could rebound on its own seemed doubtful. A public assistance package could be deemed appropriate, indeed essential. Alternatively, policymakers could point to a relatively strong economy, symbolized by Deere & Company, that required little from government. From this perspective the troubles at Rath were unfortunate, but they were part of the economic process in a private enterprise economy. As the executive vice president at the Waterloo Chamber of Commerce commented, "Maybe things will begin to break right and Rath will succeed. But our community could survive and live with a Rath failure."[47] The solution lay in the creative potential of private enterprise to readjust within a market economy.

The result was a draw—two points of orientation with quite different policy implications. While this economic setting provided the stage for policymaking, it did not determine a policy response. Which path would be followed was unclear. We must turn to the institutional level and political mobilization to complete the picture of an offset response.

Institutional System

While the process of economic accumulation set the framework, institutions in both the private and public sectors provided the immediate tools and terrain for a policy response. In Waterloo this setting provided both opportunities and obstacles to mobilization efforts and different policy strategies.

In the private sector the collective-bargaining contract provided the ground rules for the relationship between Rath management and the workforce. As with Brown & Williamson in Louisville, Rath had been a unionized company for many years. The United Food and Commercial Workers International

Union (UFCW) represented production workers at the plant and had recently negotiated a contract with the company. As in most collective-bargaining contracts, the Rath-UFCW contract covered pay scales, working conditions, and a variety of other labor-management issues. The rules and procedures embodied in the union contract set the basic content and tone of labor-management relations. And during the years of Rath's economic decline, these relations had become increasingly antagonistic as Rath workers made various concessions. For example, in the mid-1960s Rath workers made nonwage concessions to assist the company, and between 1975 and 1978 the union agreed to defer the company's required pension and retirement contributions. All of these concessions were intended to make additional operating capital available.[48] When workers received letters from management in May 1978 outlining problems at the plant, the theme was familiar. The company asked for a delay in cost-of-living adjustments, a three-month temporary cut in pay, and a one-week waiver of vacation time.[49]

This general pattern of interaction was not unlike that which took place in Louisville. Although Brown & Williamson and the tobacco workers did not operate from a history of wage and benefit concessions, they were firmly entrenched in a collective-bargaining framework dominated by wage and benefit discussions. Similarly, Rath and the UFCW were locked into a relationship measured by the financial yardstick of wages and benefits. While such issues were certainly important, they limited the nature of discussions between labor and management. Other issues relevant to the company's survival, such as product pricing and management structure, were not on the agenda created by this institutional setting. Thus, the collective-bargaining framework provided a rather limited and circumscribed setting for discussions of a possible plant closing.

The institutional role played by Rath Packing Company was shaped in part by the local identity of the company. Although Rath had facilities elsewhere in Iowa and other parts of the United States, most of the assets and workforce of the company were located in Waterloo, as was the corporate headquarters. Rath had a long history in Waterloo as an important component of the local economic base. In institutional terms this meant that corporate decision-making at Rath was undertaken primarily by individuals who lived in the community and within a corporate structure that recognized the Rath facility as the primary asset of the company. While this setting did not predetermine the outcome of corporate decision-making, it did make the company more open to local influences and pressures.

However, Rath's organizational abilities were significantly compromised by its lack of financial resources. Unlike Brown & Williamson in Louisville, Rath lacked its key organizational asset — investment. As Roger Friedland, Charles Lindbolm, and others argue, control over investment is the major power resource for a corporation. Whereas Brown & Williamson still controlled its investment strategies (witness the new plant in Macon, Georgia, and retention of headquarters in Louisville), Rath's control was significantly diminished.

The financial demise of Rath was recorded earlier in this chapter. For over fifteen years the company had faced financial insecurity and mounting operating losses. Reliance on factor financing (Talcott, Inc.) put constant pressure on the firm to realize short-term gains, to the detriment of long-term capital improvements. Facing possible backruptcy, by 1976 Rath turned to the federal government to assist in maintaining an investment level necessary for ongoing operations. With its privileged position in the local economy faltering, the company was in a weak institutional position to actively participate in the policy process.

On the public-sector side the institutional environment contained a variety of constraints and opportunities that affected the policy process. In terms of constraints, the city of Waterloo and Black Hawk County had few policy tools and limited staff expertise in the area of plant closings and business retention. Even more than in Louisville, city and county policymakers had little to draw from. There was no ongoing business loan program, nor was there a separate economic development office in the city or county.

The major tools for economic development that existed in 1978 included tax incremental financing and industrial revenue bonds. A tax incremental finance district in downtown Waterloo had been in existence for four years, and the city was initiating an industrial revenue bond program.[50] However, neither were likely candidates for a response to a plant closing. A tax incremental district was based on the need for public infrastructure improvements, which was not applicable to the problems at Rath, and the revenue bond program was just beginning, with the first bond issued in February 1978 for improvements at a hospital. Issuing a revenue bond for Rath was unlikely. As one Waterloo City Council member recalled, the first bond proposal in 1977 was turned down by the council because it would give an unfair competitive advantage to a private company. A similar argument could be made in a debate over a revenue bond for Rath.

Staff expertise was also limited. Black Hawk County supervisors were part-time officials with limited staff assistance, and the county did not have a separate economic development office. In Waterloo, city council members were also part-time, and the mayor had only limited staff available for this type of activity. The primary economic development unit within the city was the Community Development Board. Created in 1959 as the Urban Renewal Board, the board served as the city's recipient agency for federal funds. In this capacity the board and its staff worked in the area of housing rehabilitation, urban renewal, flood control, transportation development, and industrial development. However, the board had no experience in the area of plant closings.

While these institutional constraints were significant, they were not insurmountable. As local officials argued, with federal assistance they could play a role in preventing the shutdown of Rath. For example, in the UDAG application filed in October 1978, city officials emphasized their experience with federal funds and general economic development — community-development block grants, urban renewal projects, and the downtown tax incremental district. In addition, the city noted the recent federal approval of a UDAG for a downtown project. The $3.3-million grant was leveraged with $15 million in private funds for improvements in a downtown bank and hotel district. Although not involving a plant closing, this experience was given as evidence of the city's economic policy capabilities.

The policy process was also shaped by the institutional environment at the federal level. In the case of the UDAG used to assist Rath, this was particularly true. Consistent with the Department of Housing and Urban Development's standards, officials at HUD would not approve a grant to the city until a private match for the city's loan to Rath was assured. This matching requirement proved to be a major stumbling block for the local response. Local policymakers spent several months unsuccessfully seeking a private party to purchase Rath, followed by over a year spent designing an employee stock ownership plan that would provide wage deferrals as the private match.

The employee ownership strategy faced another institutional hurdle when the federal Department of Labor refused to approve the first plan. The Department of Labor treated the proposal as a pension plan and refused to waive requirements that limited a plan's holding of company stock.[51] To meet these requirements the plan was redrafted by the union and finally approved in mid-1980 by the Department of Labor. Again administrative procedures in the institutional environment proved critical in shaping the policy response.

Although these constraints were important, there were also important opportunities in the institutional setting. Perhaps the most important was the generally cooperative relationship between the city of Waterloo and Black Hawk County. Unlike the fragmentation of government units in Louisville that handicapped collective policymaking, Waterloo and Black Hawk County officials faced the possible closing of Rath without jurisdictional conflicts based on tax revenues and political responsibilities. Although the Rath plant was within the city limits, tax revenues were shared by both the city and county. Officials at both levels of government recognized the plant as important to their policy concerns. In fact, the primary government unit involved in the offset response — the county Economic Development Committee — was composed of officials from both city and county government as well as other municipalities in the area and the private sector. The EDC represented a political bridge across governmental subdivisions; it served as a forum to join the resources of government units throughout Black Hawk County. Even though the EDC was an advisory body with few resources, it provided a potentially important forum or platform for policymaking. To note a contrast, in Louisville, at the time of the Brown & Williamson closing, the city and county operated separate economic development units that often competed with one another.

Thus, the institutional environment in Waterloo, whether in the public or private sector, helped shape the possibilities for a response to the problems at Rath. The collective-bargaining contract, for example, limited early discussions between Rath and its workers to wages, benefits, and work rules, while the county Economic Development Committee represented a forum for much broader discussions. The ultimate effect of this institutional setting can not be fully assessed without examining the political dynamic in the Waterloo community. For that, we turn to alliance formation and mobilization as the third level of analysis.

Political Alliance Formation and Mobilization

Whereas the circumstances surrounding the Brown & Williamson closing were characterized by a lack of mobilization, in Waterloo the story was quite different. Here, alliance formation and mobilization played a central role in the local response. In particular, the mobilization of local and federal resources by government leaders proved critical. Facilitating this effort was a problem definition, established primarily by the feasibility study, that called for community mobilization. However, before turning to this mobilization effort by government, a brief assessment is needed of efforts in the private sector.

In general neither labor nor management were in a position to mobilize political and economic resources during the early stages of the community response. As indicated in the previous section, labor and management operated from a collective-bargaining relationship that tied discussions to wage and benefit concessions sought by management. Given this institutional setting, the union's mobilization strategies emphasized resistance to concessionary demands. In response to the May 1978 letter asking for concessions, the union balked. As the president of the union local commented, "We look at it [concession demands] as a strong-armed tactic — one of using community fear and pressure on the people to cover up for their failures."[52] From the union's perspective, wage cuts were not the solution. Rather, the company needed a long-term plan that included financing and changes in management, not temporary concessions from labor that treated only the symptoms.

However, the bargaining table was not conducive to such discussions, and the union leadership was skeptical of the Economic Development Committee. The union representative on the EDC subcommittee described the body as a "pressure group to get the union to agree to concessions." The union did support applications for federal grants, but the EDC was a political arena foreign to the union's collective-bargaining instincts. Thus, during 1978 and early 1979 the union's mobilization efforts continued to be focused on resistance to wage and benefit cuts.[53]

On the side of management Rath's ability to mobilize political and economic resources was greatly diminished owing to its financial condition. As noted earlier, Rath's ability to act was compromised by its lack of investment resources. Still, while Rath was crippled as an economic actor, it was not powerless. From the outset Rath's cooperation with government and labor was important. Rath accepted government assistance and participated in the work of the EDC. Had this cooperation not been forthcoming, the policy response might have taken a quite different path. In this sense Rath still played a major role. However, there were few options left to the company; it had become a follower rather than a leader in the policy process. Thus, even when Rath management disagreed with findings and recommendations in the feasibility study, it was reluctant to voice such concerns. As one company official noted, we "had to be supportive," since all the politicians were using the feasibility study as the framework for government assistance. The company was not in a position to lead the adjustment process.

Beyond Rath management and the union, there were a limited number of other groups or organizations on the private side of the political economy that were capable of helping with political and economic resources. One candidate was the Waterloo Chamber of Commerce and its financial arm, the Waterloo Industrial Development Authority (WIDA). In fact, in 1976 the chamber and WIDA supported Rath's application for the EDA-guaranteed loan. Not only did the Chamber and WIDA assist Rath in arranging a consortium of local lenders, but WIDA guaranteed the 10 percent of the loan not covered by the federal government.

However, by 1978 the local business community was less receptive to efforts to save Rath. To many on the chamber the 1976 loan was legitimate "assistance," but now, in 1978, Rath was involved in a bailout. Philosophical opposition to government bailouts, political "turf problems" with Democratic County Supervisor Lynn Cutler, and the limited resources of WIDA combined to diminish the chamber and WIDA's active role. Mobilization of resources would not come from this organization.

The critical role of bringing key actors and resources together in Waterloo was performed by local government leaders. However, to perform this role they needed a guide; they needed an assessment of the problems at Rath that would support a mobilization strategy. The feasibility study provided just such an assessment.

Problem Definition

The feasibility study established a definition of the plant closing that proved critical; the study was, as one local official commented, a "keystone" element in the community's response. The engineers, economists, and business management experts who conducted the study assumed ownership of the problem definition. They established a standard of judgment, specified causal responsibility, and presented options for remedial action. Most important, the study provided a critical context for the mobilization of resources needed to save Rath.

According to the feasibility analysis the standard of judgment was clear: Could Rath survive in a competitive market economy? Rath's operating structure, costs, and physical plant were compared to others in the industry. The bottom line was production efficiency and profit potential. Success would come only if Rath faced its competitors with a viable, cost-efficient production strategy. Thus, any mobilization efforts required a close working relationship with Rath.

Based on this standard of judgment, causal responsibility was attributed to both labor and management as well as to the nature of the physical plant. As noted earlier, labor practices such as plantwide seniority were criticized as disruptive and costly for the firm's operations. On management's side a variety of business decisions, such as poor pricing practices, were added to the list of causal factors. Indeed, in assessing Rath's operations the study noted that "Rath's management lacks either the sophistication or the desire for so competitive a business."[54] And finally, the physical plant itself was no longer efficient for competing in the industry. Observed one of the consultants in a preliminary assessment of the plant, "The buildings here have little value, except sentimental."[55]

Given this broad causal interpretation the feasibility study specified a course for remedial action that touched each area — restructuring management practices, altering labor costs, and building new facilities. As noted in Table 4.1 three options were presented to avert a plant closing. From short-term financing to constructing a new plant, the feasibility study offered a menu for policy discussions. Furthermore, the study emphasized the importance of cooperative action to address the problems at Rath:

> The solution to Rath's problems will be difficult. It will require the combined efforts of management, the employees, the community, and the federal government. Though it will not be easy, with a concerted effort over the next few years, recovery is possible; however, if any one of the four groups refuses to cooperate in the overall plan, the result will severely impact the Waterloo community.[56]

Clearly, mobilization of key resources and actors was the critical task facing the Waterloo community.

This problem definition received wide support because it offered a frame of reference that fit within the existing economic and institutional environment. For example, the conclusions of the feasibility study were generally compatible with existing economic conditions. The study did note the potential economic consequences of a Rath closing, but it did not provide a broad-based critique of capitalism, which would have been out-of-place given the expansion at Deere and general strength of the local economy. Furthermore, in the area of institutions, the study highlighted problems at Rath, particularly in management practices and the condition of the facility, that were generally accepted in the broader community. This definition also recognized the availability of government resources, particularly at the federal level, to address the problems at Rath. Perhaps most important, in the area of mobilization, this definition recognized the presence of many factions in the community — labor, management, government — that were interested in helping Rath. Joining these groups in a collective response was posed as the challenge for political mobilization.

Political Leadership in Waterloo

To build upon this problem definition became the strategy of local government officials, and the feasibility study quickly became the guide. Two individuals were candidates for wearing the mantle of leadership — Leo Rooff, the mayor of Waterloo, and Lynn Cutler, county supervisor. Neither faced the institutional obstacles evident in Louisville. First, there were no legal restrictions on reelection. Leo Rooff was in his third two-year term as mayor, and Lynn Cutler was making a reelection bid for a second four-year term on the county board. In addition, also unlike Louisville, neither official was embroiled in a major legal or political controversy with their peers. While partisan differences existed, Waterloo was not the site of impeachment inquiries. This was fertile ground for political leadership.

Leo Rooff was a well-known local civic and political leader. Twice elected to the county board in the 1960s, Rooff resigned in 1973 to move into the mayor's office. In a reputational survey of local elites, Mayor Rooff ranked third in the voting, behind the manager of the Deere Works and the president of the local broadcasting company. Describing himself as a conservative Republican, Rooff was active in local civic groups — Elks, Masons, Kiwanis, and the Chamber of Commerce.[57]

Rooff's political philosophy was rooted in a tradition of limited government. In an interview with the *Waterloo Courier,* Rooff took pride in his administration's ability to contain government growth. He commented that the primary responsibility for city government was to provide a "safe, sanitary and healthy place to live . . . to give people the most out of government at the least possible cost."[58] A limited government was one that did not hinder the workings of a private market economy. Said Rooff in a later interview, "Government ought to keep its nose out of private enterprise."

Given this conservative orientation, Mayor Rooff faced a dilemma when the future of Rath appeared to be on the line. Philosophically he was opposed to government intervention, but the consequences of a closing for the community required second thought. As he admitted in an interview in early 1979, "Although this [UDAG] is in opposition to my personal philosophy, it's in the best interests of the community to keep Rath going."[59] At city council meetings and other public forums the mayor defended his support for government assistance as the least-cost strategy to protect the community and encourage private investment. After the council voted to seek a UDAG, he remarked, "Whichever costs less to government is certainly the way to go."[60]

Although the mayor played an important part in Waterloo's offset response, he did not assume the key role. A continuing ambivalence toward government assistance compromised a leadership position. Although he says he was the "first one to lead the pack to get that grant," his support appeared less entrepreneurial than he would have us believe. The driving force for the policy response lay elsewhere.

By most accounts Lynn Cutler provided the critical ingredient in the offset response. In 1978 Cutler transformed the county Economic Development Committee from a weak advisory body to the primary stage for policy discussions and action. Under Cutler's leadership the EDC divided into subcommittees, hired its own staff, and over a period of two weeks legally incorporated as well as applied for and received a $3-million federal grant. In addition, Cutler used her political contacts to smooth the way for federal grants. Democratic party contacts in the White House as well as the legislative branch proved critical. Said one city council member, "Lynn obtained that [EDA] grant for Rath single-handedly." In classic fashion, Cutler was the political entrepreneur. Guided by the problem definition from the feasibility study, she mobilized local and federal government resources to achieve an outcome that would benefit the community as well as her own political future.

Cutler's interest in politics, both locally and nationally, was well established. A list of her civic and political affiliations covered considerable ground — United Way, Chamber of Commerce, County Board of Social Services, County Council on Aging, League of Women Voters, NAACP, and the local Democratic party.[61] Outside the Waterloo community Cutler served on the Advisory Commission on Intergovernmental Relations and the National Association of Counties while also attending various national Democratic party functions. Her electoral career began with a position on the county board of supervisors in 1974 and included a period as chairperson of the board in 1975 and 1976. By 1978 a survey of local influentials ranked Cutler tenth in the Waterloo community.[62]

Government assistance to save Rath fit the pattern of Cutler's political affiliations and orientation. From Cutler's perspective, government should serve an active and positive role to improve the welfare of the community. This orientation extended particularly to minorities and others disadvantaged in political and economic affairs. Cutler's political philosophy provided considerably more room than that of Mayor Rooff for an active government policy. As she later recalled, her reaction to the possible closing of Rath was, "Why don't we fight it!" Preventing the closure of Rath or minimizing a closing's consequences on the community called for political leadership and active government intervention that well suited Lynn Cutler's view of public policy. In addition, the leadership role Cutler assumed complemented her national political connections as well as electoral agenda. With Democratic party contacts in both the Carter White House and key executive agencies, Cutler served as the lead representative in Waterloo for the federal assistance effort. As Leo Rooff noted in frustration, he received much of his information on federal activities regarding the UDAG through Cutler rather than direct contacts. Newspaper articles that followed the federal role typically recounted federal action through reports Cutler made.

The "electoral impulse" was also important for Cutler. On June 6, shortly after the Rath Study Subcommittee was formed, Cutler was renominated in the Democratic primary for the county board of supervisors. In the November general election she was the top vote-getter in winning her second four-year term. The interest in electoral office continued. In 1980 and 1982 Cutler ran against Republican Cooper Evans for Iowa's Third District seat in the U.S. House of Representatives. Although Cutler fared well among voters in Black Hawk County, she received less support in outlying areas and lost both elections. Shortly after the 1982 loss Cutler left Waterloo and moved to Washington D.C., where she continued her involvement in the Democratic party.

Lynn Cutler's role as political entrepreneur did not come without friction. Throughout much of the 1978–79 period there was an underlying tension between Cutler and Rooff over respective roles in the policy response. For example, when the city's UDAG application was initially approved in 1979, Cutler argued that the county Economic Development Committee should have responsibility for monitoring the loan. Leo Rooff objected and insisted that the grant go through the city's Community Development Board. After a period of debate a compromise was struck that included both agencies. This competition between the two political leaders was captured by a *Waterloo Courier* cartoon that pictured two annoyed Santa Clauses ringing bells and holding contribution kettles with the same inscription on each kettle — "WE want to help Rath."[63]

Not only was Cutler's leadership role built upon her political contacts and political philosophy, but it also benefited from interest and support generated during an election year. As a local labor leader commented, "Had it not been a political election year, I don't think it [government efforts to save the plant] would have happened." While perhaps exaggerating the importance of the electoral impulse, this comment does reveal an important element in the response. Cutler was standing for reelection, as was fellow Democrat Dick Clark, a first-term U.S. senator from Iowa. Supporting Clark's reelection was near the top of the list at the Carter White House. A local initiative from Iowa, such as the Rath proposal to the EDA, was likely to receive prompt and favorable consideration in these circumstances. Thus, Cutler's mobilization efforts benefited not only from her own contacts and interests but also from the timing of an election year.

In summary, political alliance formation and mobilization played a critical role in this policy reponse. The inability of management and labor to address the problems at the company provided considerable space for political leadership. Lynn Cutler quickly filled that space. Using the problem definition established by the feasibility study, Cutler pointed to the possible economic consequences of a Rath closing and took advantage of flexibility in the institutional environment to assemble an assistance package designed to keep Rath open. In rebuilding the Economic Development Committee, Cutler engineered what might be called an entrepreneurial leap — "an act that either creates or elaborates an organization in unforeseen ways such that major existing allocation patterns of scarce public resources are ultimately altered."[64]

LIBERAL POLITICS AND PUBLIC POLICY

Liberal Politics and Waterloo

The policy response in Waterloo exemplifies the essence of liberal politics. The government assistance package to save jobs at Rath was based on the liberal goal of supporting actions that would overcome political and economic barriers restricting opportunities for individual betterment. As one student of liberal politics notes, "Economic and political arrangements, whatever their specific form and nature, must offer individuals both the opportunity and the incentive to make their own choices and to develop themselves freely and fully."[65] A plant closing can represent a restriction of these opportunities and choices.

In liberal politics public debate and government action are acceptable mechanisms for ensuring individual opportunities. Unlike the conservative's distrust and suspicion of public solutions, the liberal recognizes public discourse and government action as appropriate and often necessary for securing individual freedom and general community welfare. Social, economic, and political impediments to individual self-determination should be minimized. Positive government action serves to overcome impediments and promote both individual freedom and the common good.

In the economic realm a liberal society aims to improve access to and production from a market economy. As Alford and Friedland note, "Liberal politics assumes that the market can be made to work more democratically and hence more efficiently."[66] Government has a legitimate role to facilitate and promote greater democracy and efficiency in private markets. Importantly, government actions are intended to support markets, not replace them. Liberal politics is not a debate over a command economy; it is a debate over the different ways government can identify and rectify market problems.

The Waterloo experience described in this chapter was premised on a liberal faith in positive government action and public debate. The possible closing of Rath Packing Company represented an impediment to the realization of worker, manager, and community welfare. While support for government action may have waned at times among certain parties, the overall theme was one of acceptance and reliance on public policy to address problems facing the community. This policy approach to the problems at Rath was structured around a community dialogue through the Rath Study Subcommittee and the Economic Development Committee. Participation by labor, management, government, and others in the community provided a forum for public discussion and debate. Maintaining the economic welfare of the community was a public as well as private responsibility.

Public Policy as Consensus Building

In liberal politics public policy is dominated by consensus-building strategies. Instead of emphasizing private actions, policy formation within liberal politics is characterized by compromise and mutual adjustment forged in public arenas. Public discussion and debate provide a forum in which different parties to the issue at hand can reach a point of consensus around a common denominator. This is a dynamic that relies extensively on existing political institutions and processes.

Consensus building as a characterization of liberal policy formation is discussed in much of the pluralist literature. *Classical pluralism* as Robert Waste defines it "holds that public policy is a tug of war between various interest groups that often ends in a delicate balance or compromise."[67] Policy consensus in this process emerges from a competition of interests, no one of which long dominates the policy arena. As Charles Jones outlines the process, public policy involves a "highly relative and pluralistic decision-making system characterized by compromise, incrementalism, and continual adjustment."[68] Government policymakers facilitate this adjustment process while also representing the interests of the broader community.

In the offset policy response in Waterloo, consensus building was indeed the dominant theme. While different parties to the Rath situation had quite different interpretations of the problem, as with labor's critique of management's decision making and management's analysis of financial markets,

establishing a common point of understanding was the key task in policy formation. In this regard the feasibility study served a critical role. It reinforced
the emerging consensus around the financial needs of the company. With
capital requirements as a common denominator, each party to the policy
response could play a part: management agreed to organizational restructuring and key equipment investments, labor accepted wage deferrals and an
employee stock ownership plan, and government provided two loans to increase production and modernize the plant.

Equally important, this consensus-building process was structured around
existing political institutions and processes. The Economic Development Committee, for example, provided an important forum for discussion and resolution of differences. While the EDC was legally incorporated and reinvigorated
for purposes of the Rath situation, it had been in existence since 1972 and
was well within the mainstream of policymaking institutions. The feasibility
study with its expert analysis was also a well-accepted tool for policymaking.
And the federal grant application process provided a point for common effort that was within the norms of existing policy patterns. This reliance on
existing political institutions and processes served well an offset response,
but it also revealed the limits to policymaking in a liberal society.

Liberal Politics and the Limits of Consensus Building

Within liberal politics there are limits or boundaries to the reach of public
policy. Although government serves a valuable purpose, there is ambivalence
as to how far the arm of government should extend, particularly in economic
affairs. Undue expansion of the public sector can pose a threat to economic
freedom and competition. Government may serve to ensure equal opportunity and protect freedom of choice, but overzealous government policies
can undermine the individual and competitive basis of economic society. Thus,
respect for and preservation of a private market economy is part and parcel
of liberal politics.[69] In addition, as indicated above, liberal policymaking
reflects a preference for incremental problem-solving. In this regard political
and economic boundaries tend to remain unchallenged. Social protests and
other nonincremental challenges to the consensus-building process are "defined as either illegitimate, unrealistic, or utopian."[70] In short, consensus
building is a slow process that favors existing institutions and processes.

In the Waterloo experience several aborted policy options suggested the
limits of liberal policymaking. Each involved a situation in which policymakers might have extended the reach of government beyond existing political
and economic boundaries. In one example there was a flurry of discussion
in September 1978 around the possible formation by the city of a nonprofit
corporation to construct a new meatpacking plant and lease it to Rath. This
option, which was outlined in the feasibility study, was seen as a long-term

strategy to replace the existing facility.[71] If this strategy had been pursued, the city, as owner of the facility, might have played a significant role in the operations of the company. While Mayor Rooff and others discussed this option, it never went beyond the idea stage. The costs involved and lack of support for this degree of involvement by the city derailed it.

In another example there was periodic discussion, particularly in 1979, about a city official taking a seat on the Rath board of directors. A city official in this position would provide a public-sector voice in decision making by the firm as well as an information link to the city council. As with the nonprofit corporation, this policy option would stretch the arm of government farther into the private world of a capitalist economy. However, this option never materialized. Questions concerning the city's legal liability and general opposition by existing Rath board members sidetracked this policy possibility.

And finally, both the city of Waterloo and the county Economic Development Committee were in a position, by virtue of their loans to the company, to play a role in the firm's decision making. As part of the loan agreements, the city and county EDC held collateral in Rath's plant, equipment, and inventories. This collateral provided both groups with a continuing interest in Rath's success. Beginning in October 1978 the Long-Range Financial Planning Committee of the EDC met every seven to fourteen days to monitor progress by the company and union in implementing the feasibility study's recommendations. The city's Community Development Board also monitored its loan to Rath according to six spending categories outlined in the UDAG. Although this monitoring presented an opportunity for government input into the firm's recovery strategy, such involvement was limited. The government officials involved generally lacked technical expertise in the meatpacking business, and Rath management resisted a government role beyond periodic reports and reimbursement procedures.

Each of these options offered an opportunity for increased government input into economic decision-making. However, each was sidetracked by a combination of financial, legal, philosophical, and political concerns. Importantly, each stretched liberal policymaking beyond the boundaries of general acceptability. Government influence through close monitoring of expenditures, a seat on the Rath board, or a nonprofit corporation could pose a threat — as public infringements — to the existing line of demarcation between the public and the private.

Thus, in Waterloo, public policy remained within the bounds of liberal politics. A positive offset government role, based on the leadership of local government officials and in conjunction with a public consensus-building process, was the dominant response. Policy options to place government policymakers further into the decision-making world of the corporation failed to gain support. While untried in Waterloo, efforts of a similar vein have occurred in other instances of plant closing (see Chapter 5).

UPDATE

Rath Packing Company

Did Rath remain open? The financial offset package—$3 million from the county Economic Development Committee and $4.56 million from the city of Waterloo—provided an important boost to the company, but the struggle for survival was just beginning.[72] As a shakeout continued in the meatpacking industry, Rath turned to its employees for assistance. From June 1980 to May 1982 workers deferred approximately $20 per week per person to purchase stock in the company, providing a total of almost $6 million in assistance. Although employees became 60-percent owners in Rath, and an employee involvement system was established, Rath's troubles continued.

The downward spiral started in full swing in 1981 as operating losses totaled $9.6 million. In September 1982, as wage deferrals continued, the union accepted termination of the pension plan under the umbrella of the federal Pension Benefit Guaranty Corporation. In another important change, in late 1982 the president of the union local, Lyle Taylor, resigned and assumed management responsibilities at the plant. While some welcomed this move as beneficial to the company, others were suspicious and critical.

Despite these changes the economic slide continued. In February 1983 a $2.50 hourly wage deferral was accepted by the local union, yet the company's operating statement showed a $13-million loss. As one union representative stated, "Rath went to a plus $14 million net worth with the pension plan termination. Yet, from October 1982 up to October 1983, they managed to lose all of that net worth plus the continuing deferrals."[73] In November 1983, when Rath was unable to increase its line of credit, the company filed for Chapter 11 bankruptcy. In the following month the labor contract, which was to increase hourly wages to $10.24, was declared void by the bankruptcy judge. By the end of 1983 Rath was in bankruptcy court and workers were without a labor contract. In 1984 the economic downturn continued as worker discontent grew and layoffs mounted. Production continued to decline until finally, in December 1984, the plant closed.

Still, many Rath workers and members of the community refused to resign themselves to a permanent closing. Lyle Taylor and a management team proposed a plan to reopen Rath as a regional packer with 500 employees. In a competing proposal an Employees Reorganization Committee (ERC) formed and presented a $15–20 million plan to reopen the plant with 1,200 workers.

For both proposals the critical element was financing. While the ERC raised local pledges of $900,000, it, as well as the management group, were unable to secure long-term financing commitments.

The final blow came on May 1, 1985, when the bankruptcy judge approved the sale of Rath's trademark and patents to another meatpacker. The judge commented in his decision, "The prospects for reorganization at the current time are fainter than the glow of a candle on a hillside."[74] During seventeen months of bankruptcy proceedings sixteen individuals and groups expressed interest in Rath, but none arranged a viable plan. The judge concluded, "There comes a time when the memories of a grand past and the tantalizing promises of a better future must be squared with the hard realities of the present. That time has arrived in this case."[75] With those words the bankruptcy court began to prepare for liquidation.

Waterloo, Iowa

For Waterloo and Black Hawk County, the gradual demise of Rath was accompanied by a severe economic downturn in the local economy. Between 1980 and 1984 manufacturing employment declined by 9,000 workers. Although employment in service and finance sectors remained steady, total employment in the county declined by over 10,000. By 1982 the unemployment rate in Black Hawk County reached 12.1 percent and remained in double digits for the next four years.[76] Home foreclosures rose sharply as the county's population declined. As a sign of the times, in December 1984 the local newspaper offered $1,200 for the best ideas on "how to get the Black Hawk County economy moving ahead once again."[77]

Although the problems at Rath contributed to this economic decline, the major source was the plight of Deere & Company. The optimism expressed in 1979 for Deere's expansion was quickly lost amid the general decline in the farm economy and subsequent drop in farm implement sales. After a 1979 peak employment level of 16,100, layoffs became the order of the day. By May 1985 employment at Deere's operations in Black Hawk County had declined to 7,800.[78] This sharp drop in employment had a ripple effect through the local economy. As noted in a local news article, "when the company [Deere] is healthy, the metro economy is robust. When the company feels ill, the economy has a bout with indigestion."[79]

Although the numbers involved were much higher than those at Rath, the policy response by local officials was of a different order. Unlike Rath, Deere was not a local company lacking capital to repair a deteriorating facility. Rather, Deere was a multinational company, headquartered outside Waterloo, facing a declining world market. Investment resources were not the issue; declining demand was.[80]

Furthermore, Deere was not asking for assistance. Layoffs had happened before. Deere workers and local policymakers hoped for a recall of workers once conditions improved. As local officials perceived the problem, there was little they could do. A Dislocated Workers Program was established in 1983 by the union at Deere (United Auto Workers) and subsequently brought under the umbrella of federal funding, but local government officials had little role in this process. Layoffs at a company such as Deere were beyond the reach of local policymakers.

Although the local role in responding to the situation at Deere was limited, both the city and county did develop new economic policy tools. The county Economic Development Committee, for example, established several programs to assist new and existing businesses. Between 1980 and 1983 a revolving loan fund provided over $500,000 in loans to 20 businesses in need of capital. The committee also provided four loan guarantees and participated in several technical-assistance projects.[81] The committee hired permanent staff to operate the loan fund and engage in other business-retention and attraction projects. In all of these activities a partnership approach with the private sector was central. As one committee report emphasized, it is "important that public solutions be decided upon jointly by the public and private sectors."[82]

City of Waterloo officials also expanded their economic policy capabilities. For example, in 1985 a "mini-UDAG" program was established to assist new or expanding businesses. Under the program, grants were made to local businesses to leverage other funds needed to open a new business or expand an existing facility. The city also established an interest write-down program to reduce interest rates on loans to new or expanding businesses.

In addition, as in Louisville and other communities, the city's use of industrial revenue bonds became an important tool to assist local businesses. From 1978 to 1985 the city issued over $53.8 million in industrial revenue bonds for thirty-five separate projects. A number of these bond issues were used to encourage local businesses to remain open.

To highlight the importance of economic revitalization, the mayors of Waterloo and nearby Cedar Falls declared 1985 "economic development year."[83] Earlier in the year the Waterloo City Council passed a resolution establishing itself as an Economic Development Committee to address economic problems in the city. An offset approach to potential plant closings remained the dominant strategy. In Cedar Falls, for example, a public-private financial package that included the city and the county Economic Development Committee was praised for saving an important local manufacturer.

The area experienced a proliferation of economic development groups. By one count, local policymakers were involved in approximately twelve organizations. These groups included a NE Iowa Saturn-GM Steering Committee, intent upon luring the Saturn plant to the area, and a newly formed Cedar Valley Economic Development Action Company. The latter group, started by the Waterloo Chamber of Commerce, began with a focus on business attraction but soon became involved in issues of business retention and expansion. Although the Cedar Valley organization had its critics, one newspaper editorial praised the group for showing that the area "is alive and working together toward a common goal."[84]

The cooperative public-private approach to economic development continued. Although the sustained downturn in the local economy left many skeptical of government efforts, the consensus-building characteristic of an offset approach to plant closings still remained. Having left the community, Lynn Cutler no longer provided a leadership role, but the tools and precedent for a public-private approach were well established. Political leadership was less critical now; the pattern was set for local governments to play an important role in addressing economic decline.

5

A "Player" Response: The Steel Valley Authority and U.S. Steel

The Monongahela River Valley (Mon Valley) extends southward from downtown Pittsburgh and was once the heart of America's steel industry. In 1900 the steel mills in the Mon Valley produced 40 percent of the nation's steel, and during World War II the mills were an integral part of the Allied war effort. Pittsburgh was aptly known as America's steel city. Today the story is quite different. The recession of the early 1980s concluded a long process of decline. Led by the U.S. Steel Corporation, the steelmakers of the Mon Valley have either diversified into other product lines, moved steelmaking elsewhere, or become mired in operating deficits. What remains in much of the area are idle mills and economically depressed communities.

Duquesne and the U.S. Steel mill located therein represent one example. Located fifteen miles south of Pittsburgh, the Duquesne mill was one of U.S. Steel's six major integrated facilities in the area. Although the mill employed 3,200 workers in 1981, by late 1983 the mill was on the company's list for closure. In 1984 the mill was closed, and the announcement was made that the "hot end" of the mill would soon be dismantled. U.S. Steel's announcement sparked a variety of responses in the community. While some in the area accepted the closing as inevitable, others pursued various strategies to reopen the mill. Among the latter responses was a campaign to create a new political organization known as the Steel Valley Authority. This authority was to be incorporated under state law and would possess a range of legal tools that could be used to prevent the Duquesne closing as well as other closings in the area. Support for this strategy was led by the Tri-State Conference on Steel, a public interest coalition of local government officials, labor, clergy, and workers. Tri-State argued for a community role in the economic future of the region. As one Tri-State pamphlet declared, "Since private industry will not rebuild our steel industry, the workers and communities of the Mon

Table 5.1 Characteristics of Selected Municipalities in the Monongahela Valley

	Population (1980)	Median Family Income[1]	Total Municipal Revenues[2]	Taxes Per Capita[1]
Steel Valley Authority Members				
Pittsburgh	423,900	17,500	285,106,000	285
McKeesport	31,000	17,100	8,784,000	168
Munhall	14,500	22,100	3,213,000	123
Swissvale	11,300	18,900	2,210,000	114
Turtle Creek	7,000	17,600	1,193,000	102
Glassport	6,200	20,400	929,000	74
Homestead	5,100	12,900	2,045,000	200
Rankin	2,900	12,900	451,000	87
E. Pittsburgh	2,500	16,100	711,000	150
Non-members				
Duquesne	10,100	17,100	3,611,000	126
West Homestead	3,100	22,300	1,110,000	270
Wilmerding	2,400	16,600	488,000	105
Allegheny County	1,450,000	16,700	429,364,000	118

[1] In dollars, in 1980; from Allegheny County Department of Planning, "Municipal Profiles," Pittsburgh.
[2] In dollars, in 1982; from Commonwealth of Pennsylvania, *Local Government Financial Statistics* (Harrisburg: Pennsylvania Department of Community Affairs, 1982), pp. 36–55.

Valley must be allowed to do it."[1] By July 1985 nine communities, including the city of Pittsburgh, voted in favor of forming this new authority.

Formation of the Steel Valley Authority represented a policy response quite distinct from the two previous case studies. This was not a response that deferred to private-sector actors, as in Louisville, nor was it a response that relied on government provision of offset resources, as in Waterloo. Rather, the Steel Valley Authority represented the beginnings of a populist player role in which government authority would challenge decisions made by private economic actors and would play a major role in guiding the investment and disinvestment process. This was a policy response that would reveal important possibilities as well as limits in American economic policymaking.

THE SETTING

The Political and Economic Terrain

In contrast to the two previous case studies, this case involves a large number of governmental actors. In addition to the nine municipalities that formed the Steel Valley Authority, several other local governments played an important role (see Table 5.1).

These Mon Valley communities include governments with a wide range of

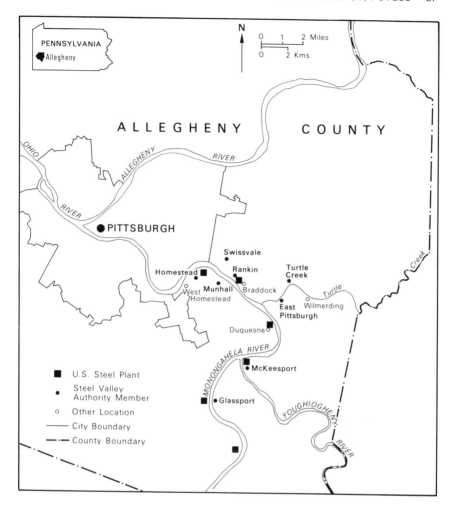

resources and responsibilities. On one end of the spectrum are Pittsburgh and Allegheny County. Both have full-time elected officials and bureaucracies with extensive expertise and experience in economic affairs. Pittsburgh, for example, is guided by a mayor and seven-member city council with access to a professional bureaucracy that includes the Urban Redevelopment Authority as the key economic development unit. Allegheny County has three full-time county commissioners supported in economic policy areas by the county Department of Development and several other county agencies. In contrast, the smaller communities in the Mon Valley have part-time elected officials with limited staff support. Duquesne, for example, has a part-time five-person city council with a mayor chosen from among the council. Primary city responsibilities are in the areas of public safety, street maintenance, and basic sanitation; economic development is not a discrete function within city government. Of the Mon Valley communities outside Pittsburgh, only McKeesport has a full-time mayor and an economic development office. In general these communities rely on Allegheny County, a regional council of governments, or other collective bodies for policy and program development.

The economy in which Pittsburgh and Mon Valley governments operate had a historical base in manufacturing. In 1960, 39.9 percent of the county workforce was employed in manufacturing plants and steel mills.[2] U.S. Steel, Jones & Laughlin, and Westinghouse were household names in the region. Pittsburgh's title as Steel City and Turtle Creek's claim as Westinghouse Valley attested to the importance of manufacturing to the area.

However, in recent years this economic base had undergone a major transformation. By 1985 manufacturing employment as a proportion of the county workforce was cut in half, down to 17 percent, as wholesale-retail trade and services became the predominant employment sectors. Between 1960 and 1985, 100,360 manufacturing jobs were lost as 172,700 nonmanufacturing jobs were created. Highlighting this trend was the demise of the steel worker. Steel employment in the county dropped from 82,900 in 1960 to 31,200 in 1985.[3] Steel City was no longer an appropriate title. Within Allegheny County, the Mon Valley was the principal victim of the general decline of the American steel industry.

The American Steel Industry[4]

As with the meatpacking industry the steel industry experienced difficult times in recent years. Indeed, as one government report noted, the steel industry had been in a "quasi-permanent recession since 1966."[5] Domestic steel production peaked in 1973 and declined in the late 1970s and early 1980s. By 1982 domestic production was well below the 1966 level. Steel mills were closed and employees laid off as the industry shrank in size. As the title of a *Business Week* article declared, "It's Every Man for Himself in the Steel Business."[6]

Attributing causation for the decline in steel is a complicated and controversial task. Depending on the point of reference, blame is variously assigned to poor management decisions, high labor costs, import competition, government policies, and the changing nature of global capitalism.[7] While this is not the place to resolve the debate, several comments are pertinent to understanding the nature of the industry's "crisis" and its implications for U.S. Steel and the Mon Valley.

Perhaps the most significant problem faced by steelmakers has been technological. Major American steelmakers have been criticized from various quarters for failing to adapt in a timely manner to changing technologies. The basic argument is that integrated steelmakers, such as U.S. Steel, relied on open-hearth and basic oxygen-production processes long after many foreign competitors and domestic mini-mills took advantage of electric arc furnaces and continuous casters.[8] The reasons for this technology lag are many, but the bottom line is a competitive cost disadvantage for major American steel producers.

In addition, the steel industry is a victim of the changing nature of the American economy. An expanding service sector and the development of materials that can replace steel have contributed to a decline in U.S. steel consumption. From a peak year in 1974, U.S. steel consumption has fluctuated depending on economic conditions but has not returned to the 1974 level. The decline in consumption is particularly apparent in light of the overall growth of the American economy. In 1984 steel consumption as a percent of real GNP was 40 percent less than the comparable measure in 1966.[9]

Accompanying the decline in demand has been an increase in both overseas steel production and imports to the United States. While annual U.S. steel production has increased very little since the 1950s, non-U.S. production has increased nearly sixfold. By 1982 the U.S. produced only 10 percent of the world's steel. The increase in non-U.S. production has led to an increase in imports to the United States. Whereas only 3 percent of new tonnage available in the United States in 1958 was from foreign producers, by late 1984 the comparable measure was 26 percent.[10]

Among other issues cited as contributing to the decline of the American steel industry is a rise in labor costs during a time of declining productivity. For most of the 1970s, compensation per worker increased at an annual rate of 11 percent, compared to 9.2 percent in overall manufacturing. By 1980 the average compensation per worker in steel was 76 percent higher than the average for manufacturing. However, during most of this period total input productivity was actually negative. Between 1974 and 1979 annual average input productivity in steel was −0.8 percent compared with a +0.6 percent in all manufacturing.[11]

The response by steelmakers to this changing environment has involved a number of paths. In one response, steelmakers turned to government for assistance. From relaxation of environmental regulations to more generous depreciation allowances on tax returns, steelmakers have sought a more supportive public policy.[12] Most noted among government policies are those pertaining to steel imports. Beginning with voluntary export-restraint agreements in 1968, import-restrictive policies have included a trigger price mechanism established under the Carter administration and a more recent return to negotiated agreements.

Another path followed by the steelmakers has been a get-tough approach with workers. Prior to the early 1980s a form of business unionism based on labor-management accord was the model for labor relations. Typifying this accord was the Experimental Negotiating Agreement established in 1973 between the major producers and the steel workers' union. This agreement guaranteed workers a 3-percent annual wage increase, cost-of-living adjustments, and productivity wage increases in return for a no-strike pledge. Noted one observer, the "steel union traded militancy for ever fatter pay packets."[13] In 1983 this system came to an end when a new industrywide contract sharply reduced the increasing rate of labor compensation. In the following year industrywide bargaining began to crumble as individual steel producers sought labor adjustments tailored to their own specific circumstances.

Steelmakers also pursued a variety of other strategies. For several companies merger was the only way to keep afloat. In 1984 LTV's Jones & Laughlin steel division merged with Republic Steel, thereby combining the third- and fifth-largest U.S. producers. Bankruptcy was another option. In 1985 Wheeling-Pittsburgh, the nation's seventh-largest steelmaker, sought to reorganize under court protection in Chapter 11 bankruptcy proceedings. Included in the reorganization was abrogation of the labor contract. And finally, diversification into other product areas was a possibility. U.S. Steel's purchase of Marathon Oil in 1982 highlighted that company's plan to diversify into energy resources and related sectors.

A common denominator among survival strategies in the industry was the closing of steel mills and related facilities. Between 1977 and 1985 approximately 200 production facilities of varying size closed as capacity in the industry was reduced by 20 percent and employment cut by 40 percent.[14] These closings and reductions in production capacity hit the Pittsburgh and Ohio regions particularly hard. In Youngstown, Ohio, for example, three major mills closed in the late 1970s. It is in this context that we turn to U.S. Steel and the Duquesne mill.

U.S. Steel Corporation

From its inception U.S. Steel Corporation has dominated the American steel industry.[15] Formed in 1901 as the world's first billion-dollar corporation, U.S. Steel merged the steel empires of Andrew Carnegie and several other steelmakers in the Pittsburgh and Chicago areas. With the company's headquarters established in Pittsburgh, the Mon Valley was the heart of U.S. Steel's empire. Six major mills along the Monongahela River represented U.S. Steel's investment in the area. By the late 1970s, however, U.S. Steel began a major campaign to reduce its steelmaking capacity in the troubled industry. As one industry analyst argued, "U.S. Steel has the greatest number of plants that would appear to be less than minimum efficient scale."[16] In 1979 a first wave of closings idled steel facilities in Ohio, Indiana, Alabama, and California. In December 1983 another wave of closings was announced.[17] By early 1985 U.S. Steel had reduced its nationwide production capacity by 30 percent and cut 100,000 workers.[18] One news article noted that "profitability was more important than preserving the empire."[19]

The company's strategy was clear: "The strategic plan called for diversification to ensure that the Company would no longer be as tied to the cyclical extremes of the steel industry."[20] The most noted example of diversification came in 1982 when U.S. Steel purchased Marathon Oil for $5.9 billion. Entry into the oil business, along with other asset sales and purchases, dramatically altered the composition of the company. Whereas in 1978, 73 percent of revenues came from steel, by 1985 the comparable measure was down to 33 percent; the oil and gas segment of the company now brought in 54 percent of revenues.[21] The 1986 decision to reorganize the company and change the name to USX put the concluding touch on corporate restructuring. U.S. Steel was no longer just a steel company. Although not abandoning the steel industry, U.S. Steel followed a pattern of selective investment and disinvestment at its facilities.[22] Under this strategy production facilities in such areas as Gary, Indiana, and Fairfield, Alabama, were upgraded, but many other plants and mills were targeted for capacity reduction or closing. From the company's perspective plant closings were necessary to reduce production in an industry already plagued by overcapacity.

The company's restructuring strategy had a dramatic impact on Pittsburgh and the steel-mill towns of the Mon Valley. Between 1979 and 1984 employment at U.S. Steel's six major facilities in the Mon Valley dropped from 28,000 to less than 6,000.[23] Steelmaking operations in the valley were reduced or eliminated as part of the company's "nationwide rationalization program." As part of this rationalization U.S. Steel announced, on December 27, 1983, the permanent shutdown of two major segments of the Duquesne works — the blast furnace, known as Dorothy 6, and the basic oxygen process furnace. Since opening in 1885, the Duquesne mill had been one of U.S. Steel's major facilities in the Mon Valley. As an integrated facility, the mill covered 260 acres and employed, as late as 1981, 3,200 workers in production operations ranging from molten iron to finished steel.

The furnaces designated for closing covered 100 acres of the mill. According to the company these furnaces no longer merited reinvestment and were not needed in the reorganization strategy for the Mon Valley plants. Furnaces at the nearby Edgar Thompson works in Braddock would satisfy the hot-metal needs of the Duquesne mill and other U.S. Steel plants in the area. On May 24, 1984, the Duquesne furnaces were closed, and in October the company announced its intention to raze the furnaces and clear that portion of the mill for development as an industrial park.[24]

THE RANGE OF COMMUNITY RESPONSES

The decision to dismantle Dorothy 6 and the basic oxygen furnace sparked a variety of reactions. While our focus is on the groups and strategies related to a player policy, there were other responses as well. To a greater degree than the two previous case studies, the Mon Valley experience encompassed a range of quite different responses, which became intertwined as the story unfolded. An introduction to these alternative strategies provides important groundwork.

Accepting the Closing

Within the Mon Valley were a number of individuals and groups that accepted the closing. Most significant among them were the public officials in Duquesne, where the mill was located. Although Duquesne would suffer the greatest immediate economic losses from the closing (see the later section on economic accumulation), several key officials regarded the closing as inevitable. One member of the city council commented that trying to revive the mill was like "kicking a dead horse." These officials accepted U.S. Steel's conclusion that the mill was no longer an efficient and productive economic unit. Another member of the council observed that the "handwriting was on the wall"; the mill had not been modernized for years.

These officials concurred with U.S. Steel's plan to build an industrial park on part of the mill site. This proposal, made by U.S. Steel in October 1984, received general support from the mayor and city council of Duquesne as well as a number of local businesses. From their perspective, broadening the economic base of the city was essential to shed the community's image as a "one-horse town." City officials initiated contacts with a number of prospective tenants, but the industrial park proposal was sidelined by U.S. Steel pending completion of feasibility studies of the mill during 1985. Although Duquesne city officials listened to proposals to revive the mill through creation of a regional authority, the consensus of the council remained in support of the industrial park proposal.

In addition to the city of Duquesne, there were others in the area, such as the Allegheny Conference on Community Development (ACCD), that accepted the closing as an inevitable part of economic change. Formed in 1943, the ACCD was generally regarded as the most influential public-private organization in the area.[25] The ACCD was directed by an executive committee composed of chief executive officers of major Pittsburgh financial institutions and corporations, including U.S. Steel. Government officials worked closely with the ACCD to, as one report described, "bring together the right combination of ideas, people and funding to improve Pittsburgh and its surrounding region."[26]

The ACCD emphasized an economic development approach in which the primary government role was development and improvement of public infrastructure. Since World War II, government authority had been used to support smoke and water pollution controls, flood controls, transportation improvements, and downtown renewal. According to a recent ACCD report, "Economic development requires, above all else, investment and risk taking. The private sector is the engine for this economic activity." The government's major role is to "reinforce private investment decisions by helping provide a supportive climate for economic activity."[27]

From this perspective, plant closings were inevitable in a dynamic economy. Although the Allegheny Conference did not take a public position on the Duquesne mill closing, it was unlikely the organization would oppose U.S. Steel's plans. Consistent with the ACCD view of economic development, the mill closing was properly a business decision.

Pressure for Public Intervention

Although some in the Mon Valley accepted the closing, others took a quite different position. Public opposition was led by a coalition that included the Tri-State Conference on Steel, members of union locals in the United Steelworkers of America (USWA), and several other groups and individuals in the area. The intensity of opposition varied, but for many the Duquesne closing represented another instance of deindustrialization in the Mon Valley. From this perspective, U.S Steel was leading a wave of plant closings that marked a decline in regional manufacturing and an abandonment of the community's economic base.

The Duquesne mill became an example and symbol for the cause. Shortly after the announcement was made to raze Dorothy 6, Tri-State called a meeting of labor leaders, U.S. congressional representatives, Pennsylvania state legislators, clergy, and numerous local government officials. By the conclusion of the meeting an agreement was reached to call for a feasibility study to determine whether or not the mill could be operated profitably. Although U.S. Steel saw no need for such a study, pressure from the USWA and Allegheny County commissioners convinced them to delay demolition.[28]

Feasibility Studies: An Offset Role?

As with the experience in Waterloo, public attention turned to a feasibility study to analyze the viability of the plant. Was the closing an economic inevitability, as U.S. Steel claimed, or was the mill still viable? Could public assistance turn the Duquesne mill into a profitable economic enterprise? While the questions were similar to those asked of the Rath plant, the study process became much more controversial and contested.

The first study began in late 1984. Conducted by Locker/Abrecht Associates of New York, the $150,000 study was funded by Allegheny County, the city of Pittsburgh, USWA, and a local utility company. The results of the study, announced on January 28, 1985, provided a mixed assessment: "Initial findings indicate that the Duquesne steelmaking facilities can be operated on a competitive basis, provided major cost reductions are achieved in non-wage related areas."[29] The study concluded that Dorothy 6 could be operated competitively, provided it was at a reduced capacity level and that the furnace was linked to rolling and finishing facilities either at the Duquesne mill or elsewhere in the Mon Valley. Locker/Abrecht estimated cost requirements for the first three years of operation at $90 million. In the event of a permanent shutdown, the study estimated a loss of 2,000 steel jobs at the Duquesne and Homestead mills, the loss of an additional 5,400 local jobs due to a multiplier effect, and numerous tax losses, including $1.2 million in tax revenues to Duquesne.

However, this analysis was not accepted by U.S. Steel. As David Roderick, chairman of the board at U.S. Steel was quoted, it would take "five minutes on the back of an envelope" to show that Dorothy 6 was not worth keeping.[30] At a press conference Roderick emphasized the point, "We all have to realize that it can't be business as usual, we're in a highly competitive market. . . . We want to be friendly, but we're not Santa Claus."[31] While continuing to delay demolition of the furnaces, U.S. Steel prepared its own analysis and on April 15, 1985, released a rebuttal to the Locker/Abrecht study:

> Our analysis indicates conclusively that there is a vastly insufficient market to support a reactivation of the Duquesne plant's hot end [Dorothy 6]. We feel that the costs associated with rehabilitating and running the facilities would prohibit any chance of success.[32]

U.S. Steel argued that a product market did not exist, as Locker/Abrecht asserted, and costs for the first three years of operations would total $243 million rather than $90 million. As a result the venture would lose $110 million in the first three years instead of earning a profit as claimed by the consultants. U.S. Steel continued to argue that dismantling the furnaces and creating an industrial park would be in the best interests of Duquesne and the Mon Valley.

The debate continued. The Locker/Abrecht report was followed by a more detailed study by Lazard Freres and Company. Commissioned by the USWA, this study considered the feasibility of reopening the Duquesne mill as well as the potential market for the mill's product. A preliminary version of the market analysis presented an optimistic assessment provided certain investments were made. In particular, a continuous caster was needed to modernize the operations and expand the market potential for the mill's products.[33]

During the remainder of 1985 the market study was further refined, and a more general feasibility analysis continued. In January 1986 Lazard Freres presented its final report. Unlike the Locker/Abrecht study and preliminary market analysis, the assessment was clearly negative.

> We conclude, reluctantly but necessarily, that Dorothy 6 cannot be re-opened unless the demand and price for steel improves substantially. Under current circumstances financing for the rehabilitation of Dorothy 6 will not be forthcoming from the private capital markets.[34]

This negative assessment was based primarily on changed market conditions. Lazard Freres concluded that a continuous caster necessary to meet the segmented demand of the market would require considerably more capital than earlier studies indicated. Higher costs for the caster, along with rehabilitation costs for the furnace, would make the operation unprofitable given current steel prices. The conclusions of the Lazard Freres study ended the already waning debate on reviving Dorothy 6 and the Duquesne mill.

An offset response to reopen the mill was not to be. In contrast to the Waterloo case, two factors proved decisive. First, business cooperation was not forthcoming. U.S. Steel refused to consider assistance packages to reopen the mill. From the company's perspective the industry already suffered from excess capacity. And second, the feasibility studies did not identify conditions amenable to improvement with public assistance. According to the Lazard Freres study the Duquesne mill was not viable under existing market conditions. In the end, U.S. Steel's argument won the day. Unlike Waterloo, grantsmanship and an offset policy would not be the local response.

FORMING THE STEEL VALLEY AUTHORITY: TOWARD A PLAYER POLICY RESPONSE

However, the community response was not over. At the same time that feasibility studies were being conducted, the Tri-State Conference on Steel and others in the community were openly questioning U.S. Steel's right to make disinvestment decisions that threatened the livelihood of workers and communities. While supporting the feasibility studies, Tri-State initiated a campaign to create a local political authority capable of preventing plant closings, even when faced with corporate opposition. The goal was a governmental unit capable of assuming a player role in the process.[35]

Building Support

From Tri-State's perspective the feasibility studies obscured the fact that the Duquesne mill was the victim of U.S. Steel's disinvestment decisions. It was

U.S. Steel, not the inexorable workings of the market that were closing Dorothy 6. Members of Tri-State argued that the Duquesne mill could be profitable if it was connected with other steelmaking operations in the Mon Valley. To save the mill, Tri-State called for alternative means of community participation to redirect economic decision-making. As longtime labor activist Monsignor Charles Owen Rice of Tri-State argued, "Capital is too powerful to be left to the care of capitalists and their compulsive search for instant, maximum profit."[36] Existing forums for participation, such as city councils, often lacked either the interest, knowledge, or ability to address the underlying nature of plant closings. Alternative forums were needed.

Early types of participation included direct action, rallies, and town meetings. In December 1984, for example, a group of workers using their own tools and supported by the union entered the Duquesne mill to winterize the furnace in an effort to prevent damage from freezing. U.S. Steel refused to support this project and required a $16,000 insurance policy before allowing the workers to enter the mill. In addition, to monitor the company's actions at the mill, workers established a twenty-four-hour watch to mobilize opposition against removal of equipment. Public rallies also provided a means of participation. In May 1985 a rally in Duquesne was organized around the theme "Save Our Jobs, Families and Communities." Although the rally gathered only moderate support, Dorothy 6 was the focus as various speakers called for community action to stop the shutdown of mills, factories, and businesses in the area. As Jesse Jackson stated at an earlier rally in January, "It's time for a new formula, a fundamental change in how the steel industry is run."[37]

Forming the Steel Valley Authority

Although important, rallies and demonstrations provided a limited and temporary base for influencing local economic change. Members of Tri-State argued for a more permanent forum, one that would possess governmental powers that spanned individual municipalities. One supporter noted that what was needed was an "intermunicipal body that would deal with plant closings not just on a plant-by-plant basis, as the crises arise, but hopefully in a more systematic fashion."[38] The Steel Valley Authority would fill that void. This new political authority was to be established pursuant to the Pennsylvania Municipality Authorities Act first passed in 1945. Under the act an authority could be formed by one or more municipalities with powers to initiate eminent domain proceedings, issue bonds and contract other forms of debt, sue in court, acquire property, and assess fees and other changes. An authority could be created for the purpose of acquiring, holding, constructing, improving, maintaining and operating, owning, leasing, either in the capacity of lessor or lessee . . . industrial development projects, including but not limited to projects to retain or develop existing industries and the development of new industries.[39]

In response to a possible plant closing, an authority might pursue strategies ranging from owning and operating the facility to assisting in finding another party to purchase the plant.

Receiving municipal approval for creation of a new authority was not an easy task. Members of Tri-State and other proponents spoke at city council meetings and public hearings throughout the Mon Valley. While support was growing, reservations were also expressed. Concerns voiced by municipal officials ranged from legal and financial liability for actions taken by the authority to philosophical opposition to interfering with private enterprise. In several communities, such as Duquesne, West Homestead, and Wilmerding, these concerns proved decisive as they declined to join the new authority.

However, nine communities did approve establishment of the Steel Valley Authority. Munhall, a borough adjacent to Duquesne, was the first municipality to hold a hearing and, on February 17, 1985, approve creation of the Authority. In subsequent months other communities followed suit. In June the city council of Pittsburgh provided an important legitimating role by joining and contributing $50,000 for operating expenses of the Authority. By the end of June, Munhall and Pittsburgh were joined by McKeesport, Swissvale, Turtle Creek, Glassport, Homestead, Rankin, and East Pittsburgh. Articles of incorporation were filed, and each municipality chose three persons for the twenty-seven-member board of directors.

For the remainder of 1985 the incorporation papers to establish the Authority were processed through state government agencies. On January 31, 1986, the Steel Valley Authority was incorporated, and the first meeting of the board of directors was held on February 18. However, by that time the debate to reopen Dorothy 6 was over. The conclusions of the Lazard Freres study, released a month earlier, ended what remained of community support to reopen the mill. The Authority had been formed to challenge plant closings, but the Duquesne mill would not be the first test. Attention turned to other plant closings in the area.

Expanding the Agenda: "Brake & Switch"

Of more immediate concern were two manufacturing plants in Swissvale and Wilmerding. Both plants were owned by the American Standard Corporation and were part of the rail products industry. Employing 3,700 production and maintenance workers in 1981, the plants were down to 2,500 by 1985.[40]

In the summer of 1985 American Standard announced its decision to phase out production at the two plants. The Union Switch & Signal plant in Swissvale would be sold, although production might continue for two more years. In October the plant was sold to Radice Corporation for future development on the site. At the Westinghouse Air Brake plant in Wilmerding, production would be reduced and employment cut to approximately 600.

In November 1985 area politicians and community groups, including Tri-State, organized the Save the Brake & Switch coalition to keep the plants open. Joining this coalition, the Steel Valley Authority at its February 1986 meeting designated the two plants as the organization's first industrial development project. These plants would be the initial test of the Authority's player role.

A feasibility study by the Philadelphia Area Cooperatives Association (PACE) set the stage for a response. The study noted that "American Standard has come to its current strategy by choice, rather than by the inexorable workings of the marketplace,"[41] and it concluded that "there is a justification, from a business standpoint, for the retention of operations in Swissvale and Wilmerding."[42] Although this problem definition was challenged by American Standard, it was a definition that facilitated a player response.

A Judicial Strategy

While other government officials, such as county representatives, pursued a negotiating strategy with American Standard and Radice, the Authority sought an injunction. Based on its power of eminent domain and the right to preserve a designated industrial project, the Authority filed suit in state court on March 24, 1986, to prevent American Standard from removing equipment. The next day American Standard and Radice, the new owner of the property (the companies were codefendants in the case), succeeded in moving the case to federal court.[43] A month later Authority members and an appraiser exercised their legal right to enter the Swissvale plant and inventory property, machinery, and equipment. In July a delegation from the Authority also entered the Wilmerding plant.

Although the suit gained considerable support, the court did not look favorably on the Authority's case. On June 17th the federal judge dismissed the suit. As the judge concluded, for the court to grant injunctive relief the Authority must "have some interest in the real estate being wasted."[44] A show of "interest" would involve a "declaration of taking" to exercise eminent domain as well as resources, particularly financial, to support such action. Said the judge, "There has been no declaration of taking and it is uncertain when, if ever, the money will be available. . . . [I]t is clear that it [the Authority] lacks the resources to condemn the plant."[45] The injunction was denied.

In July the Authority filed an appeal to the U.S. Circuit Court of Appeals in Philadelphia. The appeal challenged both the judge's decision to move the case from state to federal court as well as the conclusion that the Authority did not show "interest" and state a cause of action. In its appeal the Authority won a partial victory. Although the circuit court did not rule on the Authority's request for an injunction, it did remand the case to state courts. However, in the interim almost all equipment was removed from the Switch & Signal plant, and development plans were begun for alternative uses of the site.

Even though the Steel Valley Authority failed to prevent plant closings by American Standard and U.S. Steel, it did exemplify the beginnings of a player role. Unlike the two previous case studies, this was a role in which governmental authority was introduced to significantly shape and alter economic decision-making. The Steel Valley Authority was attempting to inject public criteria and a public voice into plant-closing discussions. Although unsuccessful in the cases cited, the experiences of the Authority provide a useful comparison to the bystander and offset responses analyzed in previous chapters.

COMMUNITY MOBILIZATION AND INSTITUTION BUILDING IN THE MON VALLEY

Formation of the Steel Valley Authority represents a significantly different political dynamic than in our previous two cases. Quite distinct from private negotiations in Louisville and more proactive than the political entrepreneurism in Waterloo, the Steel Valley Authority emerged from a long and difficult institution-building process involving actors from the public and private sectors. The Steel Valley Authority was a new institution advocating direct public intervention into the workings of the marketplace. In this institution-building process the Tri-State Conference on Steel played a critical role, but that does not tell the whole story; we must look more closely at the economic and institutional environment within which Tri-State operated and the Steel Valley Authority was formed.

The Mon Valley Economy

In the early 1980s, Pittsburgh and the Mon Valley, to an even greater degree than Louisville, were in the midst of a major economic transformation. As one academic observer concluded, Allegheny County was "caught in the eye of a world-wide economic storm." Steel mill and other manufacturing jobs were being replaced by employment in services and related areas. Between 1980 and 1985 employment in manufacturing declined from 155,200 to 93,200, a drop of 40 percent. Although job increases in the service and finance sectors partially compensated for the decline, rising from 199,900 to 244,300 over this five-year period, overall employment in the county still dropped by 30,000 workers.[46]

This transition was a difficult one. In 1981 unemployment in Allegheny County stood at 7 percent, but increased to 11 percent in 1982, 12.9 percent in 1983, and back to 11 percent in 1984. Each of these rates exceeded the national average.[47] During this period there were a number of plant closings and major layoffs. From January 1982 to July 1984 seventeen manufacturing plants closed in Allegheny County, resulting in the loss of approximately 3,000 jobs. In addition, thirty plants experienced major workforce reductions, resulting in layoffs totaling over 10,900 workers.[48] Furthermore, plant closings, layoffs, and unemployment came on the heels of a period of continuing population loss throughout the region. Between 1960 and 1980 Allegheny County lost 11 percent of its population while Pittsburgh declined by 29.8 percent. In twelve milltowns in the Mon Valley the loss was even higher, averaging 32.4 percent.[49]

While these economic trends had regional dimensions, the burdens and benefits of economic change were concentrated in different parts of the county. The area assumed a dual character. As the authors of one study noted, "Some see Pittsburgh as a bright thriving 'post-industrial metropolis'; others as a city with a troubled industrial base."[50] Both characterizations captured a part of the economic transition.

The benefits of economic change were most apparent in Pittsburgh. Whereas the city's manufacturing base was dwindling, information and service industries offered a bright future. In a city where manufacturing workers were once the largest industry group, by 1980, 46.4 percent of workers were in professional and related services, and 19.4 percent were in wholesale and retail trade, leaving the manufacturing sector with only 13.3 percent.[51] This new economy was based on educational services and corporate headquarters. On the educational side the University of Pittsburgh and Carnegie-Mellon University supported an economic agenda based on medical research and high technology. Robotics, computer software, and medical sciences became topics of discussion. Symbolizing this transition was the razing of part of the LTV steel mill to establish the Pittsburgh Technology Center. As a corporate center, Pittsburgh was home to fifteen Fortune 500 companies. Legal, secretarial, and other support occupations were becoming increasingly important in Pittsburgh. White-collar employment was estimated at 60,000 as office construction continued in the downtown "Golden Triangle."[52]

In contrast, many of the smaller communities surrounding Pittsburgh, including Duquesne, faced the full impact of the negative side of economic change. Unemployment, for example, reached depression levels in the Mon Valley. In McKeesport, home of U.S. Steel's National Works, unemployment was 7.4 percent in 1981, then rose to 17.2 percent in 1982 and 18.3 percent in 1983 before "dropping" to 12.8 percent in 1984. In the smaller communities of the Mon Valley, unemployment data were not regularly collected, but one county document listed the following unemployment rates for 1980, prior to many of the largest layoffs: Braddock – 18 percent; Duquesne – 11.8 percent; Homestead – 13.9 percent; and Rankin 15.1 percent.[53] According to one academic survey, unemployment by 1986 had risen to 21.3 percent in Duquesne and 15.1 percent in the East Pittsburgh–Turtle Creek area, home of Westinghouse factories and another U.S. steel mill.[54] One study conducted in 1985 by a regional social service agency presented an even more distressing picture. According to the Mon-Yough Community Social Services Agency, 55 percent of households in McKeesport, Clairton, and Duquesne had an unemployed member, and 46 percent of working age males were unemployed.[55]

These Mon Valley boroughs and cities often developed as "company towns" in which one plant or corporation dominated the local economy. For many communities, U.S. Steel was that company. As noted in Table 5.2, the reliance of Mon Valley governments on tax revenues from U.S. Steel captures an important element of this "company town" character. As a result of reliance on U.S. Steel, Westinghouse, and other companies, a decline in company operations had a devastating impact on the community. As one study noted, such communities suffered "population losses, a declining tax base, inadequate services, eroding infrastructure, fiscal distress and a limited capacity to participate in a comprehensive thrust for economic growth."[56]

In Homestead and Munhall, for example, employment dropped at the local U.S. Steel plant from 7,000 workers in 1980 to 600 in 1985 and had a dramatic impact on local governments. In Homestead, the more dependent of the two boroughs, declining tax revenues meant the elimination of various government services and major employee layoffs by over 50 percent in some departments. One longtime borough council member commented that "whatever U.S. Steel gave us was the budget, everything else was cream." Homestead was losing the core of its budget.

Duquesne was also a one-company town; since 1898 the mill had been the major employer in the community. The finance manager of Duquesne estimated that in the early 1980s, 50–60 percent of the city budget could be attributed to the mill. U.S. Steel paid approximately one-third of property taxes collected by the city ($300,000 out of $980,000) as well as $900,000 for water usage. In addition to these losses, the closing of the mill was reflected in other revenue sources for the city: wage taxes based on place of residence declined from $220,000 in 1982 to $130,000 in 1986, and parking meter revenues declined over the same period from $70,000 to $4,000.[57]

To summarize, the process of economic accumulation in the Pittsburgh area yielded two quite different results. On the one hand, the economic transformation of the region left Pittsburgh with a growing service and educa-

Table 5.2   U.S. Steel's Contribution to Municipal Revenues (in percentages of total)

Community	Real Estate Taxes	Wage Taxes	Community	Real Estate Taxes	Wage Taxes
Braddock	32	31	West Mifflin	21	30
Clairton	47	51	Munhall	25	35
Duquesne	44	60	North Braddock	44	31
Homestead	60	30	Rankin	55	40
McKeesport	20	57	West Homestead	37	40

Source: U.S. Congress, *Hearings on the Economic Health of the Steel Industry and the Relationship of Steel to Other Sectors of the Economy*, 97th Congress, 1st Session, 148.

tional economy. In contrast, the communities of the Mon Valley faced idle steel mills and layoffs in other manufacturing plants. This dual character, and its varying concentration in different parts of the area, provided the economic context for policymaking, the different orientations of which reflected the constraints and opportunities in each part of the local economy. Among Mon Valley officials outside Pittsburgh, some focused on the constraints, while others looked for opportunities. Constraints were most apparent in a collapsing economic base and declining government revenues; resignation and helplessness was one response. However, others looked to the possibility of an active and interventionist response to stop decline in the community; community survival was at stake.

Constraints and opportunities also existed for officials in Pittsburgh, but of a quite different order. As in the other Mon Valley communities, the traditional manufacturing base was declining, but in Pittsburgh, unlike the mill towns of the valley, this base was being replaced by a service and high technology economy. The opportunities to support this change were apparent to Pittsburgh policymakers. Establishing the Pittsburgh Technology Center and supporting downtown office development exemplified these opportunities. Although the economic context was different, the process of economic accumulation again provided the context for policymaking.

Yet generalizations must be made with caution. As indicated earlier, economic conditions provide a context for policymaking but do not predetermine policy responses. Local officials in Duquesne were not resigned to the demise of their community, nor were they supportive of Tri-State's interventionist strategies to reopen the mill. From the perspective of these officials, an industrial park on the mill site seemed a more viable strategy. This dissent is important; it highlights the range of possible policy strategies within a particular economic context.

Institutional System

Not only is the terrain for policymaking shaped by the economic setting, but key institutions within the political economy also provide a setting of constraints and opportunities. As in the two previous case studies, we turn our attention to the organizational rules, procedures, and tools within and between institutions in the public and private sectors. As an organization, the Tri-State Conference on Steel certainly plays an important institutional role, but it must be considered within the broader institutional environment.

In the private sector, labor and the business corporations were again key actors, but neither played the central role in the player response. On the side of labor, institutional fragmentation served to minimize the policy role of the United Steel Workers of America. This fragmentation was most apparent in debates over mill closings. Prior to 1984 the national leadership of the union (International) gave very limited support to local efforts to keep steel mills open. In general the International accepted the steel companies' arguments for labor concessions and supported calls for government trade assistance. The companies' claims that mill closings were inevitable in the rationalization process found general acceptance; maximizing worker benefits subsequent to a closing became the major concern of the International.[58] In contrast, many locals in the USWA were exploring different strategies to keep their mills open. For example, in Youngstown, Ohio, local discussions to keep the mills open touched on employee ownership, community ownership, legal action, and public demonstrations.[59] In Duquesne the president of Local 1256 had been talking to workers and U.S. Steel for over a year about an employee ownership program to keep the mill open. Support, however, was limited among both workers and the International. This split between locals and the International leadership was perpetuated by a top-down organizational structure within the USWA that gave local union members few opportunities for participation. Although this structure was changing, the legacy of fragmentation served to handicap labor as a key actor in the local policy response.

As for the company, U.S. Steel played a limited role in the policy response, not because it operated from a weak position, as did Rath Packing Company in Waterloo, but because it did not favor or seek government intervention. U.S. Steel's goal was simple enough — close the Duquesne mill. This goal was consistent with the company's organizational structure and purpose. As outlined earlier, U.S. Steel was in the midst of a major reorganization that shifted the focus of the company from the production of steel to a broad range of energy and natural resource activities. U.S. Steel, soon to become USX, was diversifying, and its institutional structure reflected this change. The Mon Valley mills were being reorganized to provide what the company thought would be a more efficient operating system. Closing the Duquesne mill was part of this reorganization.

The problem definition put forth by U.S. Steel reflected this organizational change. The company presented the decision to close the Duquesne mill as a purely economic one. In responding to the Locker/Abrecht study the company reiterated the position that their Mon Valley mills could support only one hot-metal facility. Based on present and future operating efficiencies, the Edgar Thompson mill in Braddock was best suited to be that mill. On economic grounds Dorothy 6 should be closed.

The importance of corporate reorganization and a reliance on economic criteria were also evident in the case of the American Standard Corporation and its plans to close the Swissvale and Wilmerding plants. American Standard argued that the closing of Union Switch & Signal in Swissvale and the partial closing of Westinghouse Air-Brake in Wilmerding were the result of changing conditions in the rail products industry, inefficiencies at the plants, excess capacity, and the need to restructure internal operations. As with U.S. Steel, a solution was best left to private parties. The Union Switch & Signal plant, for example, was sold to Radice Corporation for conversion to an office-hotel-shopping complex.

Thus, in the case of both U.S. Steel and American Standard the changing organizational purpose of each served to shape the course of the policy response. For both companies, corporate reorganizations made their respective plants expendable. Importantly, both corporations retained control of investment resources and investment decisions and thus continued to occupy a privileged position in the political economy. Although this position did not go unchallenged, U.S. Steel and American Standard retained important status in the policy-formation process. With this status both companies attempted to direct policy debates to private economic criteria and private-sector solutions.

It was the goal of another private organization in the Pittsburgh area — the Tri-State Conference on Steel — to refute those terms of debate. Tri-State had its roots in a regional effort that started in the late 1970s to prevent steel-mill closings in nearby Youngstown, as well as the construction of a replacement mill at Conneaut on the shores of Lake Erie. Under the banner of Tri-State Conference on the Impact of Steel, area labor, church, and community activists pursued a variety of strategies to prevent the Youngstown closings as well as construction of the new mill. These efforts met with mixed success — the Conneaut mill was not built, but the Youngstown mills closed. Seasoned by this regional effort, activists in the Pittsburgh area adopted the shorter title of Tri-State Conference on Steel and began meeting in 1979 to focus attention on the Mon Valley as the next area to confront major mill closings. At its first general membership meeting on January 14, 1981, ninety individuals from labor unions, churches, academic institutions, the legal profession, and other parts of the Pittsburgh community met to discuss the local effort.[60]

The institution that developed was a community-based organization with a relatively informal operating structure. A board of directors was chosen and outside foundation funding received, but Tri-State relied extensively on the voluntary donation of time and resources. As an organizaton there were few formal rules or procedures; the major constraints evolved out of the limited financial resources. This was not a rigid organization bound by a

bureaucratic tradition. In fact, the openness and flexibility of the organization supported its goal of using different strategies to mobilize workers and
the public against corporate disinvestment in the Mon Valley. In sharp contrast to business corporations, and to a greater degree than labor unions, Tri-
State required active member and community support for its success. Mobilization was central to this organization. From 1979 through the formation of
the Steel Valley Authority in 1987, Tri-State led a campaign to inform and
mobilize workers, government officials, and the general public concerning
the condition of the steel industry and options for public action (discussed
in greater detail in the next section). In this process, Tri-State was redefining
the prevailing definition of plant closings.

Redefining Plant Closings

Members of Tri-State argued that the existing debate, which lay behind the
feasibility studies of the Duquesne mill, cast a cloud of confusion over agency,
responsibility, effects, and possible solutions for plant closings. A new definition of plant closings was essential before meaningful policy discussions could
take place. This definition called for community mobilization, but equally
important, it also identified the critical role for a regional political institution.

Tri-State's redefinition emphasized three key elements. First, causal responsibility for plant closings must be understood within the context of corporate
decision making. While such market forces as supply and demand played a
part in this process, they were only one ingredient that influenced corporate
decisions. Business corporations closed plants for a variety of reasons, relating
to corporate strategies as well as the condition and profitability of a particular
plant. To understand the reasons for a plant closing, as well as the likelihood
of a plant successfully operating outside its current corporate structure, careful
analysis of the plant and the parent corporation is essential.

Second, Tri-State redefined the temporal and geographic context of a plant
closing. Rather than view plant closings as single and isolated events at one
point in time, Tri-State presented plant closings in the Mon Valley as common victims of corporate disinvestment with consequences for the entire
region. For example, the closing at Duquesne was preceded by mill closings
in nearby Youngstown and would likely be followed by other closings in the
Mon Valley. The closing of Dorothy 6 was not an isolated event; the steel
mills of the Mon Valley were part of a larger economic community involving
other industries. The announcement by the American Standard Corporation
to close two manufacturing facilities in Wilmerding and Swissvale was part
of this pattern. Deindustrialization was taking place throughout the valley.

And third, this definition pointed to a collective response and community
mobilization. If the effects of an individual plant closing were not restricted
to one city or borough, neither could a response that hoped to play a role

in shaping the local political economy. Mill towns would have to organize together if they hoped to address problems of a plant closing. As one Tri-State newsletter concluded, "Our goal has to be a commitment to maintaining a fabric — not a series of independent plant closing fights that accept the current economic chaos as a criterion for operating."[61] To support a collective response, an independent regional political authority would be essential.

Acceptance of this definition was slow in coming and only partially won. In contrast to the Louisville and Waterloo experiences, problem definition in the Mon Valley was a much more contentious affair. For example, Tri-State's definition stood in sharp contrast to that of U.S. Steel. As noted earlier, U.S. Steel emphasized economic criteria and private solutions in its analysis of the Duquesne mill, such as declining production in the steel industry and the condition of its mills, as well as an industrial park for private businesses.[62]

Tri-State refuted these terms of debate. With respect to the economic rationale for closing the mill, Tri-State not only questioned the calculations of U.S. Steel but also argued that Dorothy 6 should be considered in a broader context that included other mills in the area, not just those owned by U.S. Steel. As for a private solution emphasizing an industrial park, Tri-State prepared statistics showing an excess of existing industrial park space in the area.

In addition, and more to the heart of its efforts, Tri-State tried to cast the debate in terms of workers and communities controlling their own economic futures. As one supporter argued, many of the mills in the valley should actually have been considered community property. Citing federal dollars that went into the Homestead and Duquesne mills during World War II, and the low discount price that U.S. Steel paid for the return of the mills after the war, this supporter concluded that "as far as we're concerned, U.S. Steel is merely the groundskeeper. . . . It's just as much our steelworks as it is theirs."[63]

Although the debate over the problem definition continued, Tri-State did win a significant level of support by speaking directly to the world of many Mon Valley residents. For example, Tri-State's portrayal of regional deindustrialization was increasingly evident throughout the valley. Many workers and government officials recognized that layoffs were not temporary; manufacturing jobs were fleeing the region. Furthermore, the call for an intermunicipal political institution also fit with current realities. The inability of individual milltown governments to have any meaningful effect on the regional economy was apparent; a regional authority was a solution that merited careful consideration.

In fact, members of Tri-State became increasingly convinced that the authority of government was essential for an effective stand against mill closings and corporate disinvestment. In the Youngstown experience, for example, community efforts to form a locally owned company and secure outside financial assistance faltered when faced with company opposition and no legal mechanism to force cooperation, acquire the mills, or contract debt. Those who formed Tri-State concluded that eminent domain and a legal structure to exercise it might have led to a different outcome in Youngstown.[64] As one Tri-State pamphlet stated, "Government—acting on behalf of working people and their communities, rather than the profits of irresponsible private corporations—will have to play a larger and more responsible role if the American steel industry is to be saved."[65] Thus, harnessing the authority of government was the goal; mobilizing support from workers and others in the community would be the means.

Government Institutions and Political Authority

The Pittsburgh area offered a range of public organizations with quite different institutional capabilities—from the limited and part-time nature of mill town governments to the professional resources available to county officials. Whether the resources of any of these governments could be applied in support of Tri-State's goals was a critical question.

In the mill towns, political institutions were relatively weak in the face of economic change. Most mill town governments, including Duquesne's, were directed by part-time elected officials who had few economic policy tools at their disposal. Further weakening these governments was the general economic decline in the region. Faced with declining revenues, most mill towns had instituted budget cuts that reduced personnel and services. East Pittsburgh, for example, the home of a major Westinghouse plant, reduced its public works staff from 13 to 4, and the police department was reduced from 10 to 7. In addition, regional associations, such as the Turtle Creek Valley Council of Governments, assumed a more important role in service provision as municipalities pooled their resources.[66]

In contrast, policymakers in Allegheny County government operated in an institutional environment with considerably greater policy capabilities. For example, the county Department of Development operated several loan funds, administered an industrial development bond program, provided various businesses with assistance services, and administered several federal programs that supported economic development. Between 1980 and 1985 the department was involved in projects utilizing $38 million in public funds and $500 million in private support.[67] Also at the county level the Allegheny County Redevelopment Authority provided a variety of resources and powers for economic development projects, including eminent domain, bonding, and other finance mechanisms. In addition, at the state level the Pennsylvania Industrial Development Authority (PIDA) provided low-interest loans for manufacturing and industrial projects. In 1982, for example, PIDA made four loans in Allegheny County totaling $1.8 million.[68]

Although some of these tools were available in Louisville and Waterloo, in Allegheny County they were available to a much greater degree and had been used in a variety of circumstances, including plant closings. In Pittsburgh, for example, the county worked with city officials to prepare a loan package to help Clark Candy Company move to an alternative site within the county rather than close its plant. In another case, in the community of Jefferson, county staff assisted local officials in preparation of a UDAG application and a tax incremental finance district to develop a site on the grounds of a closed industrial facility. In a third case the county joined the city of McKeesport and private lenders in an EDA-guaranteed loan assistance package that helped workers establish an employee ownership program to reopen a steel casting company.[69]

These and other examples demonstrated the potential for government action. However, while Allegheny County or another established political institution might be sympathetic to Tri-State's goals, it was unlikely they would support a confrontational stand against U.S. Steel. As described in the next section, political leadership in the Mon Valley was constrained in a number of important ways. Still, the need for governmental authority was clear.

Two elements were recognized as critical for an effective political institution — eminent domain and a public authority structure. Eminent domain involves a legal procedure of condemnation and fair market compensation in which property is taken to serve a public purpose. As a policy tool eminent domain had been used for many years in Pennsylvania. For example, state, county, and municipal governments used it to acquire land for both highway construction as well as the expansion of private businesses. In fact, several of the steel mills in the Mon Valley were expanded during and after World War II with the assistance of eminent domain to remove houses and other existing structures. Eminent domain could play a critical part in a plant-closing; if, for example, the owner of an industrial facility refused to sell the property, and the courts accepted eminent domain proceedings as constituting a public purpose, the plant could be legally seized as an alternative to a shutdown. While this use of eminent domain would be controversial, a number of court decisions recognized this extension of the powers of eminent domain.[70]

The creation of public authorities also had a history that predated the closing of Dorothy 6. Since the 1930s, local governments in Pennsylvania had the power to create authorities that could oversee such activities as housing construction, provision of water and sewerage services, construction and operation of transportation systems, general economic development, and a variety of other capital projects. By 1980 Allegheny County had 178 authorities engaged in these activities. In the area of economic development, for example, the Urban Redevelopment Authority was created in 1946 in Pittsburgh to specifically address economic development concerns in the city.

A public authority represented an important platform for the exercise of governmental powers. Public authorities could undertake projects with bond revenues or assessment fees instead of local taxes, and they could be formed on a multimunicipal basis, thereby facilitating legal action by representatives from more than one municipality. While powers and capabilities varied, public authorities had the potential to assume significant roles in planning and implementing various projects. Although no authority had been formed in response to a plant closing, in such a situation one could, if legally empowered, provide an important means for active public intervention.

Combining these elements was the goal. The Port Authority of Pittsburgh was occasionally cited as an example. After its creation in 1956, the Port Authority used its powers of eminent domain to acquire thirty-two independent transit companies and merge them into one urban transportation system. In this instance the authority of government was used to rationalize an economic activity as well as to overcome the resistance of private companies.

In the case of a regional steel valley authority, the enabling statute to support a like-minded effort was the Pennsylvania Municipality Authorities Act of 1945. As mentioned earlier, an authority could be formed under the act with the power to initiate eminent domain proceedings, issue bonds and contract other forms of debt, sue in court, acquire property, and assess fees and other charges. Although enabling state legislation was present, the institution-building process was neither simple nor easy. Creating the Steel Valley Authority as a new political institution required a careful crafting of powers and limitations to meet the concerns of local political officials. To understand the successes and failures in such an effort requires that we look outside the level of institutions to that of mobilization and alliance formation.

Political Mobilization and Alliance Formation

Just as Lynn Cutler served as the political entrepreneur in Waterloo, the Tri-State Conference on Steel played the entrepreneurial role in the Mon Valley. Since its inception in 1979, Tri-State had engaged in informational and mobilizing efforts to raise public awareness of disinvestment in the area. Pamphlets, newsletters, public rallies, press releases, and city council hearings were the arenas for action. Mobilization and alliance-building were fundamental to the organization. As described in Tri-State's first newsletter, the organization was dedicated

— to build a grassroots organization to oppose current corporate disinvestment/shutdown policies . . .
— to educate the public on the causes of plant shutdowns and how they have affected the local communities, the corporate/government response to the problem (Renaissance II), and possible alternative solutions . . .
— to expand the work of the four steelworker unemployed committees to other mills and plants . . .

—to expand the religious network of Tri-State [and]
—to link up with . . . other concerned organizations throughout the frost-belt in order to more effectively combat the governmental/corporate bias towards disinvestment and abandonment of our region.[71]

This call for mobilization was premised on Tri-State's definition of plant closings. As noted earlier, central to this definition was the use of governmental authority to influence investment and disinvestment in the area. However, mobilizing support was a long and difficult process. Prior to forming the Steel Valley Authority, Tri-State was involved in several attempts to use an authority structure and/or eminent domain to prevent a plant closing.

One of the first attempts occurred in early 1982 in Midland, a small steel town of 5,300 residents in western Pennsylvania. The Crucible steel mill in Midland, which employed over 4,500 workers in 1979, had reduced production and was targeted for shutdown by conglomerate owner Colt Industries.[72] After the company's efforts to sell the mill to private parties failed, several members of Tri-State presented to the borough council a plan in which either an existing or newly created authority would use eminent domain and sell bonds to buy the plant. The borough council considered the proposal but declined to act. Members of the council continued to hope for a private sale of the plant and were also concerned about financial liability and the appropriateness of taking over a steel mill.[73]

A second opportunity came in the fall of 1982. In October Nabisco Brands announced its intention to close a 650-employee plant in Pittsburgh. In response Tri-State and thirty other community and labor groups organized the Save Nabisco Action Coalition.[74] Strategies against Nabisco included a consumer boycott, corporate campaign, strike threat, and a proposal for the use of eminent domain. The coalition presented eminent domain as both a threat to force the company to reconsider its decision as well as a tool to be used if the plant closed. According to the plan, Pittsburgh's Urban Redevelopment Authority would serve as the vehicle to exercise eminent domain.[75] Although the Redevelopment Authority was skeptical, statements of support were received from city council members. However, this use of eminent domain was never put to a test; on December 21 Nabisco announced it would not close the plant.

In the following year a third opportunity to prevent a plant closing arose, this time in West Homestead. Mesta Machine Co., one of the largest employers in West Homestead, had experienced financial losses since 1979 in its production of steelmaking machinery. In February 1983 the company filed for Chapter 11 bankruptcy protection. The local steelworkers' union began to explore an employee ownership buyout, and the Save Mesta Committee was formed by Tri-State and other local groups. The committee organized a campaign against local banks that foreclosed on loans to Mesta and presented a proposal to the borough council to assume control of the plant. On April 12 the borough council approved a resolution to study the feasibility of "creating a municipal authority for the purpose of acquiring private properties by the process of eminent domain." On June 21 the borough council approved creation of a nine-member authority, but the mayor vetoed the resolution. The mayor argued that not only did a municipal takeover lack general community support, but the municipality did not have the expertise to become involved in such an undertaking, and a new owner had been found for the plant.[76]

By late 1983, as U.S. Steel was preparing to make public its plan to close the furnaces at Duquesne, Tri-State could look back on several years of publicity campaigns and organizing efforts. In October the Conference on the Revitalization of Pittsburgh's Steel Industry, sponsored by Tri-State, provided a forum to review and assess these efforts. Shortly after the conference Tri-State published a booklet summarizing a strategy to save the local steel industry.[77] Central to that strategy was creation of the Steel Valley Authority. As one proponent argued, the Authority would "open the door to the political stage for working people and their allies in the community and churches. It [would] allow them to stand squarely on center stage and become active participants, instead of passive bystanders."[78]

Although Tri-State was dedicated to mobilizing support for a regional authority, the critical question was whether such an alliance of groups and individuals could be put together. To be certain, the Pittsburgh area was not a quiescent community; a wide range of mobilization activities already existed in the area. Whether support could be won for formation of a new regional redevelopment authority was uncertain, however. To consider this question, we need to look at other groups and organizations in the area. What was the status of major alliances and coalitions in the public and private sectors?

In the public sector, government officials could be important allies if not leaders in mobilizing political resources. As the experience in Waterloo demonstrated, this element could be critical; Lynn Cutler played the entrepreneurial role in assembling resources for the offset response in that community. However, in Pittsburgh the story was quite different. In this case study a player policy role would place quite different demands on political leaders. In particular, to confront and act against the stated interests of one of the largest corporations in the area would be a difficult step for public officials. While government policymakers in the Pittsburgh area displayed a range of leadership skills, few were willing to take that step. Those who were willing did so with caution and from a limited power base. Nearly all were circumscribed by existing political and economic institutions, albeit in quite different ways.

Among officials of Allegheny County and the city of Pittsburgh, political leadership was present, but it was generally crafted within existing boundaries of the local political economy. These boundaries were shaped in large part by a regime of public-private partnerships that dated back to World War II. Under the postwar sponsorship of Mayor David Lawrence and financier Richard King Mellon, the city of Pittsburgh worked with the newly created Allegheny Conference on Community Development (ACCD) to address pollution problems and other environmental issues and to support downtown development. Known as Renaissance I, this partnership established a pattern of public-private cooperation to support private economic growth. In 1975 this approach was revived as Renaissance II by Mayor Richard Caliguiri to further develop the downtown area.[79] The partnership approach set a general tone for public-private interaction. As one writer noted, the Pittsburgh area was dominated by a "corporatist mode of public-private arrangements [in which] efficient private growth" was the central value.[80]

Exemplifying this approach, the Allegheny Conference in 1984 released its blueprint for revitalization of the regional economy. Called *A Strategy for Growth: An Economic Development Program for the Pittsburgh Region,* the report was premised on the theme of efficient private growth. The report emphasized the "inevitability of change" and the need to diversify beyond steel and other "sunset" industries. According to the report, the region needed a balanced economy driven by entrepreneurial energies. Government would play a facilitating role, but private "innovation and risk-taking—the hallmarks of the entrepreneur—will be keys to success."[81]

While not rigidly bound to this framework, regional political leaders were unlikely to stray far from the partnership model. For example, the mayor of Pittsburgh, Allegheny County commissioners, and presidents of the University of Pittsburgh and Carnegie-Mellon University presented a proposal in 1985 for revitalizing the region's economy. Called "Strategy 21," the proposal outlined a $425-million package to take Pittsburgh and Allegheny County into the twenty-first century. Relying extensively on state government funds, the proposal called for a partnership of government, university, and private sector to create a "diversified economic base [that would include] light as well as heavy manufacturing [and a] new mix of large and small businesses marked by a renewed spirit of entrepreneurship and university-linked research and development."[82]

In a similar tone Allegheny County's *Overall Economic Development Program,* released in April 1986, emphasized the changing nature of the local economy and the need to retain key industry groups with growth potential as well as foster an environment for new business ventures, advanced-technology industries, and the service sector. Again public-private partnerships would be critical. As Tom Foerster, chairman of the Board of County Commissioners remarked in an earlier congressional hearing, there was a "symbiotic existence of the private and public sectors" in economic development.[83]

These proposals were indicative of political leadership and mobilization attentive to regional issues and generally supportive of a public-private partnership approach to economic development. From such a perspective the Mon Valley was problematic. The idle and aging manufacturing plants in the valley were a reminder of what many political leaders were trying to move away from. There was, as one Pittsburgh official admitted, an "absence of leadership in dealing with economic *decline*." Economic growth was a more compelling topic. For example, in the county's *Overall Economic Development Program,* highest priority was given to attracting new firms, developing high technology industries, and expanding professional employment.

In contrast, the Mon Valley was not a popular subject. While a metals retention/reuse study was proposed to inventory steel production sites and identify which facilities had future potential, emphasis was typically on worker dislocation programs and new business-support facilities and services. As for specifics on the issue of reopening the Duquesne mill, silence or neutrality was typical. "Strategy 21," for example, recognized the "controversy surrounding the future of Dorothy 6" and proceeded to propose infrastructure and highway-access improvements to make the site more attractive for whatever future development occured.

Thus, at the regional and countywide level there were boundaries to the leadership and mobilization that would be forthcoming for the Duquesne mill and for Tri-State's goal of creating a regional political authority. While Caliguiri, Foerster, and others supported the feasibility studies, they were less supportive of efforts to form the Steel Valley Authority. An offset role guided by a feasibility analysis would be acceptable, but exercising eminent domain against the wishes of U.S. Steel did not fit into a public-private partnership approach to economic development. Support for reopening Dorothy 6 began to fade. U.S. Steel continued its opposition to reopening the mill, doubts about the economic viability of the mill became more pronounced as the Lazard Freres study dragged on, and public pressure for government action declined. These were not favorable circumstances for the exercise of political leadership to revive the mill.[84]

Among government officials in the small mill towns of the Mon Valley, economic circumstances were quite different, yet mobilization and alliance building were also circumscribed by political and economic interests, albeit of a different order. In particular, as noted earlier, mill town governments possessed few economic policy tools and had very limited expertise to draw upon. In addition, many political officials in the mill towns were skeptical and hesitant when it came to discussions of creating new political institutions, such as a regional redevelopment authority. Thus, although less bound by a past pattern of public-private partnerships, mill town officials operated in an environment characterized by the fragmentation of political authority and limited political and economic capabilities.

As an example, financial concerns were foremost in the minds of many mill town officials. One organizer for the Steel Valley Authority reflected that "the major concern of . . . municipalities was their possible financial liability."[85] Municipalities did not want to assume liability for any actions an authority might take, such as defaulting on a bond issue, nor did they want to be assessed for operation of the organization. Said one official, "We want to get it in writing that it won't cost the borough any money; we can't go along with any costs."[86] In addition, many municipal officials were concerned about the possible loss of local control. There were many questions: Could an authority initiate a project in a municipality regardless of the interests of the municipal council? Could the Steel Valley Authority stop a municipally sponsored project? Local officials were wary and concerned. One council member in McKeesport premised his approval of the Authority on three conditions: the Authority must give member municipalities veto power over any action; the Authority could not interfere with any actions taken by a member municipality within that municipality; and member municipalities could withdraw at any time.[87]

And finally, several municipal officials questioned the intent of the new organization and/or its effectiveness. To some, the key question was whether the Authority would actually own and operate a plant or whether it would serve as a broker by selling the plant to a private party. Public ownership raised philosophical questions. Said one mayor, "What they're doing looks a little like socialism."[88] To others, doubts centered on the effectiveness of the Authority given the existence of other, more powerful economic development organizations in the Mon Valley. From this perspective, was it realistic to expect a new political institution to succeed in attempting actions that other economic development organizations declined to undertake?

Given these concerns and others, including personality conflicts, the city of Duquesne and several other municipalities declined to join the Authority. For others, however, the Authority was a collective response that deserved a chance, provided it was structured to meet these basic concerns. From this perspective there were few other viable options available to these depressed communities. Declining tax bases and limited institutional capabilities made it difficult, if not impossible, for individual mill towns to address broad problems of industrial decline.[89] As one mayor put it, without a regional effort the mill towns were "still at the mercy of these corporations without any recourse . . . frustrated with no tools or avenues" to address problems of economic adjustment. Thus, the idea of a regional industrial authority to help rebuild the local manufacturing base appealed to many officials. Two borough council members concluded that "most were for trying anything[;] without the Steel Valley Authority, nobody was going to try."[90]

However, while support was won from nine municipalities, few Mon Valley officials were in a leadership role. To many the Steel Valley Authority was worth a try but only if it did not jeopardize the limited power local officials still retained. Hence, the Authority was structured in a manner that limited its ability to act. For example, to meet financial concerns, the Authority's Intermunicipal Agreement and By-Laws protected individual municipalities from financial liability for Authority actions and also restricted the Authority's taxing and assessment powers. To protect local autonomy a municipality could veto a project that involved property within its borders. Mill town officials were generally supportive but often were hesitant allies for Tri-State.

Organized labor also played a part in the mobilization and coalition-building process, but it too was qualified. By 1984 the International of the USWA was under new leadership that encouraged rank-and-file participation and provided more support to local efforts to stop plant closings.[91] However, while the International provided financial support for feasibility studies of the Duquesne mill, the union leadership was less supportive of public rallies and demonstrations sponsored by Tri-State. An offset strategy would not be politically difficult, but a new political authority with the power of eminent domain was a concept the International was not yet prepared to embrace. After reading the negative conclusion of the Lazard Freres study, the International wrote in its newsletter that "there are too many forces working against Dorothy 6 to make it a profitable operation again."[92]

Labor support also was fragmented because many workers at the Duquesne mill accepted contract closing benefits as the best-case alternative to a long and questionable fight to reopen the mill. The contract between the steelworkers' union and U.S. Steel contained an array of provisions covering pensions, supplemental unemployment pay, health insurance, and severance pay. Particularly for senior workers at the mill, these provisions addded up to an attractive package that would carry them into their retirement years. Further hindering collective action were personality conflicts and differences in personal politics among various individuals in the labor community.[93] The result was a fragmented union ill-prepared to play a leadership role. With respect to efforts to form the Steel Valley Authority, members of the labor community were most effective as part of Tri-State.

Building support among labor organizations and local officials was complicated, both positively and negatively, by the presence in the Mon Valley of a growing critique of capitalism. This critique, quite unlike any debate that took place in Louisville or Waterloo, included fundamental questions about the nature of a private enterprise system. As a banner in the McKeesport offices of the Mon Valley Unemployed Committee stated, "If you think this system is working, ask someone who isn't." Such questions were raised by a number of groups in the Pittsburgh area that criticized, through a wide range of tactics, the disinvestment actions of Pittsburgh corporations.

Among the most visible were two affiliated groups known as the Denominational Ministry Strategy (DMS) and the Network to Save the Mon/Ohio Valley. The DMS was formed in 1979 by a group of Lutheran and Episcopal ministers, while the Network was formed in 1982 as a partial merger of DMS and labor activists. The common agenda of both organizations was a campaign against the investment strategies of U.S. Steel, Mellon Bank, and other local "power elite" that were, from the organizations' perspective, responsible for unemployment in the area. The DMS and the Network initiated tactics ranging from lobbying to direct confrontation. Confrontation, however, soon became their trademark. The groups gained notoriety for such tactics as placing dead fish in Mellon Bank deposit boxes and throwing skunk oil on business leaders during a Christmas service.[94]

By most accounts the tactics of the DMS and the Network alienated more people than they brought into the movement. For the DMS, bitter disputes within church congregations and church hierarchies led to defrockings, and several ministers received jail sentences for their activities in the organization. By April 1983 the Lutheran synod and Episcopal diocese as well as Methodist and Presbyterian hierarchies had withdrawn support. With respect to the Network, local unions were split, some joining the demonstrations and others choosing to distance themselves. As the president of the Clairton steelworkers' local commented, once the DMS and the Network turned to confrontational tactics, "I lost interest in that movement."[95]

For the Tri-State Conference on Steel and its efforts to form the Steel Valley Authority, the DMS and the Network were a mixed blessing. On the negative side Tri-State was continually distancing itself from the disruptive tactics of the DMS and the Network. Observed one Tri-State supporter, the DMS and the Network may have "raised the consciousness about unemployment, but in a negative way. Some who may have been inclined to help, won't now."[96] Commented another supporter, "The public is lumping us together, and that causes problems about how we're perceived and received."[97] However, on the positive side the disruptive tactics employed by the DMS and the Network made Tri-State's campaign and proposal for the Steel Valley Authority appear reasonable in comparison. As two academic observers noted, "What is striking about the DMS' ideology is that it contains no major role for government in the economy, despite its demands that 'something be done' about the problem of unemployment and its consequences."[98] In contrast, Tri-State was explicit as to what needed to be done. The Steel Valley Authority appeared as a legitimate effort to use the tools of government to address the region's economic problems. Ironically, the DMS and the Network, by their extremism, helped lay the groundwork for a player response that might have appeared too "radical" without the contrast in strategies and tactics.[99]

Although the issues raised by the DMS and the Network may have helped facilitate Tri-State's efforts, mobilizing support for the Steel Valley Authority remained a very difficult task, requiring extensive coalition-building. Public officials, as already noted, were often skeptical or opposed. Still, enough support came from mill town officials and several other political officials to form the Authority. Democratic state representative Tom Michlovic stated that citizens of the Mon Valley would have to change some long-held beliefs, including "an unquestioned reliance on company decisions as good ones" as well as the "pervasive sense of helplessness" that hit Mon Valley communities.[100] To Michlovic and a number of other public officials the Steel Valley Authority deserved a chance. As Father Garrett Dorsey of Tri-State concluded, "There's so much at stake we have to try. We don't want to be silent spectators to a continuing tragedy. We don't buy the theory that heavy industry is dead in the Mon Valley."[101]

Thus, Tri-State assumed the leadership role in mobilizing support for the Authority. In the terminology of this study, Tri-State's goal was one that touched both levels of analysis above that of mobilization. That is, Tri-State was attempting to build a new "institution" that could influence the process of "economic accumulation." Building support for such an attempt goes well beyond the liberal politics identified in Waterloo, Iowa; it represents another form of politics that merits closer scrutiny.

POPULIST POLITICS AND PUBLIC POLICY

Populist Politics and the Duquesne Mill Closing

The policy response outlined in this chapter exemplifies much of what I have called populist politics.[102] As the term is used here, *populist politics* has three core elements. First, populism is an attack on the concentration of privilege in American society; antielitism is a fundamental tenet. As Jack Newfield and Jeff Greenfield argue, "Wealth and power are unequally and unfairly distributed in America today."[103] Rectifying this inequality is central to populism. Of particular importance is the concentration of power held by those controlling the investment of economic resources. Just as the "Money Trust" was a primary target of nineteenth-century populists, so the control of economic investments by today's major corporations perpetuates a system of privilege criticized by contemporary populists.[104]

Second, to address problems of inequality, populism identifies government as the key tool. Martin Carnoy and Derek Shearer, for example, argue that "government — at all levels — is the key arena in the struggle for economic democracy."[105] Only through the power of government will the general public be able to reduce the concentration of privilege. As Mark Kann concludes, "The common thread of understanding [in new populism] is that mass movements can win state power and then use it to transform social life according to egalitarian norms."[106]

And third, populism is premised on an active and involved citizenry. Public participation in community affairs is seen as basic to individual growth and the general welfare. Participation is particularly important in the workings of government; government is not to be a distant bureaucracy. "The populist program is based on a very old American set of insights: for government to work there must be a solid citizenry that is educated, organized, and empowered."[107]

Each of these tenets of populist politics was evident in the Duquesne experience. Antielitism, for example, was an underlying theme in much of the local organizing. Tri-State's long-standing attack on U.S. Steel was aimed at the company's investment patterns that were, according to Tri-State, leaving the Mon Valley an economic wasteland. Elite control of investment meant that economic assets were dedicated to serving the profit motives of capital owners rather than workers and communities. Through this control a system of privilege in the valley was perpetuated.

Clearly Tri-State and other like-minded supporters saw government as the necessary tool to address economic problems. However, since existing governments in the Mon Valley were unable or unwilling to play the role, the Steel Valley Authority was created to harness the power of government to serve workers and communities. Tools of government—eminent domain and an authority structure—were central to Tri-State's efforts to give communities and the general public a voice in economic affairs.

And finally, the efforts of Tri-State and the Steel Valley Authority were premised on public participation. Tri-State supported public rallies and demonstrations to protest mill closings and led efforts at town meetings to create the Steel Valley Authority. The Authority itself was a platform for twenty-seven community representatives to serve the interests of the general public. The goal in both organizations was to expand citizen participation in the political process.

Public Policy as Democratic Transformation

In populist politics, public policy is intended to democratically transform the American political economy. This is not a strategy of revolution; but neither is it simply the consensus-building process of liberal politics. Rather, public policy in a populist mold works within generally accepted political institutions and norms, but with the goal of transforming relations to eliminate elitism and privilege while facilitating public participation. In essence populism "aims at identifying with the political system, capturing it, and using it as a mechanism for democratic change in America."[108]

This view of public policy takes an important step beyond liberal politics and policymaking. Whereas liberal policies use offset strategies to reach a consensus within existing capital-labor relations, policies inspired by populism involve a player government role to transform existing capital-labor relations such that workers and communities have a voice in critical economic decisions. From the populist perspective, inequalities prevalent in contemporary American society cannot be overcome simply by consensus building; institutional change is needed. However, the populist policy agenda does not call for a socialist revolution. It occupies a "radical democratic space," but one in which "private initiative and public control can be contested and potentially made to complement one another."[109] Private enterprise and profits are not eliminated. Rather, the goal is to make the market work democratically as well as efficiently. From a populist perspective this can be achieved without revolutionary change; populists "justify winnable reforms today, which empower people to win more extensive changes tomorrow."[110]

In this case study the Steel Valley Authority was the primary instrument for democratic transformation. Energized by popular participation, the Authority's goal was to transform, at least in part, the prevailing mode of market relations. In particular the Steel Valley Authority used its popular base to challenge the economic "right" of U.S. Steel and the American Standard Corporation to unilaterally make investment and disinvestment decisions. Thus, public policy via the Steel Valley Authority had a somewhat radical goal — a public voice in investment decision-making — but utilized fairly conventional means — an authority structure, eminent domain, and a court injunction against American Standard. This was not a revolutionary policy, nor was it simply bargaining. The Authority sought an important change in the normal conduct of economic affairs.

Barriers to Democratic Transformation

While goals were relatively clear and legal tools were available, policy efforts of the Steel Valley Authority faced very difficult, some would say insurmountable, hurdles. Democratic transformation was far from a simple task. One important barrier or limit involved the Authority's use of existing policy tools. This was truly a two-edged sword. While eminent domain, court injunctions, and authority status provided legitimacy and important avenues for policy action, there was a cost. Having been created to serve purposes within existing political and economic relations, these policy tools contained an inbred bias that was contrary to the Authority's goal of challenging private disinvestment decisions.

A legal strategy exemplified this problem. By seeking a court injunction against the American Standard Corporation, the Authority gained legitimacy in the public eye, but it also entered a terrain quite protective of business interests. In the American legal system the public interest must be unequivocal before the rights of private property are compromised. In this arena protection of property is primarily procedural, leaving open the purpose to which property is used. The Steel Valley Authority was challenging these premises. It was claiming a primacy for community interests over those of the corporation. From the Authority's perspective, private property was to serve interests of the broader community rather than perpetuate a system of inequality and privilege. The Steel Valley Authority was focusing on purpose rather than procedure.[111]

In the Steel Valley Authority's case this issue never received a full hearing. While the Authority was recognized as having legal status to pursue an injunction, the claim was dismissed owing to a lack of resources and plan of action. However, the likely problems were evident in another court case related to the earlier Youngstown, Ohio, plant closings. In this case a federal judge recognized the relevancy of a community interest in a plant closing but ultimately ruled that current legal codes provided no basis for a "community property right" that challenged private disinvestment decisions.[112]

Although such legal challenges may be looked upon more favorably in the future, this strategy has important hurdles to overcome. As Alford and Friedland argue, as long as private control of investment and production are the basis for government revenues and general economic prosperity, "political issues questioning that control are extraordinarily difficult to raise."[113] Politics is not irrelevant, but the "structural barrier" created by the private control of investment is formidable.[114] Thus, as part of the existing political economy, courts provide difficult policy terrain for the realization of populist goals.

Policy efforts aimed at democratic transformation are also likely to face barriers in the areas of organizational resources and ideological compatibility. This is particularly true in the case of a new organization, such as the Steel Valley Authority. As to its organizational resources, the Authority had limited staff support. Prior to hiring its first staff person in 1987, the Authority relied on volunteers and assistance from Tri-State. In addition, the resource weakness cited most often by proponents and opponents alike was financial. As one member of the Authority's board recognized, "money is power." And as the federal court emphasized in the decision denying an injunction, it was a power the Authority lacked. Although the Authority possessed bonding authority, it was doubtful bonds backed by a plant identified for closure by a private firm could be sold on the open market. By this dimension the Authority was clearly at a disadvantage when compared with other economic development organizations.

The institutional design of the Authority also posed limitations. With a multiple-veto structure created to assuage fears of concentrated power, the Authority was limited in its ability to make decisive and quick action. A veto by a municipality in which a plant was closing would render the Authority powerless. Further, the legal structure that isolated the Authority from resources of member municipalities contributed to staff and financial weaknesses already cited.

In addition, to a significant degree the Authority was ideologically isolated in the existing political economy. In part this was due to its recent origin; but equally significant was the Authority's "radical" agenda that alienated other organizations. The Authority's agenda did not follow the dominant public-private partnership model; nor did it adhere to the rational planning approach advocated and followed by more traditional economic development groups. In the local development community it was viewed by some as a marginal participant with no "practical capability." As others phrased it, lacking the "right connections," the Authority existed in "relative isolation" in the economic development community.

These various weaknesses and barriers posed major challenges for the Steel Valley Authority. Other organizations and governments with a similar agenda may face comparable hurdles in the policy process. Indeed, building a player role in the populist manner is not an easy task. As one writer comments, the populist impulse is to "create a new freedom that preserves — yet redefines — the vital elements of the old. This is an institutional as well as intellectual project."[115] And to the Authority's credit, it raised an alternative conception of public action and responsibility in a changing economy. Noted one supporter shortly after the organization was formed, the Authority "is an idea, not an entity in the sense of being a major actor." While the Authority attempted to build its capabilities as an "actor," its role as a purveyor of ideas was perhaps its first accomplishment.

UPDATE

U.S. Steel and the Duquesne Mill

The Duquesne mill closed by U.S. Steel in 1984 never reopened. Throughout 1985, plans to dismantle the hot-end (Dorothy 6) of the mill were delayed as the feasibility studies were conducted. But even in 1986, after efforts to reopen the mill were abandoned, the mill remained standing. Disagreements between U.S. Steel (now called USX) and the demolition company postponed the project.

In mid-1987 USX transferred development responsibilities for the site to the Regional Industrial Development Corporation (a quasi-public county organization) and Allegheny County.[116] Since that time several development plans have been proposed, including a small-business assistance center, but the rusting blast furnace as well as the rest of the idle mill remain standing.

The closing of the Duquesne mill was only one step among many taken by the company to restructure its operations. While much of USX's Mon Valley operations were idled as part of this restructuring, the company did not abandon the steel industry. USX was, however, determined to reduce its costs in steel manufacturing. In mid-1986, contract negotiations with the United

Steelworkers Union broke down and led to a six-month work stoppage involving over 22,000 active workers. While the company sought wage and benefit reductions, the union emphasized the need for job security. The January 1987 contract settlement was a complex document in which workers accepted an 8-percent wage and benefit reduction, the permanent loss of 1,300 jobs, and the closure of a number of facilities. In return the company agreed to restrictions on outside contracting, an early retirement program, profit-sharing, and investments at several of its facilities.[117]

Although the six-month strike contributed to losses in 1986 of $1.37 billion in steel operations, USX emerged with what market analysts described as a leaner and more productive operation. In February 1987 the company announced additional layoffs and production cuts. By May 1987 the company's steelmaking capacity was 35 percent less than what existed just six months earlier. With less capacity and fewer workers, USX improved its productivity to four man-hours to produce a ton of steel — two man-hours below the industry average and well below the company's 1983 level of ten man-hours.[118] By the end of 1987 steelmaking operations were on a profitable basis. In 1987 the steel segment reported an operating income of $125 million compared to the previous year's loss. The return to profitability was partly attributable to modernization efforts, but reductions in employment costs and production capacity were important contributors.

For the Mon Valley this meant a dramatic drop in steel production as other facilities, particularly in the Gary, Indiana, area, became the focus of steel operations. Of the six major USX mills and 30,000 workers in the valley in 1978, parts of only three mills remained in operation, employing 3,600 workers, by 1988.[119] Steelmaking may have returned to profitability for USX, but the Mon Valley was no longer a beneficiary.

Switch & Signal Plant in Swissvale

The court battle between the Steel Valley Authority and the American Standard Corporation (and Radice Corporation, the new owner) over disposition of the Switch & Signal plant in Swissvale continued through 1987. As mentioned earlier, the Steel Valley Authority's effort to prevent removal of equipment from the plant reached the federal circuit court in Philadelphia. While the court did not rule on the merits of the Authority's cause for action, it did remand the case to state courts where the Authority filed its initial complaint. Plans were made to continue court actions, but by mid-1987 almost all equipment had been removed from the plant. Further litigation was avoided when American Standard and Radice paid the Authority compensation for legal fees in an out-of-court settlement.

During this period of litigation, plans for development of the Switch & Signal property proceeded. As noted previously, American Standard sold the facility to Radice Corporation in October 1985 but continued to lease the building as it phased out operations. In the interim Radice began planning for alternative development. In December 1986 Radice unveiled a plan to replace most of the existing structure with a new retail-office-hotel complex.[120] Although some in the community supported this project, the Steel Valley Authority continued to argue for retention of industrial manufacturing on the site. However, before Radice could act on its proposal, the company entered bankruptcy court. As part of that action the property was sold to Oxford Development. Oxford also proposed a retail-office development, but the proposal remains at the planning stage.

Steel Valley Authority

Economic development in the Mon Valley continued to be the central focus of the Steel Valley Authority. To publicize its agenda for economic action, the Authority (along with the Tri-State Conference on Steel) published "A View from the Valley" in 1987. In this report the Authority continued to support steel and manufacturing but recognized that many mills and factories in the Mon Valley would never reopen.[121] It stated that the future lay in successful development of product niches and integrated use of existing facilities; idle manufacturing plants that could not be reused should be razed and alternative development encouraged. According to the report an emphasis on business retention was needed, as was effective use of community development corporations and other forms of community participation.[122]

In the spirit of this agenda, the Authority pursued a number of projects to revive potentially viable elements of the region's manufacturing base. One of the most important projects concerned the steelmaking operations of the LTV Corporation. In 1985 LTV closed its steel plant on Pittsburgh's south side, and in 1986 the company filed Chapter 11 bankruptcy. The Steel Valley Authority joined Tri-State and others in the area in an effort to reopen the relatively new electric furnaces at the mill. Several citizen committees were established to support reopening the furnaces and financing a worker-community buyout. This effort has continued into 1989.

The idle USX Homestead mill, only a few miles from the Duquesne mill, was also on the Authority's agenda. Having closed the mill in 1985, USX announced in late 1987 its intention to sell the mill to the Park Corporation of Cleveland. Whether the Park Corporation intended to demolish the mill or redevelop parts of the facility was unknown; the Steel Valley Authority and others argued that parts of the mill could be profitably reopened. Since Park would not announce its plans, the Authority sponsored two community meetings to discuss possible courses of action.

At the first meeting a Pennsylvania state representative suggested the Authority's power of eminent domain be used if Park planned to raze the site.

At the second meeting, with other representatives from state government in attendance, an executive from Park announced the company's intention to develop the site as industrial property. As a local news reporter concluded, it was the Authority's legal ability to "force the issue" that proved instrumental in this resolution.[123]

The Authority also looked beyond specific industrial projects. In the context of bankruptcies and major restructuring in the steel industry, it (along with Tri-State) proposed a national holding company — AMSTEEL — composed of steel properties taken over by the federal Pension Benefit Guaranty Corporation during bankruptcy proceedings. Beneath the umbrella of this holding company, regional authorities, such as the Steel Valley Authority, could consolidate steel operations in an area using facilities formerly owned by different private companies. For example, the LTV electric furnaces and parts of the Homestead mill could be part of a consolidated operation.

In addition to the need for a national approach to the problems of steel and other major manufacturing industries, the Authority also sought state assistance, particularly in the area of investment capital. As the court case with American Standard made clear, the Authority needed financial resources if it expected to play a major role in local economic development. As one step toward that goal, the Authority and Tri-State worked with state officials to introduce legislation creating a Pennsylvania Industrial Development Finance Corporation. Introduced in May 1987, the bill proposed an initial state investment of $10 million to be combined with private monies in an equity investment program to support the revitalization of manufacturing businesses. The corporation could invest in local industrial projects or in local industrial development bodies like the Steel Valley Authority. An investment from the corporation could, for example, be used to assist in reopening the LTV electric furnaces. In its first test, the bill passed the House Business and Commerce Committee by a vote of 16-2.[124]

To support these and other activities the Authority slowly expanded its staff, membership, and financial resources. In late 1987 a full-time outreach coordinator was added to complement the existing position of executive director. In addition, the membership of the Authority expanded when the city of Clairton voted to become the tenth municipal member. On the financial side the Authority won a major victory in October 1987, when it received $590,000 from the Duquesne Light Company as part of that company's economic development program mandated by the Pennsylvania Public Utilities Commission. This grant was targeted for staff support, feasibility analyses, and other activities involving the LTV electric furnaces project. For day-to-day operations the Authority continued to rely on a $50,000-per-year grant from the city of Pittsburgh. To augment these funds the Authority also received a $25,000 grant from the Pittsburgh Foundation.

While these activities and the growing organizational base represent important accomplishments, the struggle for recognition has been a slow one for the Steel Valley Authority. Many in the area remain skeptical of the Authority and its policy efforts. As one member of the Authority conceded, the organization is still "not taken seriously" by some local government officials. Yet others credit the Authority with considerable influence. Two supporters argue, for example, that "the ultimate success of the Authority remains to be seen, [but] already Tri-State and the Steel Valley Authority have transformed the debate about reindustrialization in the Pittsburgh area."[125] Somewhere in the middle ground may be the most accurate assessment; the jury is still out on the success of the Steel Valley Authority as an economic player in the local political economy.

6

Comparing Policy Responses in Louisville, Waterloo, and the Mon Valley

Case studies capture the complexities and subtleties of politics and policymaking, but the lessons of each are best revealed through a process of comparison. Comparing the three adjustment experiences highlights a number of key questions: How important are economic conditions in shaping policy responses? Are local governments weak as organizational actors in the urban political economy? Can political leadership and coalition building overcome institutional and economic constraints in an urban setting? How important is problem definition in shaping responses to plant closings? In a community where several problem definitions compete for acceptance, how is the "winner" determined?

LEVELS OF ANALYSIS, PROBLEM DEFINITION, AND PLANT CLOSINGS

The framework introduced in Chapter 2 offers one way to address these questions. Using levels of analysis and problem definition, this section compares the three plant-closing experiences to identify key insights and lessons from each study. Table 6.1 offers a preview and summary.

Economic Accumulation

At the most general level of analysis, economic accumulation highlights the way in which society is organized to meet its material needs. As is evident in each case study, in the United States this task is achieved through a capitalist economy characterized by the private ownership and control of economic resources. A private economy is the fundamental setting that shapes American urban communities and provides the broadest parameters within which organizations and individuals pursue their many goals.

126

Table 6.1 Three Responses to Plant Closings

Community Response	Louisville *Bystander*	Waterloo *Offset*	Mon Valley *Player*
Economic Accumulation	*Stable economy* manufacturing weakening, but services and downtown development strong	*Traditional economy* strong manufacturing base, but potential losses if Rath closes	*Dual economy* depression in Mon Valley, but recovery in Pittsburgh
Institutional System	*Business-dominated* strong business influence (B & W); weak and fragmented government units	*Government-brokered* weak business firm (Rath); coordinated, although weak local government units	*Business-led* strong business firm (U.S. Steel, American Standard); strong county government, but weak local units in Mon Valley *Institution-building* creation of the Steel Valley Authority
Political Alliance Formation and Mobilization	*Passive* feuding among city and county officials; no examples of mobilization around economic issues	*Entrepreneurial* county official (Cutler) seeks federal and local cooperation	*Restructuring* regional support for creating SVA; builds upon previous efforts and other critiques of capitalism
Problem Definition	*Business-driven* established by B & W; closing dictated by market conditions; adjustment through collective-bargaining relationship	*Expertise-driven* established by feasibility study; threatened closing due to labor, management, market problems; save plant through local-federal cooperation	*Politically-driven* redefinition by Tri-State; closing due to business decisions; adjustment through community control of economic decisions

This level of analysis proved critical in at least two ways. First, in each community local policymakers were necessarily closely attuned to the health of the local economy. Maintaining a healthy local economy is an "imperative" or "constant element" in the urban policy environment.[1] The private economy is a major source of local government revenues as well as the basis for general community prosperity. In economic prosperity or economic decline, policymakers cannot afford to ignore the local economy.

Second, any policies, institutions, and political alliances designed to protect and strengthen the local economy will be compatible with the private nature of capitalism. A business assistance program that provides financial and other forms of assistance will be careful to respect the decision-making autonomy of private businesses; a public redevelopment authority may provide incentives for particular types of economic actions but will leave primary investment decisions to private actors; public-private alliances will emphasize the supportive and supplementary role public organizations play in a predominantly private economy. Even in periods of economic decline, policy discussions tend to be cast in language compatible with a private economy. While this is not always the case, and those deviant cases can be the most illustrative, the presumption is that the private control of investment and other economic resources is a nonnegotiable, fundamental element that limits other policy options.

These characteristics of economic accumulation framed the policy process. In each community the health of the local economy set the stage for policy considerations, while substantive policy discussions in most instances respected the autonomy and private character of economic institutions and practices. For policymakers in Louisville, Waterloo, and the Mon Valley, these features of capitalist accumulation set the boundaries for legitimate action.

In Louisville, for example, the general strength of the local economy in 1978 put little pressure on policymakers to intervene in the economy. While the economic losses from the Brown & Williamson closing were not insignificant, neither did they appear catastrophic. Brown & Williamson was the fourth-largest employer in the county, but the size of the total economy made the closing appear less critical. The loss of approximately 3,000 production-related jobs represented well under 1 percent of employment in the county. In light of the labor-market assistance provided by Brown & Williamson, it was reasonable to conclude that the economy could absorb the change. As for government revenues from the plant, tax losses were not inconsequential, but the estimated $1.1 million in losses from workers was just over 1 percent of total revenues collected by the city. Perhaps even more critical was Brown & Williamson's decision to keep its corporate headquarters in Louisville. This meant the continuation of approximately 2,000 white-collar jobs that complemented the general trend in the local economy toward service and trade employment. Thus there was not an economic imperative for government intervention. The equilibrating dynamic of the private economy appeared intact; a bystander role for local governments would suffice.

In Waterloo the local economy also played a critical role in framing the policy process. Existing economic conditions, based on a traditional manufacturing economy, were generally favorable, as in Louisville, but anticipated economic losses proved critical in shaping the debate. On measures of current economic health Black Hawk County and Waterloo were as strong as Jefferson County and Louisville. Furthermore, the largest employer in the county — Deere & Company — was in the midst of a planned expansion that pointed to a bright future for Waterloo and Black Hawk County. Judged by these measures, a response similar to that in Louisville might be expected.

However, the future health of the local economy was also critical to policymakers. From this perspective, Rath posed a major problem. Unlike conditions in Louisville, economic losses from a Rath closing would take a considerable toll on the community. Furthermore, such losses were well publicized and often cited by public officials. In the area of employment, for example, the Rath workforce represented 4 percent of workers in the county and, according to a local study, multiplier effects from a Rath closing would lead to county unemployment rates of 8 to 15 percent. Tax losses would also be significant. In addition to tax revenues that would be lost from unemployed workers, Rath property taxes represented 5.7 percent of city property taxes, and the sewerage rental fee was the single largest source of support for the city's sewer system. Based on these anticipated losses, an offset government role to preserve the health of the local economy was a strong possibility.

Not only does this level of analysis help us to understand the reason for an offset response, but it also helps explain the form the response takes. As emphasized in Chapter 4 the Rath rescue effort was carefully crafted within the boundaries of a private economy. For example, the Black Hawk County Economic Development Committee was a public-private alliance that played a supportive, not directive, role as the company tried to return to profitability. Also, the financial assistance packages to Rath were set up with the company as the primary decision-maker in the economic recovery of the firm. The boundary line between the public and private sides of the political economy was well respected; offset policies were intended to support and strengthen the private character of the local economy.

In the Mon Valley, economic accumulation as a level of analysis also proved critical in helping to explain why an even more interventionist player government role was the result. Unlike Louisville and Waterloo the Mon Valley was in the midst of a severe economic downturn that appeared to have no end in sight. Although Pittsburgh was touting the benefits of a growing high-tech and service economy, the mill towns of the Mon Valley saw little of this positive side of "creative destruction." In these mill towns, economic conditions had reached depression levels, with unemployment estimates ranging from

15 to 40 percent. As many concluded, the private economy was failing their communities. For the Mon Valley this was not a simple market failure that could be remedied with an offset response. Putting communities back on their economic feet required a stronger government role, so the Steel Valley Authority with its player agenda had a strong appeal.

However, the Steel Valley Authority represented an explicitly political effort to return the local economy to a condition of prosperity. This effort raised questions at the level of economic accumulation that challenged the dominant position of private enterprise in a capitalist economy. The Tri-State Conference on Steel and the Steel Valley Authority attacked the social irresponsibility of private corporations, particularly U.S. Steel, and asserted that the community had a right to guide, if not control, the use of economic resources.

The difficulties in such a challenge were discussed in Chapter 5. For example, a number of local officials simply refused to support Tri-State and the Steel Valley Authority. While reasons varied, for many the challenge to private enterprise presented by the Authority, Tri-State, and others was simply unacceptable. Particularly in Duquesne, a city in which 50 to 60 percent of the city's budget could be attributed to the presence of the U.S. Steel mill, the refusal to follow the Steel Valley Authority's player strategy, preferring instead to work within options established by U.S. Steel, was significant. Furthermore, those municipalities that did join restricted the legal and financial abilities of the Authority; government officials were protective of their limited resources and autonomy. Also in its court strategy against the American Standard Corporation, the Authority faced a legal system structured around the protection of private property. The Authority's advocacy of a "community right" in economic development lay outside the bounds of this legal system. Such obstacles highlight the difficulties of challenging the prevailing process of economic accumulation and its attendant institutions.

To summarize, this level of analysis offers an important vantage point for understanding the urban policy process. The economic conditions in a community set the stage for subsequent policy debate. Maintaining a healthy local economy, and doing so by supporting private enterprise, are major starting points for urban economic policymaking. However, the manner in which policymakers respond is less clear from a focus at this level of analysis. While dire economic conditions may be associated with more interventionist government strategies, this is not always the case, as Duquesne and West Homestead demonstrate. As Todd Swanstrom concludes, "In the final analysis, local government policies are never 'determined' by economic pressures. No one puts a gun to the heads of local policymakers."[2] The choice of policy roles—whether bystander, offset, or player—may be framed by the policy concern for a healthy economy, but it is also a political choice. To look closer at that process of choice, we need to consider other levels of analysis.

Institutional System

Business corporations, labor unions, community organizations, and governmental units represent different settings of resources and behavioral standards that influence the policy process, and that are in turn shaped and constrained by the nature of a private enterprise economy. In each case study,
analysis at the institutional level adds to our understanding of the respective
policy responses.

In Louisville the institutional system was dominated by the Brown & Williamson Corporation. The decisions to close the Louisville plant, expand the
Macon plant, and retain its headquarters in Louisville were all decisions
made within the company's organizational setting of goals and resources.
Furthermore, the collective-bargaining relationship between the company
and its unions constituted an important institutional relationship that guided
the adjustment process. To be certain, the institutional role played by Brown
& Williamson was supported by its status as a private corporation in a capitalist economy; the institutional level is clearly "nested" within that of economic accumulation. However, closing the Louisville plant was not the company's only choice: Brown & Williamson could have modernized the Louisville
facility, expanded production at its Petersburg plant, or chosen another in-
vestment/disinvestment strategy. To explain the actual closing decision as
well as the negotiations that led to the Settlement Agreement requires close
attention to the nature of the Louisville plant, decision making within this
multinational firm, and the company's relationship with the tobacco workers' union. These features cannot adequately be considered at the broader
level of economic accumulation, although they certainly are conditioned by
that environment.

Although the private side of the political economy dominated the institutional level in Louisville, analysis of the public side was still important. In
particular, several features of the government setting pointed to a limited role
in plant closings: fragmentation and competition between the city and county
on economic development activities, relatively new and weak economic policy tools, little continuity between city government administrations, and limited previous experience with plant closings. Although not precluding a more
active role, these features would have posed significant challenges to policymakers seeking to pursue an offset or player role.

In Waterloo the institutional level of analysis provides important insights
for understanding the role of government as well as actors in the private sector. On the government side the organizational environment included several
important features that were supportive of an active, offset government role.
In particular the prior existence of the Black Hawk County Economic Development Committee offered a platform for a policy response to the problems
at Rath. Although the Economic Development Committee was weak as an

institution (e.g., its staff and financial resources were limited), it did provide a forum within which city, county, and private parties could discuss economic issues. Transforming the committee into a stronger organization to respond to the problems at Rath was not a simple step, but át least the foundation was in place. Complementing the Economic Development Committee was the presence of several federal grant programs (U.S. EDA and HUD) that offered a means to overcome limited local fiscal resources. Although these federal programs were available to policymakers in Louisville and to a lesser extent in the Mon Valley, their availability in Waterloo could be particularly significant, since they compensated for a critical offset resource—money—lacked by the Economic Development Committee. These federal programs were central to the brokerage role played by local governments.

However, government agencies also demonstrated numerous obstacles to an active government role. As in Louisville, one could cite a number of impediments to an offset role: few government policy tools to assist ailing businesses, limited professional staff in economic development, and little previous experience with plant closings. These obstacles posed a considerable challenge to policymakers intent on keeping the Rath plant open. Thus, there were both constraints and opportunities on the public side of the institutional environment.

With respect to the private side of the political economy, an institutional level of analysis is also important for understanding the actions of Rath Packing Company and the United Food and Commercial Workers Union. In the case of Rath, years of operating deficits significantly reduced the flexibility of the company. Quite unlike Brown & Williamson, Rath had lost control over its own economic future. While the company still played an important role in deciding how government loans would be spent, Rath had to settle for an agenda set, in part, by private consultants through the feasibility study. In the policy debate, Rath operated from a much weaker position than Brown & Williamson, U.S. Steel, and the American Standard Corporation.

From an institutional level the labor union at Rath also operated from a weakened position. The initial response by the United Food and Commercial Workers Union was to treat the company's call for labor concessions as another issue to be settled over the collective-bargaining table. As in Louisville the labor contract was the institutional framework for business-labor discussions. The resource base of the union—its membership—was oriented to this collective-bargaining structure. However, the policy process very quickly deviated from this arena; first as members on the County Economic Development Committee, then as partners in an employee ownership effort, the union ventured into arenas quite different than collective bargaining. While the union adapted to its new roles, these were difficult transitions.

Finally, an institutional perspective is central to understanding the player response in the Mon Valley. The Mon Valley experience actually is a case study in institution building. When the fragmentation of individual mill towns made a coordinated response to regional economic decline very difficult, the Steel Valley Authority was created as an intermunicipal body supported by local government officials as well as private community groups. In creating the Authority the focus was on two key organizational components – eminent domain and a governmental authority structure. Based on these components the task was to build a new institution that could play a strong role in economic change while representing the interests of the Mon Valley mill towns.

An institutional level is invaluable for understanding the basic nature and strategies of the Steel Valley Authority as well. For example, to protect their own autonomy and financial well-being, policymakers in member municipalities were reluctant to grant the Authority broad organizational capabilities. Thus, the Authority's financial base was limited, and its ability to pursue development projects was restricted by voting procedures. These organizational weaknesses were most apparent when the Authority was compared with other, more established governmental actors involved in economic development.

On the private side in the Mon Valley, as in Louisville and Waterloo, the decisions and actions of private businesses set the immediate stage for the policy response. Here, the investment and disinvestment strategies of U.S. Steel and American Standard were key. For both companies the closing decisions were based on business calculations to ensure the long-term survival of the corporation. U.S. Steel, for example, was diversifying its holdings and significantly reducing its presence in the steel industry by eliminating what it described as excess capacity. However, U.S. Steel was not exiting the industry; the company intended to remain competitive in steel. Such organizational rationales are important for understanding the company's role in the closing process. For U.S. Steel, as with Brown & Williamson, there was no interest in maintaining production at a facility that only added to the excess capacity problem. Thus, U.S. Steel opposed efforts to reopen the Duquesne mill. The Waterloo experience is the obvious contrast, since Rath Packing Company was actively seeking ways to remain open. As economic organizations Rath, U.S. Steel, and Brown & Williamson had quite different resources and goals.

To conclude, the institutional environment in urban America is a complex setting of public and private organizations with quite different resources, capabilities, and goals that shape the course of public policymaking. In the case of plant closings, corporations are typically the most critical organizations. Based on their control of economic resources as well as their specific corporate goals, businesses set the initial terms of a plant-closing adjustment process. Brown & Williamson and U.S. Steel were in the strongest position in this regard, but even Rath was instrumental in shaping the adjustment process. Business corporations continue to occupy a privileged position in the urban political economy.

Although local governments are in a weaker institutional position, they nevertheless can play an important part. For example, the Black Hawk County Economic Development Committee played an instrumental role in Waterloo's offset response. The limited resources possessed by the EDC were augmented by federal grants that allowed the committee to take a lead role in the response. However, the lack of resources can be a major stumbling block; the early setbacks faced by the Steel Valley Authority could be attributed in large part to financial weaknesses. Building an organizational base of staff, financial, and other key resources is a major challenge for local governments. To meet this challenge often requires alliance building among various parties, which in turn directs us to the third level of analysis.

Political Alliance Formation and Mobilization

Although the levels of economic accumulation and institutions identify important structural features in the environment, alliance formation and mobilization capture the changing dynamics of the policy process. Whether dominated by government officials, business leaders, labor leaders, or community organizers, alliance formation and mobilization are critical components in urban economic policymaking.

The Louisville case, however, actually exemplifies the absence of such strategies and activities. In neither the public sector nor the private sector were there significant efforts to form political alliances or mobilize resources to alter the plant-closing process. Interest and attention were elsewhere. In the private sector, for example, there were no political efforts on the part of labor, community groups, or the company to alter the existing process. In general the closing was accepted by all parties as an unavoidable fact. The labor union lamented the loss of jobs, but the Settlement Agreement provided a good benefit package for workers, and the union would still represent workers at the new plant in Georgia. Brown & Williamson, far from seeking new alliances and political coalitions, wanted to avoid any such happenings. The company viewed the closing as a private matter that did not require government intervention.

Given the lack of pressure for government action, it is not surprising that political leaders in the area showed little interest in taking a part in the closing process. The county/judge executive, Republican Mitch McConnell, was an ambitious politican (he currently serves in the U.S. Senate) whose style of leadership was premised on a reactive approach; he was unlikely to challenge or confront a major corporation that was not seeking government assistance. The mayor, Democrat William Stansbury, who was absorbed in an ongoing controversy with the city council, was also unlikely to intervene. For both political officials "risk avoidance" best describes their political styles.[3] Neither were likely candidates to challenge Brown & Williamson's closing plans.

Thus, at the level of alliance formation and mobilization, neither private sector groups nor key government leaders had an interest in mobilizing resources to change the plant-closing process. For government officials a bystander role was sufficient as the collective-bargaining table became the center of attention. The adjustment process in Louisville would be determined by the institutional arrangements between labor and management, not by the formation of new political alliances or mobilization of resources.

If Louisville exemplifies the absence of mobilization, the Waterloo experience highlights the potential role of government leaders in mobilizing resources and forming alliances. In particular, the offset response in Waterloo was led by Black Hawk County Supervisor Lynn Cutler, who, with her history of partisan activities, political affiliations, and electoral goals, assumed the role of local political entrepreneur. Cutler used her position on the county Economic Development Committee to reconstitute it as a platform for the community's response, and with her direction and through her contacts, the committee received federal grants. Thus, a personal agenda and political connections proved critical in mobilizing resources for this offset response.

There were other candidates for political mobilization in Waterloo, but they were more often constrained by the institutional environment within which they operated. Organized labor, for example, was interested in keeping Rath open, but their initial response was structured around the collective-bargaining relationship with the company, rather than a comprehensive strategy to save Rath. The company was also a candidate to mobilize resources, but it was weakened by its poor financial standing. Lacking investment resources and showing a negative operating record for a number of years, Rath was in a poor position to take a lead role in building community support. Thus, even though both labor and management were receptive to alliance-building efforts, they were not in the lead — that role being filled by Cutler and other government officials.

In the Mon Valley, the Tri-State Conference on Steel provided the key political catalyst. The institution-building process that resulted in the Steel Valley Authority was predicated upon an extensive campaign to mobilize government and community support. Tri-State and other like-minded supporters relied on a lengthy campaign that included lobbying government officials, attending town meetings, sponsoring public rallies, and providing information to the public. This mobilization effort was led by a group of workers, lawyers, academics, and clergy dedicated to a community-based strategy to stop deindustrialization.

The campaign to create the Steel Valley Authority also benefited from previous efforts to mobilize political support for community control of economic resources. Although unsuccessful in terms of implementing specific actions, these mobilization efforts in Midland, West Homestead, and Pittsburgh provided useful learning experiences. In addition to Tri-State, other groups in the Mon Valley—for example, the Denominational Ministry Strategy, the United Steelworkers Union and its various locals, and the Mon Valley Unemployed Committee—raised the level of awareness as to the need for political alliances and mobilization to stop deindustrialization.

Government leaders played a limited role in this mobilization effort. Active political leadership was common in Allegheny County and in Pittsburgh, but it was leadership premised on a public-private partnership approach to economic development that had characterized the Pittsburgh region since the mid-1940s. Tri-State's advocacy for community control of economic resources and the use of eminent domain against uncooperative corporations did not fit into this model. In the smaller Mon Valley communities many government leaders were less concerned about antagonizing large corporations, but they had limited economic resources at their disposal and questioned whether the Steel Valley Authority represented a viable strategy to stop deindustrialization. The player response that developed drew support from some of these officials, but they did not lead the mobilization efforts; more often, they were brought into the process by labor and community activists.

In summary, government officials (such as Lynn Cutler) or community groups (such as the Tri-State Conference on Steel) play a pivotal role in policymaking when they mobilize key resources and establish alliances of support for policy goals. If the goal is an offset response, as in Waterloo, the primary task is to obtain needed resources and build a consensus around a government assistance package. If the goal is a player role in the populist manner, as in the Mon Valley, the challenge is formidable; resources must be identified and support garnered for policies that challenge the private control of economic resources. As the Mon Valley experience makes clear, such challenges face numerous legal, financial, organizational, and ideological obstacles.

Problem Definition

A critical step in most mobilization efforts is the establishment of a supportive problem definition. Problem definitions set the language of debate among policy actors and can be critical in shaping policy responses. As R. J. Lustig reminds us, "It is an old truth of politics that power is revealed not by those who have the ability to provide answers but by those who frame the original questions."[4] In each case study, how the "original question" was framed proved critical in molding the respective responses. Different parties to the plant closing process, whether in the public or private sector, attempted to frame the closing problem in ways advantageous to their goals. As noted in Chapter 2 this framing process typically involves three dimensions—a standard of judgment, explanation of causation, and assignment of remedial responsibility. A quick review reveals the diverse nature of problem definitions.

Standards of judgment varied quite dramatically in the case studies. One standard that appeared prominently in both Louisville and the Mon Valley was corporate profitability. Brown & Williamson emphasized this standard in its decision to close its tobacco products plant, and U.S. Steel argued that the Duquesne mill no longer fit in the corporation's balance sheet. For both companies the economic success of the corporation served as the standard. However, in sharp contrast to this standard, the Tri-State Conference on Steel used community welfare as its standard of judgement. From this perspective, deindustrialization in the region, including the closing of the Duquesne mill, was undermining the economic base of Mon Valley communities. Community welfare, not corporate profits, was the key standard. A third standard, prominent in the Waterloo case, focused on economic efficiency. Although similar to corporate profitability, this standard focused less on the circumstances of an individual firm and more on the general requirements to successfully compete in an industry. In Waterloo this standard was applied by outside consultants to Rath Packing Company, revealing a number of conditions that undermined the firm's competitive position.

Explanations for the cause of the plant-closing problem also varied. As might be expected, blame was often spread among labor, management, and general market forces. In all three case studies, proponents of a market explanation could be found. U.S. Steel cited excess capacity in the steel industry; Brown & Williamson complained of soft sales in the cigarette industry; Rath emphasized the cyclical and competitive nature of meatpacking. Alternatively, management was cited as the culprit. The Tri-State Conference on Steel pointed to U.S. Steel's choice to disinvest from steel and expand in other industries, while Rath management was criticized by its workers and outside consultants for poor pricing practices, marketing strategies, and other management practices. And finally, labor was often blamed, for demanding work rules and/or wage levels that could cause a plant's unprofitability. This was true in Waterloo and to a lesser extent in Louisville.

The third dimension in problem definition — remedial responsibility — involved the assignment of responsibility to alleviate the problem. There were a number of candidates in the problem definitions put forth in the case studies. In Louisville, Brown & Williamson, by its own definition, shared responsibility for the adjustment process with the labor union and general market forces. Each would play a part in helping workers and the general community adjust to the closing. Corporate responsibility was also evident in U.S. Steel's establishment of a workers' assistance center and its pledge to help Duquesne create an industrial park on the site of the mill. Certainly, government was also a prime candidate for assuming remedial responsibility. The Tri-State Conference on Steel, for example, emphasized that government would have to play a major role if the problem of regional deindustrialization was to be addressed. Perhaps the broadest assignment of responsibility came in Waterloo when the outside consultants declared that labor, management, and government would each need to play a part if the problems at Rath were to be solved.

Which problem definition survived set the basic terms of debate in each community. In Louisville, Brown & Williamson's version of the plant closing framed the policy process; in Waterloo the definition outlined in the feasibility study was generally accepted; and in the Mon Valley the problem definition established by the Tri-State Conference on Steel received substantial, although qualified, support. While in some instances, as in the Mon Valley, this was a highly contested process, in others, as in Louisville, there was less controversy. Why one definition succeeded over another raises significant questions for studying policy responses. Although there is no simple answer, several common features tend to characterize the dominant definitions.

First, the definitions that survived presented comprehensive interpretations of the problem. These definitions were most specific in stating a standard of judgment, explaining the events that led up to the problem, and presenting a remedial strategy. In particular, offering a solution to the problem was critical. Without a coherent and viable solution the problem definition had little chance of gaining government support and molding the policy process.[5]

In the Mon Valley, for example, both Tri-State and the Denominational Ministry Strategy presented critiques of corporate actions, but the DMS did not present a clear solution to the problem it identified. Tri-State, however, was explicit about the actions needed, such as creation of the Steel Valley Authority. Tri-State's ability to build support was predicated on the comprehensive nature of their definition. In Waterloo both Rath workers and the feasibility study identified corporate mismanagement as part of the problem, but the workers did not have a solution that appeared viable given the condition of the company. The feasibility study, on the other hand, was very explicit in its call for government action and support for a comprehensive remedial strategy.

In addition to their comprehensive nature, these definitions stood above the rest because the proponents of each could make a claim of authority or knowledge to legitimate their interpretation. This basis proved important in winning general support. Brown & Williamson, for example, implicitly rested its definition on economic science and the authority the market brings to economic interactions. The "laws" of the market — the imperative to meet supply and demand — were presented and generally accepted as the authoritative context for understanding the plant closing. In Waterloo the basis of authority was the expertise of outside professional consultants. The individuals who conducted the feasibility study were described as business and engineering experts qualified to judge and evaluate the situation at Rath. Although not everyone agreed with the consultants, the claim of expertise served to legitimate the conclusions of the study. In the Mon Valley a base of authority or knowledge was more problematic. Tri-State could not speak with the authority of government, and furthermore it was presenting a problem definition that challenged U.S. Steel and other prominent organizations in the area. However, Tri-State did win support by using its knowledge of the steel industry and U.S. Steel to explain how the Mon Valley was a victim of corporate disinvestment. To add to this and give its definition a base of future authority, Tri-State presented the Steel Valley Authority as a legitimate governmental entity incorporated under state laws with the purpose of representing the mill towns in the area.

And finally, each definition that shaped the policy process had a significant degree of political acceptability. In particular, each definition met the interests of a large number of people and did so within the prevailing biases of the community. Each definition called for a government role that was appropriate and acceptable within the context of that community. Thus, in Louisville, Brown & Williamson's definition explicitly recognized the interests of its workers to receive closing benefits, and it also recognized the needs of the community by retaining its corporate headquarters in the city. In this definition government action was unnecessary, a position that fit with the basic interests of local policymakers. In Waterloo, the feasibility study was also very explicit about sharing the burden of the problem and trying to meet the needs of all parties. Labor, management, and government were given a role in this plant closing definition. The fact that government would take an active role was also acceptable given the interests of politicians such as Lynn Cutler.

In the Mon Valley, Tri-State's definition of the problem was certainly challenged, but it became evident to many that assertive action was needed if their communities were to survive. Depression-level conditions in the valley were hard to ignore, and the interest in survival made a stand such as Tri-State's appear increasingly acceptable. Even though the government role advocated by Tri-State received guarded support, it was still acceptable given the needs of the Mon Valley mill towns.

Summing Up: Business Power and Political Action

In comparing these three plant-closing experiences, two broad themes capture our attention. First, private business corporations occupy a powerful position in the urban political economy. It bears repeating that capitalism has bestowed upon the business corporation a position of privilege. This position can be challenged and weakened, but it usually remains intact. Second, politics and alliance building can play a significant role at the urban level, but they do so within a mediated setting; economic and institutional environments structure the form and nature of politics.

The Louisville experience provides a clear example of the power of the business corporation. Through its control of financial investments and the established relationship with organized labor, Brown & Williamson was able to steer the adjustment process to suit its interests. As argued earlier this privileged position was rooted in both the economic and institutional levels of analysis. Supporting this position of power was a problem definition that conformed to the circumstances of the Louisville economy as well as to the interests of many involved parties. In this definition Brown & Williamson was able to define government as essentially irrelevant to the plant-closing process. The weakness, indeed absence, of politics and political mobilization was most apparent in these circumstances. When the adjustment process is so deeply embedded in private-sector institutions, the result is typically a conservative brand of politics in which local governments assume a bystander role.

The Waterloo experience provides a useful counterexample by tempering the conclusions drawn from Louisville. More specifically, while the business corporation still occupies a powerful position, weaknesses are apparent. In this case study the corporation, Rath Packing Company, lacked control over its financial future and was demoted as an actor in the urban political economy. While the company still played a role in determining its own recovery plans, it did not control the problem definition and terms of debate. In politics as well, Waterloo provides a contrast to the Louisville experience. Here, urban politics and political mobilization made a difference, as demonstrated by Lynn Cutler's effective offset response. The liberal politics of compromise and consensus have a place at the urban level.

And finally, the Mon Valley experience brings us back to a middle ground. When politics and political mobilization directly confront a business corporation, the result is likely to favor the corporation, although politics can make a difference. Supported by the tenets of capitalism, U.S. Steel and the American Standard Corporation set the initial agendas in their respective plant closings and continued to shape the policy process. As in Louisville both companies controlled their investment resources, yet, unlike Louisville, their privileged position was challenged by outside parties. In general they held up to this challenge, but not without making compromises along the way. Those compromises reflected the potential for political mobilization. The Tri-State Conference on Steel succeeded in adding a new actor to the institutional system and raising to the public agenda a challenge to business control of investment. The aspirations of the Steel Valley Authority to be what I call a populist player represent a significant institutional change in the urban political economy. The compromises and limitations that confronted the Steel Valley Authority attest to the difficulties of the task, but a populist brand of politics is possible in urban America.

THE DEPENDENT CITY?

Thus, we return to a question introduced early in the book: Is the American city a dependent city? That is, are urban government officials so constrained by the legal, financial, political, and economic setting that they have little policymaking autonomy and flexibility? This issue of urban dependence merits reconsideration in light of the experiences in Waterloo, Louisville, and the Mon Valley. Based on a study of the plant-closing responses in these communities, how does the theme of urban dependence fare?

The short answer to the question is yes — policymakers in the three communities were dependent on and constrained by numerous outside forces. The claims of "dependent city," "city limits," and similar descriptions of urban policymaking are generally supported in this study. Yet such generalizations can be misleading. Urban dependence and policy constraints are real, but generalizations obscure their complexity. Urban dependence has a number of different dimensions.

At the level of economic accumulation, dependence is quite evident in the reliance government officials place on a healthy private economy. The private economy serves as a major source of government revenues as well as the basis for a community's prosperity and welfare. In each of the communities studied here, policymakers recognized the importance of the private economy and adjusted their needs and actions accordingly. This was true whether the local economy was strong, as in Louisville, or relatively weak, as in the Mon Valley. Supporting an already healthy economy or reviving a faltering one were imperatives for urban policymakers.

In the course of supporting a private economy, government officials were also constrained in the types of policies they could initiate. More specifically, urban economic policies had to conform to the basic nature of a private enterprise economy, particularly the private control of investment. Without such conformity, local officials faced the possibility of further disinvestment. As Charles Lindblom argues, "Any change or reform they [businessmen] do not like brings to all of us the punishment of unemployment or a sluggish economy."[6] Bystander and offset roles fit easily within these constraints, but the interventionist nature of a player government role is more problematic. In essence the level of economic accumulation highlights a systemic bias in which urban policymakers — whether they are aware of it or not — are constrained by the need to support a private enterprise economy.[7] Policymakers operate under the assumption that the role of government is to support the local economy, resulting in what Lindblom calls a "policy prison" — a range of political and economic issues are effectively removed from policy consideration for fear of disrupting or otherwise damaging the local economy.[8] In Waterloo, for example, placing a local government official on the Rath board of directors was dismissed because it challenged private control of the firm, and in the Mon Valley the use of eminent domain to prevent the closing of an industrial plant would have constituted, as many local officials argued, an inappropriate use of government power against a private firm.

Urban dependence is also apparent in the institutional system. In the world of public and private organizations, local policymakers are dependent on the availability and use of key organizational resources needed for effective policymaking and implementation. In the public domain the case studies revealed a number of institutional constraints. In Louisville, for example, economic policymaking was fragmented between the city and the county; in Waterloo, limited local economic development tools and federal grant requirements shaped and delayed the policy response; and in the Mon Valley the limited jurisdiction of individual mill towns weakened local policy efforts and highlighted the need for a regional entity to play a role in economic development. Dependence at the institutional level is evident with respect to private-sector organizations as well. In particular, local policymakers are dependent on the investment and disinvestment actions of individual business firms. This dependence, which is a direct consequence of economic dependence at the level of accumulation, highlights the financial resources of individual business organizations and the resulting privileged position that businesses occupy. Thus, in Louisville, Brown & Williamson's investment and disinvestment decisions established the basis for the adjustment process; in Waterloo, Rath's financial needs became the central concern of policymakers; and in the Mon Valley, U.S. Steel's insistence on dismantling the Duquesne mill set the stage for a player response to reopen the mill.

Importantly, this dependence on private businesses does not require participation in the policy process by members of the business community. Business firms can exercise "power without participation."[9] The knowledge by policymakers that a firm can withdraw investments from the community may be sufficient to influence the policy process in directions favorable to the interests of business. In Waterloo, for example, the initial government response to the problems at Rath was not generated by Rath's participation or lobbying but by the fear of economic losses that would accompany a closing. Business firms need not act to exercise this form of power; it is inherent in the financial resources they control.

At the third level of analysis, local policymakers are dependent on the political alliances they form and the community support they mobilize. Neither task is simple. Alliance building often entails compromises that can dilute the purpose and strength of a project. For example, the Steel Valley Authority's powers were diluted by the various compromises required to ensure its creation; the alliance-building process among the nine member municipalities was essential for establishing the Authority. Holding community support at the ballot box is also a decisive factor for many local officials. In Waterloo, Lynn Cutler's electoral interests helped to shape her response to the problems at Rath. Such constraints exist to a greater or lesser degree in many communities.

And finally, our discussion of problem definition adds an additional dimension to urban dependence. Problem definition reveals the important role ideas and belief systems play in the policy process.[10] As Jeffrey Henig notes, "Those who wish to motivate others to action err if they proceed as if the battle for power can proceed in isolation from or prior to the battle of ideas."[11] Thus, in Louisville, the laws of the market became an important constraining force on the policy process, while in the Mon Valley a belief in public-private economic partnerships limited the role many policymakers were willing to grant the Steel Valley Authority. In both cases, the range of policy options depended on prevailing ideas and beliefs. Indeed, a critical step for Steel Valley Authority was to change the prevailing set of economic ideas and interpretations that constrained policymakers in confronting plant closings.

Of course, even as urban dependence is a major theme, politics and political action have their place. After all, Lynn Cutler's entrepreneurial strategies in Waterloo and the efforts by the Tri-State Conference on Steel to mobilize citizens in the Mon Valley cannot be explained solely by the dimensions of urban dependence. The goals, strategies, and actions of individuals and groups engaged in the policy process must be assessed; different responses to plant closings entail quite different political skills and capacities. As I suggest in the concluding chapter, this range of political strategies and actions, particularly in offset and player responses, is an indispensable key to our understanding of the urban political economy.

7

Responses to Plant Closings: The Challenge for Local Governments

In this chapter we will look at the general nature and characteristics of the bystander, offset, and player responses. In particular, our focus is on the questions local policymakers face: What are the typical decisions and choices in each type of response? What skills and resources are required for each? Which responses are likely to succeed? These questions pose an important challenge for local officials. Particularly in offset and player responses, government officials engage in activities that test their skills, knowledge, and expertise. Finding grants, interpreting federal and state laws, understanding industry trends, reading corporate balance sheets, and mobilizing general political support are but a few of the tasks faced by local officials.

To provide a broader base for understanding these challenges, additional examples of each type of plant-closing response are discussed below. In introducing additional examples two points become readily apparent. First, each policy type is more complex than an individual case study would indicate. Although each policy type is organized around common characteristics, there are variations as well; rarely are two plant-closing experiences that fit under one policy type exactly alike. And second, it is often the case that actual plant-closing experiences are a composite of two or three of the policy types rather than a "pure" case of only one type. Reality rarely conforms to descriptive typologies. This mixed nature was noted in the Mon Valley case study and is true in a number of the cases cited in this chapter.

BYSTANDER RESPONSES

In a bystander response, attention is focused on private-sector actors rather than on government officials. As in the Brown & Williamson closing in Louisville, local policymakers play little role in the adjustment process, although federal and state governments may facilitate the private adjustment process, such as through the legal framework for union-management collective bargaining. Thus, in a bystander response, private actors, such as the business firm and labor organization, identify adjustment options and determine the distribution of costs and benefits from a plant closing. As noted in Chapter 3, the result is a process of privatism in which public purposes are defined through private interests and goals.

The exact form of privatism varies from case to case, but three elements are common. First, in most bystander responses the business corporation assumes the dominant role; corporate policy guides the response. In the Louisville case study, for example, the Brown & Williamson Corporation successfully defined the plant closing problem and set basic boundaries for the adjustment process. There was little challenge, from either labor or government, to the company's decision to close the plant or to the company's benefit plan for workers.

A second frequent element of privatism, also evident in the Louisville case, is the central role of union-management relations. In Louisville the contractual relationship between Brown & Williamson and the Bakery, Confectionery, and Tobacco Workers Union provided the framework for adjustment. Government policymakers had no role in this process beyond support for national labor-management law. In other plant-closing cases as well, the labor contract plays an important part by stipulating advance notice of the closing and various employee benefits, such as severance pay, supplemental unemployment benefits, and job search assistance.

And finally, a third element found in several bystander examples, although not in the Louisville case study, is broad-based community action to shape the closing response. Although the labor union may participate, the focus is not on the labor contract. Rather, proposals such as community/employee ownership are considered outside the collective bargaining context as a means to keep the plant open. Alternatively, if adjustment to a closed plant is the goal, community-based organizations could lead labor retraining and general economic development efforts. Although community action has a populist tone, the distinguishing characteristic in these cases is the minor role played by government. Private action remains the overriding theme.

Corporate Policy

This element is present in almost all bystander examples, yet there are some cases in which it is more prominent. In particular, if the closing involves a firm in which workers are not unionized, the business corporation is unlikely to be constrained by labor contract obligations. In addition, since very few communities or states have plant-closing laws or ordinances (discussed later in this chapter), there are no legal strictures on what the firm must do during a closing process. Thus, in many plant closings the business firm is free to shape the adjustment process according to its own corporate policies.

The results vary. In positive examples corporate policies can lead to an array of valuable services and compensation benefits for laid-off workers and the community.[1] As in Louisville the adjustment process is cushioned by advance notice, reemployment assistance, financial benefits, and other corporate actions. Alternatively, the business firm can close the plant with little or no notice and leave workers and the community without compensation. In such cases the power of the corporation appears in its most negative light; workers and communities are left with few resources for economic adjustment.

Several plant-closing cases illustrate these possibilities. A recent example that captures the positive side of corporate responsibility is the closing of the International Business Machines (IBM) plant in Greencastle, Indiana.[2] With 985 employees in 1986 the IBM distribution center in Greencastle was the largest employer in this town of 8,400, and with a payroll of $38 million and property tax bill of $800,000, the company was central to the local economy. This situation was soon to change. In November 1986 IBM announced the closing of its plant, as part of its consolidation of facilities around the country. However, IBM did not simply close its doors and leave the community. Taking pride in its tradition of "no layoffs" and corporate responsibility, the company implemented a series of measures to lessen the impact of the closing on its workers, who were not unionized, and the community. For workers the company offered transfer rights to other IBM facilities, along with a moving allowance. For most of those employees who chose to transfer, the company also purchased their houses in Greencastle. Alternatively, for those nearing retirement, an early retirement package with up to two years' additional salary was available. In addition, job-retraining grants were available for workers leaving the company.

For the community, IBM chose, as the *New York Times* noted on March 27, 1988, "to play Santa Claus." It gave the city $1.7 million to offset lost taxes and agreed to continue its annual $120,000 United Way contribution for three years. The company lent two corporate executives to the community to assist in the transition. In addition, IBM offered to give the entire office and warehouse facility to the city. Commented a professor at nearby DePauw University in the *New York Times* on November 18, 1986, "IBM has always been a good corporate citizen." In this closing process government officials played little role, supporting the company's actions and accepting its corporate largesse. As a private corporation IBM benefited from a legal system that protected the right of corporations to close plants and otherwise dispose of assets. IBM's dominant position was well rooted in the framework of government laws and legal principles.

Although a bystander role was dominant for much of the closing process, an offset strategy later developed in which local government officials worked with IBM and local businesses to replace economic losses to the community. To coordinate this effort a Greencastle Development Center was established to attract new businesses. Within months of IBM's closing announcement, over seventy companies contacted local officials. By early 1988 six companies made commitments to move operations to Greencastle. One of the companies purchased the IBM plant for $700,000, the proceeds of which were turned over to the city. Although the transition period remained difficult for the community, Greencastle was on the road to recovery.

In sharp contrast, the closing of the Wisconsin Steel mill in Chicago, Illinois, exemplifies the negative side of corporate power.[3] Wisconsin Steel was one of the original steelmaking complexes on Chicago's south side. Owned by International Harvester since 1902, the mill was the economic lifeblood of the South Deering community. The mill was modernized through the early 1960s, but Harvester's problems in the farm implement business, as well as competition in the steel industry, had negative consequences for the Wisconsin mill. As production declined in the 1970s, Harvester sought an outside buyer. In 1977 the mill was sold to Envirodyne Industries, but operating deficits continued. Although workers knew the mill was in trouble, the closing came without warning. On March 28, 1980, the announcement was made that the mill would close the next day; 3,400 steelworkers were out of a job.

Unlike IBM in Greencastle, Wisconsin Steel workers and the South Deering community received little support from Envirodyne. The company was in bankruptcy court and cited various clauses in its purchase agreement with International Harvester as reason for ending all employee benefits. International Harvester, for its part, denied any liability. The result: Wisconsin Steel workers lost all vacation pay, severance pay, hospitalization, supplemental unemployment benefits, pension supplements, and early retirement pensions. As one final blow, for many workers their last paycheck bounced. Altogether, union members lost $29.2 million in benefits. The only financial compensation came when the federal Pension Benefit Guaranty Corporation assumed responsibility for existing basic pensions.

The union at the mill, the independent Progressive Steelworkers Union, played little role in assisting the workers. Instead the Wisconsin Steelworkers Save Our Jobs Committee formed in 1981 to gather support for reopening the mill as well as securing pay and benefits due to workers. The Save Our Jobs Committee sponsored marches and meetings with government officials and established a food pantry and counseling services for workers. In 1981 a class-action suit was filed to recover lost benefits, which in 1988 resulted in a court-ordered $15-million payment from International Harvester to the workers.

Government officials played a part in the closing process, but their efforts yielded mixed results. The most important government action involved a federal EDA loan guarantee in 1979. This 90-percent loan guarantee was intended to support a facility modernization plan. While an important offset step, the effort did not avert the closing that came six months later. After the mill closed, policymakers at local, state, and federal levels espoused ideas to reopen the mill, but to no avail. A state-supported Cooperative Service Center provided food, medical services, and general information on available services, but this was more in the spirit of general social services than a coordinated offset response. In summary, the actions of Envirodyne and International Harvester guided this policy response.

Collective Bargaining Contracts

In recent years collective-bargaining contracts have played an increasingly important role in plant closings. In this form of privatism the labor-management contract shapes the response, as in Louisville. This contractual relationship establishes an important environment for discussion of adjustment options to either avert a closing or minimize negative consequences of a closing. Efforts to avert a closing often take the form of concessionary bargaining. Unions accept wage and benefit freezes, wage and benefit reductions, and changes in work rules in return for a company pledge to keep a plant open. Indicative of this trend, between 1979 and 1983, when threats of plant closings were commonplace, the proportion of major labor contracts containing a wage freeze or cut in the first year of the contract rose from zero to 28 percent.[4]

While negotiations over a contract may be used to avert a closing, the contract itself often specifies certain obligations for both parties. For example, unionized employees are more likely to receive advance notice of a closing than employees that lack a union contract. A recent study found that 81 percent of union blue-collar workers received advance notice, compared with only 58 percent of nonunion blue-collar workers.[5] In recent years several union-management contracts have even prohibited plant closings. Ford Motor Company, for example, accepted a "no-closing" clause in both its 1984 and 1987 United Automobile Workers (UAW) contracts. If a plant does close, labor contracts may stipulate various reemployment and financial benefits. Using the auto industry again as an example, both Ford and General Motors have UAW contracts that include a broad package of financial benefits and reemployment assistance for laid-off auto workers.[6]

The union contract can also play an important role in the allocation of decision-making rights in the plant-closing process. In particular, if the contract does not specify a union role in the actual decision to close a plant, federal courts have ruled that the company's "duty to bargain" holds only with regard to the effects of the closing. Thus, severance pay can be a mandatory bargaining item, but the actual decision to close a plant is within the managerial prerogatives of the company.[7] In response a number of unions have attempted to establish specific contract provisions to include the union in decisions that may lead to a closing.

Numerous examples, including the Louisville case study, exemplify this collective-bargaining approach to plant closings. One such example is the closing of a Dana Corporation facility in Edgerton, Wisconsin.[8] Dana Corporation, a producer of electrical and auto products, opened the Dana axle production plant in 1972. By 1979 the company employed 1,600 people and was the fourth-largest employer in Rock County. The UAW represented the production workers at the plant and cooperated with the company in the operation of a Scanlon Plan for gain-sharing and productivity improvements. Although production at the plant increased throughout much of the 1970s, in 1979 a shrinking domestic truck market reduced demand for the plant's front axles. Layoffs began, and in May 1980 the company announced the closing of the plant. The union was not consulted regarding the closing decision, but Dana did negotiate on the effects of the closing. Union-management negotiations were facilitated by three months' notice given by Dana, which exceeded the two months' notice required under Wisconsin law.

As in Louisville, the closing agreement contained a number of provisions to buffer the impact of the shutdown. For each worker, Dana agreed to extend medical benefits for up to one year, and for those hourly workers with one year or more of service, an additional eleven months were added to their seniority to make them eligible for pensions. For workers wishing to relocate to other Dana plants, the company agreed to a preferential hiring system for up to five years and relocation assistance of two months' pay.

To assist workers in finding new jobs, Dana established and funded a Job Search Program. The main element in the program was a five-day training session that included skills assessments, job search techniques, résumé writing, and financial planning. The company also assisted by typing job résumés and providing free long-distance telephone service. While these financial and reemployment benefits were important to many workers, Dana did not go as far as IBM did in Greencastle. In particular, the company did not provide severance pay or a special community assistance fund.

During the closing, government officials played a minor role. At the state level the regional Job Service office cooperated by training and assisting Dana staff who were to conduct the Job Search Program, but the Dana program was kept separate from ongoing state Job Service activities. Local officials in the small community of Edgerton (population of 4,000) were even less involved. As one study notes, the local government response was "largely passive"; municipal officials "believed that the shutdown agreement involved only the Dana Corporation and the UAW."[9] This was an adjustment process in which government policymakers allowed private actors to determine the distribution of costs and benefits.

Another example of a plant closing in which the collective bargaining relationship played the central role was the closing of the Armco steel mill in Houston, Texas.[10] Built in the early 1940s the mill was expanded and modernized as employment reached a peak of 4,500 workers in the mid-1970s. However, in the recession of the early 1980s, and along with rising steel imports, production at the mill declined. A productivity improvement program was instituted in July 1983, but to no avail. On October 24, 1984, the company informed the remaining 1,100 active workers that the plant would close the following January.

The major program response to the closing was establishment of the Armco-United Steelworkers of America Worker Assistance Center. Supported in part by a federal grant, the assistance center provided worker assessment, assistance, and referral. Operated at the plant by the company, union, and outside consultants, the center provided an orientation session to explain available company and community services, as well as providing worker-needs assessment, counseling, and referral to other agencies for retraining or social services. The center remained open for eight months after the closing. Limited community services and the lack of a community response team created a void that was filled by the AFL-CIO Community Services Office. The Office initiated an emergency food program and ran a workshop that explained various benefit programs, such as food stamps, and provided information on mortgages, loans, utilities, and resources for medical, alcohol, and other problems.

In the way of financial benefits, the company provided up to two years' severance pay and health care insurance was extended for up to one year. For those workers nearing retirement the company improved its pension plan to make retirement an attractive option. A relocation policy for salaried workers also assisted a number of Armco employees.

As with the Dana closing, government officials primarily played a supporting role. Although there was a significant offset element — a $300,000 federal JTPA Title III grant for the Worker Assistance Center — the basic adjustment process was determined by the company and the union. Local officials did not form a special response group, as in Waterloo, nor did they assume a role in guiding the overall closing process. The federal grant served to facilitate a privately negotiated adjustment.

Community Action

A third possible element in a bystander response highlights actions by private community groups to either avert a plant closing or minimize negative consequences of a closing. Of the two possibilities, keeping the plant open is the likely goal. A common scenario is for local activists and plant employees to put pressure on the company to remain open or sell the plant to an outside buyer or to an employee-community coalition. The degree to which government officials become involved determines whether this remains a bystander response or becomes an offset or even player response.

One example in which government officials played a relatively minor part in comparison with private parties is the employee buyout of Bridgeport Brass in Seymour, Connecticut.[11] Founded in 1878 Bridgeport Brass was one of the area's major employers in a slowly declining brass industry. In early 1984 the conglomerate owner of the plant, National Distillers and Chemical Corporation, announced its intention to either close or sell the 230-employee plant. In response the leadership of the UAW local that represented production workers suggested that employees consider buying the plant. The UAW turned to two community groups for assistance. First, the Industrial Cooperative Association of Boston, which specialized in consulting for worker-owned companies, was asked to discuss with workers the possibilities of an employee buyout. And second, the Naugatuck Valley Project, a local association of workers, religious leaders, and citizens, was asked to assist in the project. After a meeting with workers and interested managers, the decision was made to pursue an employee buyout.

Although skeptical at first, National Distillers agreed to delay the closing and, with broad community support evident, contributed $25,000 toward a feasibility study of a buyout and reduced the asking price for the plant from $13 million to $11 million. An ad hoc buyout committee of workers and managers was expanded to a steering committee that further divided into subcommittees to search for new management, explore production changes, develop a financial plan, and establish an employee education network. The Industrial Cooperative Association continued with the feasibility analysis, and the Naugatuck Valley Project focused on educational and organizing efforts.

By May 1985 the buyout was complete—Seymour Specialty Wire was the name of the new company. To finance the purchase an employee stock ownership plan was established with 100 percent pass-through of voting rights and ownership. In addition, a new labor contract was negotiated that lowered wages by 10 percent, eliminated 40 jobs, and changed various work rules. Although the new company increased production and eventually restored the wage cut, instituting a participatory organizational structure was not a simple task. In 1986 a new cooperative work system was established to address workplace problems at the plant.

Throughout this process government officials provided general support. For example, to help finance the feasibility study the State of Connecticut contributed $7,500 and the Town of Seymour $3,000. However, the majority of financial support for the study came from private parties. Similarly, the buyout itself was funded by private parties (a bank and workers), and the impetus for action and ongoing project support was the result of employee and community efforts. Thus, while the state role had elements of an offset response, the key role played by workers and community-based organizations marked a private approach to the adjustment process.

Local Government Role

The dominant characteristic in a bystander response to plant closings is the reliance on private actors to allocate the costs and benefits of the closing. This faith in private actors to resolve community differences — privatism — is deeply rooted in the American political tradition. Negotiations and compromises among private parties are accepted as legitimate ways to strike a balance among conflicting interests. Thus, corporate policies, labor-management contractual agreements, and community activism are all recognized as mechanisms for a private settlement. Although the consequences of such a settlement can vary, as the IBM and Wisconsin Steel cases exemplify, such results are part of the private dynamic.

With respect to the public domain, the role for local officials is limited. Whereas national and state governments support the private settlement process through "housekeeping" policies such as the protection of private property, local policymakers are primarily bystanders. In such an observer status the demands on local policymakers are few. Still, there are several activities that are appropriate. In particular, local policymakers that adopt a bystander role should be aware of corporate policies, labor-management contracts, and other private mechanisms that could guide a plant closing. While a bystander role does not require intervention in these areas, it would be useful for local officials to know what the responsibilities of private parties are in the event of a plant closing. In this regard, local policymakers need to be knowledgeable in the areas of private-sector labor-management law and corporate decision-making. A reminder by government officials to the company or union that contractual obligations exist may save the community from a very difficult economic transition. In fact, an interest by local officials in the what and how of private settlements may actually serve as a stimulus for the formation of new or more extensive private adjustment arrangements. Statements by local policymakers could encourage private-sector responsibility for the adjustment to economic change. Business corporations, unions, and citizen groups could be challenged to assume responsibility for the adjustment process. Although policymakers could intervene to compensate for missing components or otherwise influence the course of events, and thereby assume an offset role, that need not be the case. Reliance on a private-sector dynamic is a legitimate course for public policy.

Local officials nonetheless must be able to withstand pressures for government intervention. In a plant closing, demands for government support can come from various directions. The business firm, for example, might seek public loans or other types of assistance, while labor and citizen groups might lobby for support of their position. In either case local policymakers must be prepared to deny these demands for government action. To do so is not easy, particularly given the dependence of local policymakers on business tax revenues as well as citizen votes, but it is part of the bystander role.

As a final note it should be mentioned that although demands on local policymakers in a bystander role are few, the costs can be significant. As in the Wisconsin Steel experience, a rise in unemployment, decline in income, and other losses to the community are possible outcomes. One critic comments that in this type of response "private corporations have acquired the power to issue birth certificates and death certificates to entire communities."[12] In effect there is no separate platform for the expression of public purposes that deviate from those agreed on among private parties. If such a platform is desired, policymakers will need to look to offset strategies as a way of introducing public goals and purposes.

OFFSET RESPONSES

As already indicated, in an offset response local policymakers play a more active role in the adjustment experience. Whether the goal is to keep the plant open or minimize negative consequences from a closing, government officials provide key resources to private parties to bring about a successful adjustment. In this process government policymakers seek a consensus to rally support for a policy acceptable to all parties involved in the plant closing.

Although consensus building is the common theme, the task is quite different depending on the policy goal. If the primary effort is to avert a closing, as in Waterloo, Iowa, resources are identified and agreements struck to address the specific problems at the plant. In most cases this becomes a financial offset strategy in which loans, grants, and cost reductions become the focus, with government policymakers, company officials, and labor leaders working together to identify and implement a plan of action. In contrast, if minimizing negative consequences from a closing is the goal, the policy typically becomes a labor offset strategy in which reemployment and other worker assistance efforts are the main concern. Consensus building in such cases is a quite different task, with labor, management, and government contributing to the support of worker services and community rebuilding.

In recent years both versions of an offset response have become popular among local, state, and federal policymakers. In developing either type of offset response, a common starting point in many communities is the formation of a rapid-response team. As with the county Economic Development Committee in Waterloo, a rapid-response or economic action team provides a single forum to coordinate the strategies and actions of labor, government, and business.[13] Consensus building is the primary challenge in this forum as goals and strategies are considered to avert the closing or mitigate a closing's consequences.

State governments, in particular, have taken a lead role in fostering rapid-response teams and offset strategies. California, for example, established one of the first rapid-response teams.[14] Formed in 1981, the California Economic Adjustment Team (CEAT) coordinates the use of federal, state, and local resources to address specific plant closings. With a grant and loan fund for business and worker assistance, CEAT works with local government officials, employers, and workers to fashion a closing response. While efforts might be made to keep a plant open, the typical response is a reemployment center that provides job search assistance, education/training, counseling, and other support services. Although CEAT has been less active in recent years, it still represents an important model. According to one study, over twenty states have followed this pattern by establishing rapid-response teams.[15]

In recent years the federal government has also been supportive of rapid-response teams. Pointing to the Canadian Industrial Adjustment Service as a model, the Department of Labor emphasizes the importance of an early needs assessment of the company and employees along with a cooperative government-labor-management effort to meet those needs.[16] In 1983 the Department of Labor established its own industrial adjustment service, and in 1985 it joined the National Governors' Association to introduce the Canadian model to state governments. An orientation was held in 1986 for thirty-three states, and six (New York, New Jersey, Michigan, Vermont, Ohio, and Iowa) were chosen for demonstration projects during 1987 and 1988.[17] Again the common theme was early intervention and an offset role for state and local governments.

A Financial Offset Approach

In a number of plant-closing situations the initial effort is to reopen or keep open the plant. In the Waterloo case study, for example, keeping the plant open was the major focus of local and federal policy efforts. Although one subcommittee of the Black Hawk County Economic Development Committee did consider retraining and reemployment needs, the clear emphasis of the committee was to save the Rath plant. In such cases the primary concern is identification of specific problems at the plant and viable solutions. As in Waterloo, a feasibility study is often instrumental in this identification process. Government policymakers often provide critical financial resources to support such a study and implement its recommendations.

The possible closing of the Wilson Foods' meatpacking plant in Albert Lea, Minnesota, provides a case in point.[18] With 1,900 employees in 1983, the Wilson plant was the major employer in this southern Minnesota community. The plant, however, was an older structure, similar in many ways to the

Rath plant in Waterloo. In addition to an aging facility, Wilson Foods faced general financial problems in the competitive meatpacking industry. In April 1983 Wilson entered Chapter 11 bankruptcy, unilaterally cut workers' wages, and went through a three-week strike before raising wages again, but still below their prebankruptcy level.

At the prompting of labor and management, the city of Albert Lea assembled a financial assistance package to modernize the plant. This package included a $1-million grant from the state of Minnesota to offset sales and property taxes, $1.2 million in loans from the city, and $2.5 million in loans from fifteen private banks in Freeborn County. Since Wilson was reluctant to modernize the facility and was willing to sell the plant, the package was offered to a prospective buyer. Although the deal was near completion, background checks on the buyer revealed a negative credit and personal history; the assistance offer was withdrawn. With a financial package but no buyer, city officials extended their role beyond the typically reactive nature of an offset response and sought a new owner. A local business person accepted the financial package and purchased the plant, changing the name to Farmstead Foods. A marketing agreement was arranged with Wilson to ensure sales for part of the plant's production. Later in 1984 the plant was sold again, and in 1985 an $8–$10-million modernization project was begun.

This was a policy response in which all parties played a part, albeit in rather different ways. Wilson Foods and the union were not principals in assembling the financial package, but they did play a facilitating role. The union and the company agreed to a one-year moratorium on a possible Albert Lea plant closing, and the labor contract contained a provision requiring six months' notice of a closing. In addition, severance payments and other closing costs made a plant closing unattractive to Wilson. All of these provisions and agreements provided the critical time needed to assemble an offset package.

As in Waterloo, public officials played the entrepreneurial role to save the plant. Commented the eventual purchaser of the plant, the mayor of Albert Lea "led the whole thing and made it possible."[19] In addition to the mayor the governor of Minnesota held two press conferences in Albert Lea and helped in securing a $20-million line of credit for the new company. Federal assistance was sought (an EDA loan guarantee), although unsuccessfully — the Reagan administration had significantly reduced this type of government assistance.

The success story in Albert Lea has been repeated in other communities. In Dubuque, Iowa, for example, city officials assembled a financial package that helped revive the meatpacking plant in that community. In 1982 the city secured a $3-million federal UDAG and combined it with $500,000 in federal Community Development Block Grant (CDBG) funds as a loan to FDL Foods, a new company created by Dubuque Packing Company. Along with wage reductions and private loans, FDL Foods reopened the former Dubuque plant as a pork production facility. As another example, in Gillett, Wisconsin, the state and federal government played an important offset role in reviving Linwood, Inc.[20] In 1984 the parent company of Linwood entered Chapter 11 bankruptcy and soon closed this hardwood products plant. With the support of state officials a loan package was assembled that included $800,000 in federal EDA funds, $623,000 in federal funds allocated through a state program, and $1.3 million in private investment dollars. In addition, the state provided $15,000 to assist in establishing an employee stock ownership plan. With this financial package the plant was reopened and named New Linwood.

A financial offset approach can be successful in keeping a plant open, as in Gillett, Dubuque, and Albert Lea, but it can also have an undesirable side effect when it leads to competition between communities over retaining industrial facilities. Just as numerous states and local governments competed in the mid-1980s for General Motors' Saturn plant, communities can also compete to avoid disinvestment. If a multiplant firm decides to close a plant, communities may compete against one another to avoid the closing of their plant. Each community presents its offset package in an effort to influence the decision of the firm.

Fort Wayne, Indiana, and Springfield, Ohio, provide one example.[21] In 1981 and 1982 International Harvester, which had major production facilities in both communities, faced extensive economic difficulties that many thought might lead to plant closings. Community leaders in both Springfield and Fort Wayne discussed with the company possible assistance packages to ensure continued production at the respective plants. Although International Harvester avoided an explicit comparison of the two plants, in July 1982 it did announce that one of its plants would close. At this point competition between the two communities intensified. Each community assembled an offset package. Springfield's offer involved a sale/lease-back arrangement in which a newly created Community Improvement Corporation would purchase the Harvester plant and then lease the facility back to the company. To finance the purchase, $18.4 million was secured from private lenders and $9.2 million from the state of Ohio. To ensure private support, the state of Ohio agreed to guarantee 85 percent of the value of the loans. Fort Wayne's offset package grew over time. The initial offer involved a $9.2 million loan guarantee. This proposal was soon changed to a sale/lease-back arrangement similar to Springfield's proposal. To purchase the plant, the state of Indiana would contribute $4 million, Allen County $2 million, and the city $3 million. In another addition to the offer, $8 million in low-interest loans would be available for modernization of the facility. By the time the company made a decision, Fort Wayne's offer had grown to $31 million in loans and guarantees.

In September International Harvester made its decision — truck assembly operations would be consolidated at the Springfield plant. In the end company officials claimed that the public assistance packages from the two communities were so comparable that they were not a significant factor. The long-run competitive efficiency of the newer Springfield plant was given as the primary reason for the decision. As discussed later in this section, this case reveals the potential pitfalls of a financial offset approach — public assistance packages of dubious value and questionable benefits for the community.

A Labor Offset Approach

In this type of response the primary effort is to assist workers and the community adjust to the actual closing of a plant. This approach may follow unsuccessful efforts to keep the plant open, or it may be the policy focus from the start. In either case, consensus building is aimed at identifying and implementing an appropriate assistance package to address the needs of laid-off workers and the broader community. As noted earlier, this offset policy is usually dominated by discussions over reemployment opportunities, training, counseling, and other labor support services.

A prominent example of a labor offset response was the closing of the Ford Motor Company plant near San Jose, California.[22] Built in the 1950s, the Ford plant employed approximately 5,000 people at its production peak. However, despite an active employee involvement program and retooling to produce the Escort and Lynx, Ford announced in November 1982 that the plant would close in six months. Ford made the closing decision based on its changing position in the auto industry; it was not a negotiated decision, nor was it subject to change through wage concessions or assistance packages.

In part, the adjustment process to the closing was guided by the collective-bargaining agreement. The relevant provisions in the agreement included six months' notice of the closing; consultation with the union at the national level; company support for worker counseling and outplacement assistance; local union participation; and worker benefits that included severance pay, transfer rights, supplemental unemployment benefits, and continuation of health insurance. With assistance from the national Ford-UAW Employee Development and Training Program, a local committee was established to begin the adjustment process. To support and supplement the benefits stipulated in the labor contract, local and state government officials provided financial and technical assistance. A representative from the California Economic Adjustment Team came to San Jose the day after the announcement and provided "catalytic assistance" to the union-management effort.[23] Within one week of the announcement a community task force was in place to assist labor and management.

With Ford's financial support, an Employment and Retraining Center was established at the plant to provide a focal point for transition services. With state assistance, orientation meetings were held to explain to workers benefits and services, and individual assessments were completed to determine education and retraining needs of workers. In the period leading up to and after the closing, a variety of services were provided for workers: adult basic education, vocational exploration courses, information seminars, targeted vocational retraining, and job search assistance. Participation rates were very high. Seventy percent of workers participated in assessment and testing, and 30 percent participated in education and training courses. Most of these services were delivered at the plant site, even after the plant closed in May 1983. In addition, emergency food, clothing, shelter, and counseling were provided by several United Way agencies. To support these programs and services, approximately $4 million in federal, state, and local funds were combined with $3 million from Ford and the UAW.

The San Jose case not only illustrates an important government role but also demonstrates again the critical role a privately negotiated labor contract can play in the adjustment process. As one business publication described the experience, "The Ford-UAW job initiative was the most ambitious in U.S. labor-management history."[24] In many respects the benefits available to workers exceeded those provided in the Brown & Williamson closing. Yet government officials also played a vital part in this response.

Another example that highlights a government offset role for worker assistance involves the closing of the Empire-Detroit Steel mill in Portsmouth, Ohio.[25] The Empire-Detroit mill, a division of Cyclops Corporation, was a basic steelmaking operation that had been declining in production and employment since 1970. From an employment level of 2,630 in 1970, the mill was down to approximately 1,000 employees by 1980. In January 1980 Empire-Detroit announced the closing of the mill, and in mid-February it set a May 31 closing date. Although the closing was not unexpected, it nevertheless dealt an economic blow to this Ohio River community of 25,000.

The response to the closing comprised public and private efforts to ease the burden of transition experienced by workers. Coordinating these efforts was the Community Action Organization of Scioto County (CAO). With support from the company, United Steelworkers of America Local 2116, the Ohio Governor's Office, the Ohio Bureau of Employment Services, and Scioto County Commissioners, the CAO established and operated a Job Search Assistance Program for Empire-Detroit employees. Services and benefits were available for hourly and salaried employees. For hourly employees a job search center was established at the union hall with job listings, telephone lines, and counseling. Since the local job market was already depressed, relocation assistance included bus trips to other communities for job searches and modest financial support to assist with relocation expenses. A six-month extension of medical insurance was also provided, as well as a supplemental unemployment benefit package. For salaried employees the company provided separate outplacement services. These services included individualized job search assistance and company contacts with other potential employers. If an employee relocated within Cyclops, the company would pay all relocation expenses. In addition, many salaried employees were eligible for immediate pensions or severance pay, and all received a six-month extension of medical coverage. As in San Jose, California, government officials played an important role in providing financial and technical support for these various services.

This type of response has appeared across the country. In Des Moines, Iowa, for example, the Mayor's Task Force on Plant Closings and Retraining was formed in 1981 in the wake of plant-closing announcements by Massey Ferguson and Wilson Foods.[26] With government funding, the Task Force established transition centers for the soon-to-be-unemployed workers. More recently state and local task forces formed in Wisconsin to consider a recovery strategy for Kenosha when the Chrysler auto plant located there closed in late 1988. A major purpose of these task forces is provision of retraining and job search assistance for laid-off autoworkers.

Local Government Role

In contrast to a bystander response, an offset government role finds local policymakers assuming a significant part in shaping and supporting the economic adjustment process. The first steps of an offset response are particularly demanding in the area of consensus building. As a rapid-response or economic action team is formed, local officials typically play a mediator role to find common ground. Conflicting problem definitions from labor, management, and others must be overcome if a coordinated offset response is to succeed. Building such consensus requires negotiation and group dynamic skills that local policymakers may lack. If those skills cannot be developed among local officials, outside consultants may be called on to facilitate the consensus building process.

As one step to reach common ground, a number of offset responses start with a feasibility study, which, as in Waterloo, identifies specific problems and remedial strategies. For policymakers, supporting the study and interpreting the results are critical contributions to the overall response. Thus, financial resources or access to financial resources to support the study are important, as are technical capabilities to interpret the results; both extend beyond the limited requirements of a bystander role.

The need for consensus building and the utility of the feasibility study are often complicated by the short time period available for each. In offset responses, particularly if the goal is to avert a closing, timing may be decisive. Once a plant closes, it is difficult to restart operations and build a customer base, and once workers have left the plant site, it is difficult to assist them in assessing their future job options. So, as in the Waterloo experience, policymakers must be prepared to act quickly. As a member of the state of Pennsylvania's Response Team commented, "The ability to move fast is the team's essential characteristic."[27]

Consensus building and quick action are important, but the demands on local officials do not end there. If the goal is to avert a plant closing, as in Waterloo and Albert Lea, local officials must become familiar with the world of corporate balance sheets and private finance. Although in an offset response business decisions are still private and are not to be preempted by government officials, policymakers should understand the needs and problems at the plant, if they are to account for any resource assistance provided.

Even more important is the ability of local officials to locate and secure financial resources to help address the problems at the plant. Since most local governments have limited financial resources of their own, numerous visits to private banks and other government offices are likely. Convincing private bankers to support a plant rescue attempt requires general knowledge of banking affairs as well as private loan criteria; securing intergovernmental assistance requires grant-writing skills and political contacts. Since the private banking community tends to be skeptical of such rescue attempts, government grantsmanship has become a trademark of officials who engage in financial offset responses. Thus, developing intergovernmental skills is often critical.

In contrast a labor offset strategy emphasizes a different set of policy tools and skills. Rather than corporate balance sheets and financial loans, the central concern in this type of response is labor market services. As in San Jose, Portsmouth, and other cities, local officials help establish retraining classes, counseling offices, job search centers, and other labor market services. To be effective, local officials need a general understanding of labor markets and the types of services needed to assist workers during a period of employment transition. To support these activities grantsmanship may still be important, but the grant requests are of a quite different nature. Instead of business balance sheets, requests for support of labor market services focus on educational and retraining issues. In general this social service orientation of a labor offset strategy is more compatible with the traditional skills and interest of government officials.

The problems and shortcomings of financial and labor offset responses should also be recognized by policymakers. In particular, a financial offset response is occasionally criticized for providing financial assistance when it may not be necessary. The intent of a subsidy package is to offset identified problems at the plant, yet business corporations may be able to extract an assistance package beyond what is necessary to keep a plant operating. Such a public subsidy, what Bryan Jones and Lynn Bachelor refer to as a "corporate surplus," unnecessarily shifts the costs of business adjustment from the corporation to taxpayers.[28] Unless policymakers are knowledgeable about the specific circumstances of an individual corporation, they are unlikely to know whether they are paying this surplus or whether the assistance package is indeed essential. This problem is particularly apparent when communities compete with different assistance packages. For Fort Wayne and Springfield, public subsidies became a prerequisite rather than a deciding factor to save a plant. The use of public subsidies in such cases can become a "beggar thy neighbor" approach to economic development.[29] As Terry Buss and F. Stevens Redburn note, "Local governments, always vulnerable to the claims of private capital, are especially so in hard times."[30] Knowledge of the plant and the relevant industry will not eliminate such pitfalls, but it will place policymakers in a better position to negotiate with private businesses over an assistance package.

In labor offset strategies as well, there are problems local officials should be aware of. In reemployment services, for example, policymakers may offer assistance that has little impact on dislocated workers. Buss and Redburn observe in another article that "programs that offer job search, retraining, and counseling across the board to any displaced worker seeking them are probably not cost-effective."[31] As the authors argue, careful targeting of worker assistance services is needed. Similarly, the types of services provided need to be evaluated. The relative importance of job search assistance versus more expensive retraining programs is one important example. In general, local officials need a basic understanding of labor market services to be informed on choices they may have to make.

Even if such problems are addressed, success is not guaranteed in either offset strategy. Particularly in a financial effort to save a plant, success, as measured by keeping the plant open, is problematic. In the Albert Lea and Gillett examples offset packages were successful, but in Waterloo an offset package ultimately failed (the Rath plant closed in 1985). Success in keeping a plant open is dependent not only on the appropriate use of a financial assistance package but also on other factors external to the offset response: national economic trends, general industry conditions, and the product mix, marketing arrangements, materials prices, labor practices, and management skills at the particular plant. Policymakers cannot control all these variables. The government's offset policy is only one component in a plant's survival effort.

So also a labor strategy may succeed or fail. Success, as measured by reemployment of laid-off workers, is dependent on the labor market services provided as well as the general nature of the local economy. Additional plant closings in the community, general economic decline, changing local industry mix, or other community wide characteristics can easily overwhelm the job search and retraining efforts sponsored by a labor offset policy. Again policy success or failure will depend partially on factors outside the reach of government policymakers.

The challenge is great. Outside factors can sidetrack an offset response, and the requisite skills for a successful response are many. In general, policy capabilities are needed to evaluate the appropriateness and effectiveness of an offset package, which is no small task for any government, particularly local governments with their limited resources. However, such capabilities are important if offset strategies are to be guided by informed policy discussions.

PLAYER RESPONSES

As in the Steel Valley Authority case this form of response involves a more interventionist role for government policymakers, with local officials using available policy tools, or creating new ones, to shape or impose an adjustment process. As noted in Chapter 1, a player role can assume two rather different forms. First, local policymakers can become players through an active and ongoing role in economic decision-making by building on the cooperative environment of an offset response. For example, public officials might participate in such key business decisions as marketing strategies, management reorganization, and product development. In recent years "social compacts" among labor, management, and government as well as more interventionist rapid-response teams point in the direction of this type of player response.

Second, a player role can be based on the authoritative actions of government. Rather than relying on voluntary compliance this player version highlights policies that mandate a change in the existing adjustment pattern to a plant closing. While this is likely to be combined with other policy strategies, the important distinction is the use, or attempted use, of political authority to specify a particular course of action or outcome. Plant-closing laws, for example, provide new boundaries or rules with which to structure the adjustment process. Alternatively, eminent domain might be used to take over a plant, or an injunction can be sought — as in the Steel Valley Authority's case against the American Standard Corporation — to prevent removal of equipment from a plant.

A Participatory Approach: Social Compacts

One means of stepping beyond the reactive nature of an offset response is through government sponsorship of social compacts. In a social compact government, business and labor agree, prior to a specific plant closing, to follow certain guidelines in the event or likelihood of a closing. These guidelines specify actions to either avert a closing or minimize negative consequences. In social compacts government policymakers play an active role through financial inducements, moral suasion, or other means to support an environment of shared responsibilities.

State governments have been instrumental in developing this type of policy response. Massachusetts initiated one of the first social compacts in 1984 as part of its Mature Industries legislation.[32] The Massachusetts Social Compact is a voluntary agreement under which businesses make good-faith efforts to provide advance notice, severance pay, health insurance, and reemployment assistance to employees affected by plant closings and major layoffs. State officials recognize that not all employers will be able to meet these terms, so government also provides supplemental unemployment benefits, reemployment services, and health care benefits when needed. In addition, the state provides financial and technical assistance to troubled firms (see below). For those companies accepting financial aid from a state agency, agreement with the Social Compact is a prerequisite for assistance.[33]

Massachusetts has been followed by other states. In 1985 Maryland initiated its version of voluntary plant-closing guidelines, and in 1986 New York announced its compact. Under the voluntary New York Compact, business, government, and labor accept certain responsibilities: business firms agree to consider alternatives to layoffs and closings (e.g., hourly reductions, early retirement) and agree to provide advance notification of closings; labor agrees to use strikes as a last resort after trying various mediation and arbitration procedures; and government agrees to target its assistance to help troubled businesses, aid workers losing jobs due to closings, and assist communities involved in shutdowns or mass layoffs.[34]

Although social compacts are relatively weak versions of a player role — that is, their implementation is dependent on the goodwill of labor and management — they do demonstrate an important step beyond the reactive nature of an offset role. Through a social compact government policymakers alter the boundary lines of debate and adjustment to a plant closing, and they create an environment of shared responsibilities in which the interests of labor and management, as well as the community, can be met. Although consensus building characteristic of an offset response remains a fundamental building block, government officials are playing an assertive role to shape that accord.

Extending the Principle of Rapid Response

Another version of an emerging player role adds a more proactive and interventionist element to the idea of rapid-response teams. An important example of this is the establishment of early warning systems. Rather than reacting to plant closings as they happen, as is typical in an offset response, a number of communities and states are developing early warning systems that allow government officials to learn of unannounced plant closings or critical situations that might soon lead to a plant closing. With early notice policymakers have more time to assist the plant's management in a recovery strategy, seek new owners, or prepare the community for the closing.

Early warning systems identify possible plant closings and firms in trouble through a variety of sources: business surveys, interviews with labor and management, corporate histories, and reviews of employment and other data provided by business firms. Information gathering relies on a mix of formal and informal contacts with community, business, and labor representatives.[35] The key warning signs of an impending closure include declining sales, changes in ownership, duplicate plant capacity, management instability, and expenditure declines in advertising, research, and development.[31]

A number of states and local governments operate either formal or informal early warning systems. In Connecticut, for example, the Department of Economic Development maintains a data base that includes profiles of plants that closed. This information is used to identify existing businesses of a similar nature likely to face economic difficulties. Field staff are then assigned to work with these companies.[37]

At the local level Chicago supported the West Side Early Warning Project in 1984 and 1985. The project was based on an employee-community network to monitor approximately fifty plants on Chicago's west side. An important step, the warning system nevertheless faced major hurdles. For example, several plants were identified as likely to close, but plant officials denied any closing plans and refused to consider public assistance. Although the city no longer provides funding for the project, the early warning system has continued under the auspices of various community and labor groups, principally the Midwest Center for Labor Research.[38]

Another extension of the rapid-response team is the use of government consultants to play a more active role in the recovery strategies of firms. One of the best examples is the Massachusetts Industrial Services Program. As part of the Mature Industries legislation passed in 1984, the Industrial Services Program was established to aid businesses and employees in declining industries. In response to a threatened or actual plant closing, staff from the program provide technical assistance to keep plants open or reemployment assistance to workers laid off by a plant's closing. In addition, an economic stabilization trust provides approximately $2.5 million annually for loans to companies that attempt to continue operations. Going beyond an offset role, consultants from the Industrial Services Program work closely with companies to prepare recovery plans and maximize the benefits derived from loan funds. Consultants advise on business plans, management restructuring, new ownership, alternative product development, or other aspects of a recovery strategy. As one consultant commented, "We will do anything within the law to save the company." As other state and local rapid-response teams expand their role, they may also assume a more active player role in helping shape economic adjustment strategies.

Emerging player roles, the various social compacts, early warning systems, and government consultants are still limited by the need for voluntary compliance from labor and the business firm.[39] Social compacts can be ignored, early warning systems can be frustrated by a firm's denial of problems, and advice from a consultant can be declined. In response to this critical weakness, government officials are turning to policies that use governmental sanctions to mandate changes in the adjustment process; these represent a second type of player response to plant closings.

An Authoritative Player Role: Plant-Closing Laws

Since the early 1970s, national, state, and local governments have entertained various proposals that place legal boundaries on the plant-closing process. Two typical elements in these laws are advance notice by business firms to workers and communities of plant closings and major layoffs and mandatory benefits, such as severance pay and health insurance, for workers losing jobs. These requirements provide both time and resources for a variety of assistance efforts to either keep a plant open or minimize negative consequences of a closing. The result can be a significant restructuring of the adjustment process.[40]

Advance notification is often the center of attention. While voluntary notification receives support from many businesses, legally mandating advance notice stirs considerable opposition. Richard McKenzie, for example, argues that notification laws are an infringement of private property rights and will have negative consequences on overall economic growth.[41] In general the business community sees mandatory notification as a straightjacket that will restrict the ability to respond to changing markets. However, mandatory notification requirements have their supporters. Proponents in both labor and government argue that notification requirements will not damage the economy and are appropriate protections for a community. Providing support for this position, several studies have identified positive effects of notification in reducing unemployment associated with plant closings.[42] While the debate continues, a number of proposals have been considered, and in some cases implemented, at different levels of the federal system.

At the local level only two communities have implemented a mandatory plant-closing law. In 1982 Philadelphia passed an ordinance requiring 60 days' notice for closings of facilities employing 50 or more persons. Between 1982 and 1986 approximately 65 firms provided notification. In the second example, the Vacaville, California, city council in 1984 passed an ordinance requiring firms accepting local development assistance to provide 90 days' notice of a closing or major reduction in the work force. The ordinance also required the filing of an affirmative action plan for hiring and training workers.[43] In January 1987 the Vacaville ordinance lapsed.

The controversial nature of local plant-closing laws is evident in the experience of Pittsburgh. In 1983, in the aftermath of efforts to keep the Nabisco plant open (see Chapter 5), the Pittsburgh city council passed, over the mayor's veto, a plant-closing law requiring three to nine months' notice, depending on the size of the work force. The ordinance also called for the establishment of a city office to investigate possible closings and develop economic alternatives. However, as a result of a lawsuit filed by a business association, state courts invalidated the ordinance as a violation of the city's home-rule powers.[44]

At the state level Wisconsin and Maine have the longest-standing notification laws. Wisconsin's law was adopted in 1976 and requires firms with 100 or more employees to provide 60 days' notice before mergers, closings, or relocations that would affect 10 or more employees. The law, which carries a $50 per employee fine for violation, stipulates that notification be sent to relevant state agencies for an assessment of economic assistance possibilities. Maine's law was first passed in 1971 and currently requires firms of 100 or more employees to provide 60 days' notice of a closing. In addition, the law requires a severance payment to workers employed over three years at the firm.[45] In 1987 the U.S. Supreme Court upheld the constitutionality of the Maine law against claims of federal preemption under the National Labor Relations Act and the Employee Retirement Income Security Act.[46]

In the early 1980s a number of other states considered plant-closing legislation, but few were willing to accept mandatory provisions. In 1983 Connecticut passed a law that did not require notification but did require employers of 100 or more who closed or relocated to pay for continuation of health insurance for 90 days (later extended to 120 days). Not until 1987 was another mandatory notification law passed. In 1987 Hawaii passed a law requiring 45 days' notification, and the Virgin Islands adopted a 90 days' advance notification requirement. In both laws guidelines were also established for mandatory severance or dislocated worker payments.[47]

The debate over plant-closing laws has extended to the national level as well.[48] Although plant-closing legislation has been introduced in every Congress since 1974, not until 1985 did a bill emerge from a congressional committee, yet it failed to make it beyond the floor of the House of Representatives. In 1988 notification legislation became a political football between President Reagan and a Democratic Congress. In May 1988 Congress sent to the president an omnibus trade bill that included a 60 days' notification requirement for mass layoffs and plant closings by firms employing 100 or more workers. In late May President Reagan vetoed the trade bill, citing the notification as a major reason: "I object to the idea that the Federal Government would arbitrarily mandate, for all conditions and under all circumstances, exactly when and in what form that notification should take place."[49] The political battle continued. After the Senate was unable to override the president's veto, congressional leaders removed the notification requirement from the trade bill and introduced it as separate legislation. In July both the Senate and the House of Representatives passed the bill by more than the two-thirds majority needed to override a presidential veto. In response President Reagan allowed the bill to become law, but without his signature.

Eminent Domain and Adjudicative Strategies

In addition to plant-closing laws that affect all businesses within a political jurisdiction (as specified by a threshold size), policymakers may turn to other forms of legal intervention in specific plant closing cases. As noted earlier, eminent domain proceedings are initiated to prevent a plant closing, injunctions are sought to prevent the removal of equipment, and lawsuits are filed to recoup economic damages from a closing. As in the Mon Valley case study, political authority is used to oppose either a business decision to close a plant or the manner in which the closing is taking place. While the Mon Valley case highlighted such a strategy by a new governmental authority, there are other examples involving existing state and city governments that capture the essence of this player response.

In recent years several communities outside the Pittsburgh area have turned to eminent domain in an effort to prevent a plant closing.[50] In New Bedford, Massachusetts, for example, the possible closing in 1984 of the Morse Cutting Tool factory prompted a strong government response. With backing from other elected officials and the plant's labor union, the mayor announced in June that the city would initiate eminent domain proceedings against Gulf & Western Corporation, the parent company, if it closed the Morse factory before a new owner could be identified. Gulf & Western did not close the plant, and a new owner was found. Although eminent domain was not actually exercised, parties to this case credited the threat of using eminent domain as instrumental in keeping the plant open.[51]

As a preliminary step to eminent domain proceedings or other legal action to prevent a plant closing, government policymakers may seek a court injunction to stop a closing or removal of plant equipment. This was the strategy employed by the Steel Valley Authority against the American Standard Corporation. As the basis for legal action state or local officials often cite government-provided benefits, such as financial assistance. According to government officials, acceptance of such benefits represents a contract or pledge on the part of the firm to maintain employment and continue operations. When a firm closes, government authorities claim a breach-of-contract.[52] With mixed success several local and state governments have pursued this strategy.

In one case the state of West Virginia succeeded in obtaining an injunction preventing the Newell Corporation from removing equipment at its Anchor Hocking glass plant in Clarksburg.[53] The plant, which employed 900 people in mid-1987, was closed by Newell in late 1987, shortly after the company purchased the plant. When negotiations with the company failed to reach a satisfactory resolution, the state of West Virginia filed for an injunction and initiated a lawsuit, claiming a breach-of-contract, and asked for $614 million in damages. As bases for their action, state officials cited $3.5 million in state economic development loans, job-training funds, and tax incentives, as well as a verbal agreement for cooperation in selling the plant. The court did issue a temporary injunction, although the company was permitted to remove equipment when it agreed to pay $1 million to assist displaced workers. The injunction was later lifted, and the plant now sits idle as state and company officials attempt to reach an agreement on disposition of the property.

In another case the city of Duluth, Minnesota, in February 1988 sought and received a temporary injunction preventing the Triangle Corporation from removing equipment from its Diamond Tool & Horseshoe plant.[54] Prompted by the local labor union the city filed suit after employment dropped from 760 in 1982 to 320 in 1988 as equipment and production were moved to a Triangle plant in South Carolina. As a basis for its action the city cited a $10-million industrial revenue bond issued in 1982 for Triangle's purchase and expansion of the plant. According to Minnesota law, equipment purchased with bond proceeds must remain in the state. The city also cited a company pledge to expand production at the Duluth plant. In a victory for the city the state district court ruled that the Triangle Corporation had acted in bad faith and that equipment removed in 1986–87 should be returned to the Duluth plant. However, the court of appeals overturned the lower court's stipulation that equipment be returned to Duluth, but the court did let stand the principle of corporate accountability for accepting revenue bonds. In June 1989 the Minnesota Supreme Court refused to hear the case, thereby allowing the continuing removal of equipment, but also allowing to stand the general principle of accountability outlined by lower courts.

While preventing a plant closing is often the expressed goal, these player strategies may result in a compromise in which the company accepts various costs associated with the closing. An example of this was a lawsuit involving the city of Chicago and a Playskool toy factory. In September 1984 the corporate parents of Playskool, Milton Bradley and Hasbro Industries, announced the closing of the 700-employee plant. Chicago officials, citing a $1-million industrial revenue bond issued in 1980, filed suit to prevent the closing. The company filed a motion to dismiss, but in January it and the city accepted a settlement under which the company agreed to retain 100 workers for an additional year, continue its outplacement center for laid-off workers, establish a $50,000 fund to aid laid-off workers, pay $500 to other companies for each former Playskool worker hired, and maintain the facility until September 1985 while assisting in finding a new owner or donating the facility for alternative use.[55]

In a number of cases restitution rather than prevention of a closing has been the explicit goal. The city of Yonkers, New York, for example, filed suit against United Technologies Corporation for closing an Otis elevator plant. In 1974, when the plant employed 1,300 workers, the city combined with state and federal governments to provide a $16-million assistance package to expand the plant. In 1975 United Technologies purchased Otis, and in November 1982 the company announced the closing of the plant, citing changing technology in the elevator-making business. The mayor formed a task force to consider a response and initiated a suit against United Technologies for *pro rata* restitution of earlier public assistance. Although the city recognized that an explicit agreement on the company's tenure had not been made, it argued a promise existed beyond the six years the company had stayed. In December 1986 the trial court ruled against the city, citing the lack of an explicit time commitment.[56]

And finally, a more recent example followed General Motors' announcement in 1986 that it would close eleven manufacturing plants across the country, including one in Norwood, Ohio. In Norwood local officials attempted an offset strategy of negotiating with the company to keep the plant open or to mitigate the consequences of the closing, but with little satisfaction. Turning to a player role the city filed suit in August 1987, claiming, among other causes for action, a breach of contract. City officials cited public improvements to support the facility—particularly those made in 1982, when General Motors was planning a $200-million modernization of the plant—as well as economic damages to the community that would result from the closing. In the suit the city asked for $68 million in compensatory damages and $250 million in punitive damages. The case was ultimately dismissed by the courts, but the vacant plant was cited as a nuisance. In response GM agreed to dismantle the plant so the area could be redeveloped.[57]

Player Responses and the Political Spectrum: Populist and Corporate Variations

By taking on a player role, government policymakers often become aligned with different groups or organizations in the community. Alignments on one side of this political spectrum yield populist responses, as in the Mon Valley case study, in which government actions favor labor and community groups and oppose the actions of the business firm. Alignments on the other side result in corporate responses in which government actions are in cooperation with or support of the business corporation and generally lack labor and community involvement. Equally important is the middle political ground of government actions supported by a combination of business, labor, and community groups.

Placing specific player responses on this political spectrum should be done with care. While some policy responses fit in a relatively clear manner, others are not as easily labeled. However, in a number of the examples cited here, including the Mon Valley case study, the populist label is most appropriate. Eminent domain proceedings, court injunctions, and damage suits are direct challenges to the business firm. The Steel Valley Authority, for example, was created as a political institution to "stand up" to business corporations disinvesting in the Mon Valley. The populist nature of these responses is fairly clear and was discussed in detail in Chapter 5.[58]

In other player responses, particularly in such participatory strategies as social compacts and government consultants, the political orientation is less clear. Although there is a corporate element in some of these, as in the consultant assistance provided by staff from the Massachusetts Industrial Services Program, most often such actions fit near the middle of the spectrum. In general, player responses in an explicit corporate mode involving active government-business cooperation are less evident in American plant-closing experiences. Speculation as to why this is raises several major points.

Perhaps most important are the very circumstances of a plant closing. When a business wants to close a plant, which is how most closing cases initially arise, there is little interest by the business firm in government assistance. The firm has chosen to close the plant and can usually do so within existing laws and public policies. Some version of a bystander or labor offset response is likely. If government officials oppose the closing, yet the business firm insists on closing the plant, a stalemate can easily develop. In this environment the cooperation that is critical for a corporate player response vanishes. If policymakers persist in their opposition to the closing, and the business firm continues pursuing its goal of closing the plant, a populist player approach becomes a possibility. However, if the business firm does seek government assistance and policymakers are interested in keeping the plant open, the foundation for a corporate player response is in place. Business representatives and government officials can work together as equal partners to shape a recovery package. Yet this rarely happens; the typical response is more closely akin to a financial offset policy, as in Waterloo. Government officials provide valuable assistance to keep the plant open but maintain an arm's-length distance from the decision-making process. For government officials to take a more interventionist player role, at least two conditions must be overcome.

First, there are significant ideological barriers to government involvement in the workings of a business firm. While such barriers are not absolute, they constitute an important division between the domain of a private business firm and the legitimate reach of public officials. In the case of Waterloo, for example, where both government and business leaders were interested in a recovery strategy, there was considerable resistance by Rath management and key public officials to a more interventionist government role. Rath management, in particular, remained opposed to extensive government involvement in the firm's restructuring strategies.

A second barrier to a corporate player approach is the weakness of government policy tools and resources. State and local governments, in particular, often lack staff, technical, and financial resources to be equal partners in the adjustment process. Providing a financial loan requires only limited technical expertise, but playing an active and ongoing role in a firm's decision making and general recovery strategy calls for considerably more knowledge and understanding of the business world. To use the Waterloo case again, county officials admitted that they lacked the basic knowledge to actively influence Rath's decisions on how federal UDAG funds were spent. In general, strengthening public policy capabilities is an important prerequisite to a corporate player role.[59]

Local Government Role

As noted, a player role can be based on direct and equal participation in the adjustment process and/or the authority of government to stipulate certain actions by involved parties. In either case the demands on government officials are formidable, and as is evident in the experiences of the Steel Valley Authority, success is far from certain. In implementing a player response, local government officials face demands that are both political and professional in nature. On the political side a player government role requires an extensive base of support in the community. In cases where government actions become aligned with particular groups in the community, as in populist and corporate versions of a player role, government officials and their support network must be able to withstand pressures and objections from opposing groups. Thus, in pursuing a populist policy government policymakers must have support sufficient to withstand the attacks of the business community, and in a corporate approach, pressures from labor and community groups must be countered.

Building the political support network needed for these player roles is quite different in each case. In a populist player role, as with the Tri-State Conference on Steel, the task involves a careful mix of compromises and concessions with different individuals and groups. Public meetings, rallies, and marches may become important in building a broad community coalition that can resist business pressures. In contrast a corporate player role involves a close working relationship with the corporate community, aligning local officials with business firms. This type of coalition is best formed in private meetings and through bureaucratic contacts.

In addition to political support, the importance of professional skills is apparent in both participatory and authoritative strategies. For example, to establish and implement social compacts, government officials need specific in-depth knowledge in the characteristics of different industries, firms, and labor unions. Technical skills are particularly important for government officials who assist ailing firms. These trouble shooters must be able to analyze a business firm and decide whether the firm can be saved and, if so, how to do it. The skills required are similar to those of a business management consultant in the private sector. Indeed, several of the consultants in the Massachusetts Industrial Services Program have had private-sector experience.

Such broad knowledge and professional skills are just as essential in implementing authoritative strategies. To draft plant-closing laws government policymakers must be able to analyze and interpret economic data presented to support or oppose a plant-closing law; to initiate a lawsuit against a business corporation government officials must locate and analyze relevant data specific to that business firm; to consider eminent domain actions to prevent a plant closing public officials must be prepared to defend their decision on the basis of the viability of the firm. In addition, adjudicative strategies require a considerable degree of legal expertise. While the legal realm is not new to public policymakers, lawsuits and eminent domain proceedings against business firms are. Legal skills are put to the test as policymakers search for precedents and arguments to support such concepts as community property right.

Given the political and professional requirements of a player role, it is not surprising that this type of response is often tentative and partial in conception and implementation. This is relatively new ground for American policymakers. Government officials often question the appropriateness of such an interventionist role; policy capabilities to effectively carry out a player role are limited; and members of the business community are often opposed to government "meddling" in corporate affairs. In player strategies that build upon participation in the adjustment process, such as early warning networks, social compacts, and consultants, tentativeness is often linked to a reluctance on the part of government officials to take actions opposed by a business firm. Fears of a negative business climate and corporate opposition can scuttle these player strategies. Thus, in the Chicago early warning network the refusal of firms to cooperate left local officials without a policy role. Similarly, in the Massachusetts Industrial Services Program the financial and technical services of the program are used only if the business firm cooperates with program staff. A player role premised on a cooperative partnership is likely to remain tentative and subject to a veto of private parties, principally the business firm.

Player roles based on authoritative government action have also been tentative and incomplete. In the case of plant-closing laws, the norm is lax enforcement of existing laws and a reluctance to accept new legislation. A recent evaluation of the Wisconsin plant-closing law concluded that only 10 percent of businesses subject to the law comply. Despite such low compliance no company has ever been fined for a violation of the law.[60] In Maine compliance is higher, but still low. Between 1975 and 1981, of those companies subject to the law, 23 percent complied with the notification requirement, whereas 56 percent complied with the severance requirement.[61] As for adopting new plant-closing laws, few state or local governments are even willing to consider such legislation. Although Hawaii recently adopted a plant-closing law, congressional debate in 1988 and subsequent narrowing in scope of the federal law highlights the reluctance to accept this type of player role.

With respect to eminent domain, court injunctions, and damage suits, a player response is relatively novel. These strategies do not have long track records, and their legal basis as well as efficacy are debated. In Boston, for example, the city's Corporation Counsel questioned the legality of eminent domain proceedings against Colonial Provisions Company, a meatpacking plant that was about to close, if the purpose was resale of the property to another private party.[62] However, in contrast, several legal reviews of these strategies, particularly eminent domain, have resulted in favorable assessments of their potential use in plant-closing situations.[63]

Thus far, these legal strategies have more often become pressure tactics to influence actions by the business firm. In the Playskool case, for example, the lawsuit filed by the city of Chicago yielded an out-of-court settlement in which the company shared the burden of economic adjustment. More recently, the state of Wisconsin threatened Chrysler Corporation with a lawsuit for breach of contract in closing its Kenosha automobile plant. However, the lawsuit was put on hold pending Chrysler's cooperation with an economic adjustment plan for the community.

The mixed success of player strategies attests to the obstacles and limitations local officials face, as does the fact that state governments, with their broader array of policy tools and capabilities, are often major participants in player responses. Still, local policymakers continue to be challenged both to read and interpret signs of change in a dynamic economy and to become key actors in shaping the community's economic future.

OPPORTUNITIES AND CONSTRAINTS IN THE URBAN POLITICAL ECONOMY

The American industrial landscape is dotted with the lessons of local policymakers responding to impending economic catastrophe. Among those lessons stand a range of bystander, offset, and player strategies, each undertaken within a complex environment of opportunities and constraints. It is the interplay of these contrasting themes — policy opportunities and urban constraints — that best portrays the dynamic of policy responses to plant closings and urban economic policymaking in general.

Each theme has its place: policy opportunities point to the various decisions and actions local officials confront in assuming different roles in the adjustment process; urban constraints highlight the dependent nature of urban policymaking and the many legal, economic, organizational, and ideological limits on what local officials can do. Constraints may loom large in the eyes of local policymakers, but opportunities for action and change can appear at unexpected and critical junctures. The range of policy options expands as key actors in the community identify and take advantage of their opportunities. Alliance formation and political mobilization, in particular, embody much of this dynamic. Whether it is a county commissioner acting as a political entrepreneur or an interest group seeking to build a new political institution, taking advantage of opportunities lies at the heart of any policy response.

This image of policymaking — creative action within an environment of constraints — characterizes the basic context for local responses to plant closings. It is within this environment that local officials attempt to balance their own goals with those of their various constituencies. It is always a balancing act: supporting the local economy and individual business firms does not always align well with protecting the jobs and employment opportunities of local residents. Policymakers must navigate this often tricky course between business and community interests. Building on the lessons of others is a start, but knowing what roles to play, as well as having the capacity to fill those roles, remains a central question on the agendas of local officials.

Notes

PREFACE

1. See Thierry Noyelle, "Economic Transformation," *Annals* 488 (November 1986): 9–17; Barry Bluestone and Bennett Harrison, "The Great American Job Machine: The Proliferation of Low Wage Employment in the U.S. Economy," prepared for U.S. Congress, Joint Economic Committee, 1986; Ronald Kutscher and Valerie Personick, "Deindustrialization and the Shift to Services," *Monthly Labor Review* 190, 6 (June 1986), pp.3–13.

2. Ronald Berenbeim, *Company Programs to Ease the Impact of Shutdowns* (New York: The Conference Board, 1986), p. 7.

3. For a recent bibliography of plant-closing literature, see Harold Way and Carla Weiss, *Plant Closings: A Selected Bibliography of Materials Published through 1985* (Ithaca, N.Y.: ILR Press, 1988).

4. Candee Harris, "The Magnitude of Job Loss from Plant Closings and the Generation of Replacement Jobs: Some Recent Evidence," *Annals* 475 (September 1984): 15–27.

5. U.S. Department of Labor, "*Economic Adjustment and Worker Dislocation in a Competitive Society*," Report of the Secretary of Labor's Task Force on Economic Adjustment and Worker Dislocation (Washington, D.C., 1986).

6. Gene Zack, "10 Million Jobs Erased by Closings and Layoffs," *AFL-CIO News* 33 (December 17, 1988): 1.

7. Massachusetts Legislative Research Council, "Report Relative to Plant Closings," Boston, June 30, 1983, p. 26.

8. Terry Buss and F. Stevens Redburn, *Shutdown at Youngstown* (Albany: State University of New York Press, 1983).

CHAPTER 1. PLANT CLOSINGS, LOCAL GOVERNMENTS, AND POLICY RESPONSES

1. Benjamin Barber, "Gaining Control over Our Economic Resources," in *Community and Capital in Conflict: Plant Closings and Job Loss*, ed. John Raines et al. (Philadelphia: Temple University Press, 1982), p. 101.

2. Paul Kantor, *The Dependent City* (Glenview, Ill.: Scott, Foresman and Company, 1988); Paul Peterson, *City Limits* (Chicago: University of Chicago Press, 1981). For a general discussion of this theme, see also Bryan Jones and Lynn Bachelor, *The Sustaining Hand: Community Leadership and Corporate Power* (Lawrence: University Press of Kansas, 1986); Stephen Elkin, *City and Regime in the American Republic* (Chicago: University of Chicago Press, 1987); Clarence Stone and Heywood Sanders, eds., *The Politics of Urban Development* (Lawrence: University Press of Kansas, 1987); Norman Fainstein and Susan Fainstein, eds., *Restructuring the City: The Political Economy of Urban Redevelopment* (New York: Longman, 1983).

3. For a general discussion, see Bryan Jones, *Governing Urban America* (Boston: Little, Brown and Company, 1983).

4. U.S. Department of Commerce, *City Government Finances in 1986-87* (Washington, D.C.: Government Printing Office, 1987), GF-87-4.

5. Jones and Bachelor, *The Sustaining Hand,* p. 4.

6. This three-part typology is derived from several sources. In part it is based on reports and news articles about actual responses to plant closings. A general survey of responses to plant closings identified a variety of local government roles. In addition, typologies proposed by several authors have been particularly useful. Two works by Robert Solo on American national government have been important: *The Political Authority and the Market System* (Cincinnati: South-Western Publishing Company, 1974), and *The Positive State* (Cincinnati: South-Western Publishing Company, 1982). Solo describes three policy roles—"housekeeping," "offset," and "planning-programming"—that serve as a point of orientation for the response types used in this study. Robert Alford and Roger Friedland have also developed a typology in *Powers of Theory* (New York: Cambridge University Press, 1985) that highlights different government roles in the economy. Alford and Friedland present a synthesis of pluralist, managerial, and class perspectives that identifies six different types of "politics." Four of these politics—conservative, liberal, reform, and reactionary—provide useful points of reference for the policy responses used here.

John Zysman, in a comparative study entitled *Governments, Markets, and Growth* (Ithaca, N.Y.: Cornell University Press, 1983), identifies three government economic policy roles that have also proved helpful. His typology—"regulator," "administrator," and "player"—captures somewhat similar policy roles to the typology presented here, although there are several significant differences. In particular, my use of "player" deviates from Zysman's focus on financial capabilities and includes a degree of public involvement in decision making not explicitly argued in his analysis.

And finally, at the urban level, Norman Fainstein and Susan Fainstein in *Urban Policy under Capitalism* (Beverly Hills, Calif.: Sage Publications, 1982) present four regime types with regard to public policy—liberal-democratic, market-conservative, social democratic, and corporatist-fascist—that also provide helpful insights.

7. Richard McKenzie, ed., *Plant Closings: Public or Private Choices?* (Washington, D.C.: Cato Institute, 1982), p. 176.

8. Joseph Schumpeter, *Capitalism, Socialism, and Democracy* (New York: Harper & Row, 1947).

9. U.S. Department of Labor, *Economic Adjustment and Worker Dislocation in a Competitive Society,* p. 16.

10. Providing a framework for the private settlement of differences is a well-established tradition in American politics. Writing twenty-five years ago, Andrew Shonfield in *Modern Capitalism* (New York: Oxford University Press, 1965) noted, "The

American instinct is non-interventionist: if public authority has a choice, it generally opts for the role of referee rather than that of manager" (p. 330).

11. Solo, *Political Authority*, p. 371.

12. Writers who describe responses to plant closings in a manner generally consistent with a housekeeping and bystander role include Ronald Berenbeim in *Company Programs to Ease the Impact of Shutdowns;* Richard McKenzie in *Plant Closings: Public or Private Choices?,* and in *Fugitive Industry: The Economics and Politics of Deindustrialization* (Cambridge, Mass.: Ballinger Publishing Company, 1984); National Association of Manufacturers in "When a Plant Closes: A Guide for Employers," (Washington, D.C., 1983); and National Alliance of Business in "Worker Adjustment to Plant Shutdowns and Mass Layoffs: An Analysis of Program Experience and Policy Options" (Washington, D.C., 1983).

13. There is a diverse body of literature comprising analyses of plant closings from a perspective similar to the offset response. From the academic community, examples include Ruth Fedrau in "Responses to Plant Closures and Major Reductions in Force: Private Sector and Community-Based Models," *Annals* 475 (September 1984): 80–95; William Whyte et al. in *Worker Participation and Ownership: Cooperative Strategies for Strengthening Local Economies* (Ithaca, N.Y.: ILR Press, 1983); J. Gordus et al. in *Plant Closings and Economic Dislocation* (Kalamazoo, Mich.: Upjohn Institute for Employment Research, 1981); Philip Langerman et al. in *Plant Closings and Layoffs: Problems Facing Urban and Rural Communities* (Des Moines, Iowa: Drake University, 1982); Robert Stern et al. in *Employee Ownership in Plant Shutdowns* (Kalamazoo: Upjohn Institute for Employment Research, 1979); Gary Hansen in *Cooperative Approaches for Dealing with Plant Closings: A Resource Guide for Employers and Communities* (Utah State University, 1984); and Warner Woodworth et al. in *Industrial Democracy: Strategies for Community Revitalization* (Beverly Hills, Calif.: Sage Publications, 1985).

Emphasizing a practitioner perspective, a number of individuals and organizations have produced prescriptive guides for successful offset responses to plant closings. Examples include Jacqueline Mazza in *Shutdown: A Guide for Communities Facing Plant Closings* (Washington, D.C.: Northeast-Midwest Institute, 1982); California Employment Development Department in *Planning Guidebook for Communities Facing Plant Closure or Mass Layoff* (Sacramento, Calif.: Employee Development Department, 1983); U.S. Department of Commerce in *Coping with the Loss of a Major Employer: A How-to Manual* (Washington, D.C.: Economic Development Administration, no date); U.S. Department of Labor in *Plant Closing Checklist: A Guide to Best Practice* (Washington, D.C.: Bureau of Labor-Management Relations and Cooperative Programs, 1985); and the United Way/AFL-CIO in *Assistance to Communities Experiencing Sudden Economic Disruption* (1979).

14. Langerman et al., *Plant Closings and Layoffs*, p. 76.

15. Gordus et al., *Plant Closings and Economic Dislocation*, p. 38.

16. Solo, *Political Authority*, p. 388.

17. Solo, *The Positive State*, p. 84.

18. Robert Solo, "The Economist and the Economic Roles of the Political Authority in Advanced Industrial Societies," in *Stress and Contradiction in Modern Capitalism*, ed. L. Lindberg et al. (Lexington, Mass.: Lexington Books, 1975), p. 102.

19. See Peter Eisinger, *The Rise of the Entrepreneurial State* (Madison: University of Wisconsin Press, 1988), and John Portz, "Plant Closings: New Roles for Policymakers," *Economic Development Quarterly* 3 (February 1989): 70–80.

20. Solo, *Political Authority*, p. 371.

21. I use the term *corporate* rather than *corporatist* to avoid identification with

European corporatism. Corporatism in Europe implies a tripartite bargaining arrangement in which government policymakers work with labor and business groups to arrive at mutually agreeable resolutions of economic problems. My use of *corporate* emphasizes that this player role is closely allied with business rather than a combination of business and labor.

22. *Populism* is a very broadly defined term that has quite different meanings in different contexts. While recognizing this definitional problem, I think the term captures the essence of the political experience discussed here. See Chapter 5 for a more detailed discussion.

Writers who analyze plant closings in a manner that reflects, at least in part, a populist player response include Barry Bluestone and Bennett Harrison, *The Deindustrialization of America* (New York: Basic Books, 1982); Samuel Bowles et al., *Beyond the Waste Land* (Garden City, N.Y.: Anchor Books, 1984); Staughton Lynd, *The Fight against Shutdowns: Youngstown's Steel Mill Closings* (San Pedro, Calif.: Singlejack Books, 1982); R. J. Lustig, "The Politics of Shutdown: Community, Property, Corporatism," *Journal of Economic Issues* 19 (March 1985): 123–152; John Raines et al., *Community and Capital in Conflict: Plant Closings and Job Loss* (Philadelphia: Temple University Press, 1982); Lawrence Rothstein, *Plant Closings: Power, Politics, and Workers* (Dover, Mass.: Auburn House Publishing Co., 1986); and Gilda Haas, *Plant Closures: Myths, Realities and Responses* (Boston: South End Press, 1985).

23. Elaine Charpentier, "Labor-Community Alliances in Chicago." *Changing Work* (Spring 1986), p. 19.

24. The corporate and populist variants of a player role tend to stress, as indicated, opposing ends of the political spectrum. The corporate version favors the conservative end of the spectrum in its close affiliation with business interests. Alford and Friedland in *Powers of Theory* describe this version as "reactionary politics," while Fainstein and Fainstein in *Urban Policy under Capitalism* use the label "corporatist-fascist." In contrast, a populist player role is based on support from labor and the general community. Alford and Friedland describe this as "reform politics," while Fainstein and Fainstein adopt the phrase "social democratic."

CHAPTER 2. EXPLAINING POLICY RESPONSES:
AN ANALYTIC FRAMEWORK

1. See Robert Waste, ed., *Community Power* (Beverly Hills, Calif.: Sage Publications, 1986).

2. For example, see Michael Dear and Allen Scott, eds. *Urbanization and Urban Planning in Capitalist Society* (New York: Methuen, Inc., 1981), and Norman Fainstein and Susan Fainstein, eds. *Restructuring the City: The Political Economy of Urban Redevelopment* (New York: Longman, 1983).

3. See Clarence Stone, "City Politics and Economic Development: Political Economy Perspectives," *Journal of Politics* 46 (1984): 286–299; M. Gottdiener, *The Decline of Urban Politics* (Beverly Hills, Calif.: Sage Publications, 1987); John Mollenkopf, "Who (or What) Runs Cities, and How?" *Sociological Forum* 4 (1989): 119–137; Clarence Stone and Heywood Sanders, eds., *The Politics of Urban Development* (Lawrence: University Press of Kansas, 1987); Elkin, *City and Regime*. For a different orientation to political economy, see Peterson, *City Limits*.

4. Tom Burns et al., *Man, Decisions, Society* (New York: Gordon and Breach Science Publishers, 1985), p. 37.

5. Stanley Elkin, "Pluralism in its Place: State and Regime in Liberal Democracy," in *The Democratic State*, ed. Roger Benjamin and Stephen Elkin (Lawrence: University Press of Kansas, 1985), p. 196.

6. John Zysman, *Governments, Markets, and Growth* (Ithaca: Cornell University Press, 1983), pp. 78–79. For a general discussion of levels of analysis, see Erik Olin Wright, *Class, Crisis, and the State* (London: New Left Books, 1978); Russell Keat and John Urry, *Social Theory as Science* (Boston: Routledge & Kegan Paul Ltd., 1982); and Alford and Friedland, *Powers of Theory*.

7. Ira Katznelson, *City Trenches* (New York: Pantheon Books, 1981), p. 6.

8. Alford, *Bureaucracy and Participation*, p. 2.

9. Stone and Sanders, *Politics of Urban Development*, p. 4.

10. John Mollenkopf, "Community and Accumulation," in *Urbanization and Urban Planning in Capitalist Society*, ed. Dear and Scott, p. 332.

11. This quotation and the two in the preceding paragraph are from ibid., pp. 319 and 320.

12. The three quotations in this paragraph are from ibid., pp. 320 and 321.

13. In Mollenkopf's framework there is a fourth level of analysis titled "Network of Social Ties," p. 334, which is concerned with how "people interact with each other on a day-to-day basis." The focus is on the interpersonal element in human behavior. For purposes of this study, I have included this level in my discussion of political alliance formation and mobilization. In addition to Mollenkopf's essay the work of Alford and Friedland in *Powers of Theory* was influential in shaping the approach I have adopted as was the methodological introduction by Erik Olin Wright in *Class, Crisis, and the State* (London: Verso Editions, 1979).

14. This theme of "business power" in a capitalist system is discussed by many writers from a variety of theoretical traditions. For a general introduction see Charles Lindblom, *Politics and Markets* (New York: Basic Books, 1977), and "The Market as a Prison," *Journal of Politics* 44, 2 (May 1982): 324–336; and Samuel Bowles and Herbert Gintis, *Democracy and Capitalism* (New York: Basic Books, 1986). For recent applications to an urban setting, see Martin Shefter, *Political Crisis/Fiscal Crisis: The Collapse and Revival of New York City* (New York: Basic Books, 1985); Todd Swanstrom, *Crisis of Growth Politics: Cleveland, Kucinich, and The Challenge of Urban Populism* (Philadelphia: Temple University Press, 1985); Fainstein and Fainstein, *Urban Policy under Capitalism* and *Restructuring the City*; Elkin, *City and Regime*; Stone and Sanders, *Politics of Urban Development*; and Kantor *Dependent City*.

15. Shefter, *Political Crisis/Fiscal Crisis*.

16. Fainstein and Fainstein, *Restructuring the City*.

17. The two quotations in this paragraph are from Mollenkopf, "Community and Accumulation," p. 333.

18. For a general discussion of this distinction, see Claus Offe, "Two Logics of Collective Action," in *Disorganized Capitalism*, by Offe (Cambridge, Mass.: MIT Press, 1985), and Roger Friedland, *Power and Crisis in the City* (New York: Schocken Books, 1983).

19. Douglas Ashford, "Political Science and Policy Studies: Toward a Structural Framework," *Policy Studies Journal* (1977): 572.

20. Shefter, *Political Crisis/Fiscal Crisis*, p. 9.

21. R. Scott Fosler and Renee Berger, *Public-Private Partnerships in American Cities: Seven Case Studies* (Lexington, Mass.: D. C. Heath and Company, 1982).

22. Harvey Molotch, "The City as a Growth Machine," *American Journal of Sociology* 82 (September 1976): 309–330; G. W. Domhoff, "The Growth Machine and the Power Elite," in *Community Power*, ed. Waste.

23. Alford and Friedland, *Powers of Theory*, p. 409.

24. Norman Fainstein and Susan Fainstein, "Economic Restructuring and the Rise of Urban Social Movements," *Urban Affairs Quarterly* 21 (December 1985): 187–206.

25. Karen Branan, "Save Our Jobs: Lessons from a Plant Closing Fightback," (Minneapolis: Working Group on Economic Dislocation, 1985).

26. Eugene Lewis, *Public Entrepreneurship: Toward a Theory of Bureaucratic Political Power* (Bloomington: Indiana University Press, 1980), p. 13.

27. John Mollenkopf, *The Contested City* (Princeton, N.J.: Princeton University Press, 1983), p. 6.

28. Jones and Bachelor, *The Sustaining Hand*, p. 13.

29. Mollenkopf, "Community and Accumulation," p. 334.

30. Ibid., p. 334.

31. See Charles Anderson, "The Logic of Public Problems: Evaluation in Comparative Policy Research," in *Comparing Public Policies: New Concepts and Methods*, ed. Douglas Ashford (Beverly Hills, Calif.: Sage Publications, 1978), pp. 19–42.

32. Joseph Gusfield, *The Culture of Public Problems: Drinking, Driving and the Symbolic Order* (Chicago: University of Chicago Press, 1981), p. 13.

33. David Dery, *Problem Definition in Policy Analysis* (Lawrence: University Press of Kansas, 1984), p. 4.

34. Roger Cobb and Charles Elder, *Participation in American Politics: The Dynamics of Agenda-Building*, 2nd ed. (Baltimore: Johns Hopkins University Press, 1983), p. 172.

35. Ibid., p. 15.

36. Ibid., p. 102.

37. Staughton Lynd, *The Fight against Shutdowns: Youngstown's Steel Mill Closings* (San Pedro, Calif.: Singlejack Books, 1982).

38. Robert Alford, *Bureaucracy and Participation* (Chicago: Rand McNally, 1969), p. 31.

CHAPTER 3. A "BYSTANDER" RESPONSE:
LOUISVILLE, KENTUCKY, AND THE
BROWN & WILLIAMSON CORPORATION

1. George Yater, *Two Hundred Years at the Falls of the Ohio: A History of Louisville and Jefferson County* (Louisville, Ky.: Heritage Corporation, 1979).

2. Population data are given for 1978 since the Brown & Williamson plant closing was announced in early 1979. In this and the other case studies, statistics and other data will generally be given for the time period most relevant to the plant closing being analyzed.

3. George Yater, "Louisville," in *Cities Reborn*, ed. Rachellle Levitt (Washington, D.C.: Urban Land Institute, 1987), pp. 55–104.

4. The major brands of the "Big Six" are (1) R. J. Reynolds — Winston, Salem, Camel, Vantage; (2) Philip Morris — Marlboro, Benson and Hedges, Merit, Virginia Slims: (3) Brown & Williamson — Kool, Raleigh, Viceroy, Bel-Air; (4) American Brands — Pall Mall, Carlton, Tareyton; (5) Lorillard — Kent, Newport, Golden Lights, True; and (6) Liggett & Meyers — Chesterfield, Lark.

5. James Overton, "Diversification and International Expansion: The Future of the American Tobacco Manufacturing Industry with Corporate Profiles of the 'Big Six,'" in *The Tobacco Industry in Transition*, ed. William Finger (Lexington, Mass.: D. C. Heath and Company, 1981), p. 161. See also David Tucker, *Tobacco: An International Perspective* (London: Euromonitor Publications, 1982); and Paul Johnson, *The Economics of the Tobacco Industry* (New York: Praeger Publishers, 1984).

6. Overton, "Diversification and International Expansion"; Robert Miles, *Coffin Nails and Corporate Strategies* (Englewood Cliffs, N.J.: Prentice-Hall, 1982).

7. Tobacco Workers International Union, "Diversification in the Tobacco Industry," *The Tobacco Worker* 16 (January 1972): 1.

8. U.S. Department of Commerce, *Census of Manufactures: Tobacco Products* (Washington, D.C.: Government Printing Office, 1963); U.S. Department of Commerce, *Census of Manufactures: Tobacco Products* (Washington, D.C.: Government Printing Office, 1982).

9. Elizabeth Tornquist, "Labor Displacement in Tobacco Manufacturing: Some Policy Considerations," in *The Tobacco Industry in Transition*, ed. Finger; *Louisville Times*, January 22, 1979.

10. Yater, *Two Hundred Years at the Falls.*

11. *Louisville Courier-Journal*, July 12, 1965.

12. Brown & Williamson Corporation, Press release, September 28, 1973.

13. "The $150-Million Cigarette," *Fortune* 102 (November 17, 1980): 121-125.

14. Overton, "Diversification and International Expansion."

15. Carroll Teague, "Easing the Pain of Plant Closure: The Brown & Williamson Experience," *Management Review* 70 (April 1981): 24.

16. *Louisville Times*, November 16, 1978.

17. Ibid.

18. *Louisville Courier-Journal*, January 19, 1979.

19. The story of the Louisville plant closing has been reported by company officials in at least two forums: hearings before the U.S. Congress, Senate Committee on Labor and Human Resources, *Hearings on Workers and the Evolving Economy of the Eighties*, 96th Congress, 2nd Session, 1980, and an article by Teague in *Management Review*. A similar account appears in "Brown & Williamson Case Study," U.S. Department of Labor, *Plant Closing Checklist: A Guide to Best Practice* (Washington, D.C.: Bureau of Labor-Management Relations and Cooperative Programs, 1985). Each account emphasizes labor-management negotiations along with financial and reemployment benefits outlined in the Settlement Agreement.

20. *Louisville Courier-Journal*, January 21, 1979.

21. "Settlement Agreement," 1979.

22. *Louisville Courier-Journal*, April 8, 1979.

23. *Louisville Times*, July 6, 1979.

24. For example, in May 1979 the Louisville board of aldermen debated an IRB issue for a printing business that employed 200 workers and planned to move to Indiana. To accommodate this company the board approved a $1-million Industrial Revenue Bond (IRB) for acquisition of a new site within the city. As one alderman commented, the closing of this company would "mean loss of jobs, loss of tax base, a loss to this community" (City Council Minutes, May 8, 1979). In another example, an IRB was used to help a local firm relocate from the county to the city.

25. U.S. Department of Labor, *Employment and Unemployment in States and Local Areas* (Washington, D.C.: Government Printing Office, 1979).

26. U.S. Department of Commerce, *County Business Patterns*, 1974, 1978.

27. *Louisville Times*, March 8, 1979.

28. Ibid.

29. Robert Bivens, "The State of Downtown Louisville," *Louisville* (March 1979): 36, 38-41; Yater, "Louisville."

30. Bivens, "Downtown Louisville," p. 36.

31. *Louisville Times*, January 18, 1979.

32. Yater, "Louisville."

33. Louisville Department of Economic Development, *Overall Economic Development Program, Fiscal Year 1978–79* (Louisville, Ky., 1979), p. 17.

34. Prior to 1978 the Tobacco Workers International Union (TWIU) represented the production workers at B & W. In 1978 the Tobacco Workers merged with the Bakery and Confectionery Workers' International Union of America to form the Bakery, Confectionery and Tobacco Workers International Union. The 1977 contract, then, was actually negotiated by the TWIU.

35. Tobacco Workers International Union, "B&W Agreement Cushions Layoff Impact," *The Tobacco Worker* 21 (May–June 1977): 1.

36. Tobacco Workers International Union, "Diversification in the Tobacco Industry," p. 1.

37. Teague, "Easing the Pain of Plant Closure," p. 26.

38. Charles Springer, "Government Reorganization: Help Wanted," *Louisville* (January 1980): 24–28.

39. Kentucky Legislative Research Commission, *The Multiplicity of Local Governments in Jefferson County*, Research Report No. 130 (Frankfurt: Commonwealth of Kentucky, 1977).

40. Yater, "Two Hundred Years at the Falls," p. 233.

41. At the time of the B & W plant closing, occupational license fees, which were the single largest source of revenue for both the city and county, were collected on the basis of the location of the place of employment. Thus, the B & W plant provided occupational license revenues for the city rather than the county. In 1986 this was changed by a Cooperative Compact that effectively froze the existing proportion of occupational tax receipts received by the city and county. The compact was part of an effort to end city vs. county competition over new businesses (see "Update" at end of chapter).

42. Louisville Department of Economic Development, *Overall Economic Development Program*.

43. Ibid.; City of Louisville, Mayor's Executive Budget, 1979–1980.

44. Tobacco Workers International Union, "Diversification in the Tobacco Industry"; Tobacco Workers International Union, "Conferences Endorse Merger Plans," *The Tobacco Worker* 22 (May–June 1978): 1, 3.

45. *Louisville Courier-Journal*, December 21, 1978.

46. *Louisville Courier-Journal*, January 12, 1981.

47. *Louisville Courier-Journal*, January 2, 1982.

48. Harvey Boulay, *The Twilight Cities: Political Conflict, Development, and Decay in Five Communities* (Port Washington, N.Y.: Associated Faculty Press, 1983).

49. *Louisville Courier-Journal*, June 17, 1979.

50. Ibid.

51. Alford and Friedland, *Powers of Theory*, p. 413.

52. Milton Friedman and Rose Friedman, *Free to Choose* (New York: Avon Books, 1979), p. 3.

53. Robert Lekachman, "How to Civilize Capital," in *Community and Capital in Conflict*, ed. by John Raines et al. (Philadelphia: Temple University Press, 1982), p. 152.

54. Sam Bass Warner, *The Private City* (Philadelphia: University of Philadelphia Press, 1968), p. x.

55. Swanstrom, *Crisis of Growth Politics*, p. 39.

56. Warner, *The Private City*, p. 3. See also Dennis Judd, *The Politics of American Cities: Private Power and Public Policy* (Boston: Little, Brown and Company, 1984).

57. Mark Nadel, "The Hidden Dimension of Public Policy: Private Governments

and the Policy-Making Process," *Journal of Politics* 37 (1975): 33; see also Nadel, *Corporations and Political Accountability* (Lexington, Mass.: D. C. Heath, 1976).

58. Nadel, "Hidden Dimension," p. 15.

59. Cited in Selznick, p. 153.

60. Ibid., p. 229.

61. Peter Bachrach and Morton Baratz, *Power and Poverty: Theory and Practice* (New York: Oxford University Press, 1970); Matthew Crenson, *The Un-Politics of Air Pollution* (Baltimore: Johns Hopkins University Press, 1971).

62. There are numerous writings on "private governments" that are generally compatible with this thesis of privatism. For example, see Grant McConnell, *Private Power and American Democracy* (New York: Alfred A. Knopf, 1967) and Sanford Lakoff, ed., *Private Government* (Glenview, Ill.: Scott, Foresman and Company, 1973). As Grant McConnell states, "The function of policy-making is often turned over to the private group in what amounts to delegation" (p. 163). The general theme in these writings is that private groups, such as labor unions and corporations, constitute "governments" that affect in very important ways the lives of their members.

63. *Louisville Courier-Journal*, September 18, 1980.

64. Ibid.

65. Thornquist, "Labor Displacement."

66. Selznick, *Law, Society and Industrial Justice*, p. 239.

67. Ibid., p. 240.

68. *Louisville Courier-Journal*, April 3, 1986.

69. *Batus 1986 Annual Report.*

70. *Washington Post*, September 8, 1985.

71. *Louisville Times*, November 25, 1983; *Batus 1982 Annual Report.*

72. Louisville Chamber of Commerce Research Department, "Plant Closings" (Louisville, Ky., 1987).

73. Jefferson County Fiscal Court, *Comprehensive Annual Financial Report for Fiscal Year Ended June 30, 1986* (Louisville, Ky., 1986).

CHAPTER 4. AN "OFFSET" RESPONSE:
WATERLOO, IOWA, AND THE RATH PACKING COMPANY

1. *Waterloo Courier*, May 5, 1978.

2. *Waterloo Courier*, May 11, 1978.

3. *Waterloo Courier*, May 14, 1978.

4. Ibid.

5. In the meatpacking industry, earnings as a percentage of sales average 0.8 to 1.0 percent. For comparison, the comparable measure in all manufacturing industries is approximately 4 percent. For meatpackers this low margin means high-volume sales are critical. In addition, packers are very susceptible to fluctuations in live animal prices, which represent approximately 80 percent of the sales dollar. See American Meat Institute, Department of Economics and Statistics, *MEATFACTS* (Washington D.C., 1985).

6. American Meat Institute, *MEATFACTS.*

7. Bruce Marion, *The Organization and Performance of the U.S. Food System*, (Lexington, Mass.: Lexington Books, 1986).

8. Kenneth Nelson, *Issues and Developments in the U.S. Meatpacking Industry*, USDA Economic Research Service (Washington, D.C.: Government Printing Office, 1985).

9. The number of plants is based on SIC Codes 2011 and 2013 as reported by the U.S. Department of Commerce, *Census of Manufactures: Meat Products* (Washington, D.C.: Government Printing Office, 1967 and 1982).

10. United Food and Commercial Workers International Union, "1985 Meat Packing Industry Fact Book," National Packinghouse Conference, Washington, D.C., April 1985.

11. Black Hawk County, *Overall Economic Development Plan* (Waterloo, Ia., 1971).

12. John Stevens, "History of the Rath Packing Company," Unpublished manuscript, n.d.

13. *Des Moines Register*, July 30, 1978; Stevens, "History of Rath Packing."

14. Stevens, "History of Rath Packing."

15. *Des Moines Register*, July 30, 1978.

16. *Rath Annual Report, 1979.*

17. Ibid.

18. *Des Moines Register*, July 30, 1978.

19. Development Planning and Research Associates, *Operation and Management Review and Evaluation, Rath Packing Company, Waterloo, Iowa: Appendix Report* (Manhattan, Kans., 1978), VIII–12.

20. *Waterloo Courier*, May 14, 1978.

21. U.S. Congress, *Hearings on Conglomerate Mergers.*

22. Black Hawk County, Economic Development Committee, "Rath Report" (Waterloo, Ia., 1978).

23. *Waterloo Courier*, May 23, 1978.

24. Black Hawk County, "*Rath Report.*"

25. Development Planning and Research Associates, *Evaluation of the Rath Packing Company, Waterloo, Iowa: Final Report*, (Manhattan, Kans., 1978).

26. Development Planning and Research Associates, *Operation and Management Review*, I–3.

27. Ibid., VII–4.

28. Ibid., VIII–26.

29. Ibid., IV–8.

30. *Waterloo Courier*, September 29, 1978.

31. Black Hawk County, Grant Application to Economic Development Administration, 1978.

32. *Waterloo Courier*, October 17, 1978; U.S. Congress, *Hearings on Conglomerate Mergers.*

33. Black Hawk County, "Rath Report."

34. *Des Moines Register*, July 30, 1978.

35. City of Waterloo, Urban Development Action Grant, 1980.

36. The difficulties in establishing the employee stock ownership plan, which would provide private leverage for federal funds, proved to be the major stumbling block. In May 1979 employees agreed to the outline of a stock purchase plan, but negotiations continued with Rath into the fall of that year. Discussions centered on balancing employee concessions (primarily in wages and benefits) with the structure of stock ownership and a profit-sharing plan. In early 1980 the plan was sent to the federal Securities and Exchange Commission (SEC) and the Department of Labor (DOL). While the SEC approved the plan, the DOL determined that the plan violated pension regulations. The union went back to the drawing board and restructured the plan to satisfy DOL requirements. In December 1980 an employee stock ownership trust was approved by the DOL and Rath employees. Purchases of stock continued until May 1982, when the trust held 51 percent of Rath stock.

37. *Waterloo Courier*, July 10, 1979.

38. *Rath 1983 Annual Report.*

39. U.S. Department of Labor, *Employment and Unemployment in State and Local Areas* (Washington, D.C.: Government Printing Office, 1976–78); U.S. Department of Commerce, *County Business Patterns,* 1976–1978.

40. Wayne Broehl, *John Deere's Company* (New York: Doubleday and Company, 1984).

41. *Waterloo Courier*, September 22, 1978.

42. Black Hawk County, *"Rath Report."*

43. City of Waterloo, Urban Development Action Grant.

44. Black Hawk County, *"Rath Report."*

45. City of Waterloo, Urban Development Action Grant.

46. Black Hawk County, *"Rath Report."*

47. *Waterloo Courier*, June 1, 1978.

48. *Rath Annual Report, 1979.*

49. *Waterloo Courier*, May 11, 1978.

50. Waterloo Community Development Board, *1983 Annual Progress Report* (Waterloo, Ia., 1983).

51. Christopher Gunn, *Workers' Self-Management in the United States* (Ithaca, N.Y.: Cornell University Press, 1984).

52. *Waterloo Courier*, May 11, 1978.

53. While the concern over concessions was the major issue for labor during the early stages of the community response, other issues soon found their way to the collective-bargaining table. In particular, the employee ownership plan was debated and eventually accepted within the context of labor-management negotiations. Beginning in March 1979 the union negotiated with the company to establish an employee stock ownership plan as compensation for wage deferrals. While arranging an employee stock ownership plan started in a collective-bargaining arena, it soon put the union on new and uncharted terrain. Unlike the prior focus of resistance to demands for concessions, stock ownership was not familiar ground. Union leaders had to become versed in the world of stocks, corporate structure, and financial plans. Mobilizing membership support for employee ownership was critical in the later stages of the response.

54. Development Planning and Research Associates, *Operation and Management Review*, VII–9.

55. *Waterloo Courier*, August 11, 1978.

56. Development Planning and Research Associates, *Operation and Management Review*, I–2.

57. Robert McCartney, *"Decision Makers II: A Comparative Community Power Study of a Mid-Western Industrial Community,"* Master's thesis, University of Northern Iowa, Cedar Falls, 1979.

58. *Waterloo Courier*, August 16, 1978.

59. *Waterloo Courier*, January 21, 1979.

60. *Waterloo Courier*, October 17, 1978.

61. McCartney, *Decision Makers II.*

62. Ibid.

63. *Waterloo Courier*, July 30, 1979.

64. Lewis, *Public Entrepreneurship*, p. 17.

65. Kirk Koerner, *Liberalism and Its Critics* (London: Croom Helm, 1985), p. 322.

66. Alford and Friedland, *Powers of Theory*, p. 412.

67. Waste, *Community Power*, p. 121.

68. Jones, *The Study of Public Policy*, p. 9

69. For a general discussion, see Lindblom, *Politics and Markets*, and Andrew Levine, *Liberal Democracy: A Critique of Its Theory* (New York: Columbia University Press, 1981).

70. Alford and Friedland, *Powers of Theory*, p. 420.

71. Among its list of options, the feasibility study proposed that the city of Waterloo form a nonprofit corporation to buy land, construct buildings, and purchase equipment for a new packing plant. The nonprofit corporation could supervise construction of the new facility and lease the building to Rath; the company could provide operating capital. In the time line for this option the nonprofit corporation would be formed in early 1979, construction of the new plant would take place over the succeeding two years, and Rath could lease the new facility in October 1981.

72. The following narrative is based on accounts in Gunn, *Workers' Self-Management*; Tove Hammer and Robert Stern, "A Yo-Yo Model of Cooperation: Union Participation in Management at the Rath Packing Company," *Industrial and Labor Relations Review* 39, 3 (April 1986): 337–349; Christopher Meek and Warner Woodworth, "Worker-Community Collaboration and Ownership," in *Industrial Democracy: Strategies for Community Revitalization*, ed. Warner Woodworth et al. (Beverly Hills, Calif.: Sage Publications, 1985); Gene Redmon et al., "A Lost Dream: Worker Control at Rath Packing," *Labor Research Review* 6 (1985): 5–23; *Rath Packing Company 1983 Annual Report*; interviews conducted in Waterloo; and news clippings from the *Waterloo Courier*.

73. Gene Redmon et al., "A Lost Dream: Worker Control at Rath Packing," *Labor Research Review* 6: 20.

74. U.S. Bankruptcy Court for the Northern District of Iowa, "Orders Approving Sale of Trademarks," Rath Packing Company — Debtor, May 1, 1985, p. 4.

75. Ibid., p. 7.

76. U.S. Department of Commerce, *County Business Patterns*, 1980, 1984; U.S. Department of Labor, *Employment and Unemployment*.

77. *Waterloo Courier*, December 2, 1984.

78. Black Hawk County, *Overall Economic Development Program: Annual Report and Program Update — FY 1985* (Waterloo, Ia., 1985).

79. *Waterloo Courier*, September 24, 1984.

80. *Deere & Company Annual Report*, 1982–84.

81. Black Hawk County, *Overall Economic Development Program*, 1984.

82. Black Hawk County, *Overall Economic Development Program*, 1985, p. 34.

83. *Waterloo Courier*, June 11, 1985.

84. *Waterloo Courier*, April 10, 1985.

CHAPTER 5. A "PLAYER" RESPONSE:
THE STEEL VALLEY AUTHORITY AND U.S. STEEL

1. Tri-State Conference on Steel, "Steel Valley Authority: A Community Plan to Save Pittsburgh's Steel Industry," 1984, p. 6.

2. Allegheny County Department of Development, *Overall Economic Development Program, 1986–1988* (Pittsburgh, 1986), p. 106.

3. Ibid.

4. In 1983 the major U.S. steel producers were (with U.S. market share): U.S. Steel (16.7 percent), Bethlehem Steel (12.9 percent), Jones & Laughlin Steel (8.6 percent), National Steel (6.0 percent), Republic Steel (7.1 percent), Inland Steel (7.1 per-

cent), and Armco (6.4 percent). All of these companies were integrated steelmakers involved in a broad range of steelmaking operations.

5. U.S. Department of Commerce, *The U.S. Primary Iron and Steel Industry Since 1958*, Studies in the Economics of Production by Office of Business Analysis (Washington, D.C.: Government Printing Office, 1985), p. 133.

6. *Business Week*, June 3, 1985.

7. U.S. Department of Commerce, *Iron and Steel Industry*; Jack Metzgar, "Would Wage Concessions Help the Steel Industry?" *Labor Research Review* 1, 2 (Winter 1983): 26–37; Tom DuBois, "Steel: Past the Crossroads," *Labor Research Review* 1, 2 (Winter 1983): 5–25; Robert Crandall, *The U.S. Steel Industry in Recurrent Crisis* (Washington, D.C.: Brookings Institution, 1981).

8. The discussion in this paper focuses on integrated steelmakers, such as U.S. Steel, rather than the newer mini-mills. Integrated steelmakers are involved in each stage of steel production—mining iron ore; combining ore and other materials in a blast furnace to produce pig iron; converting pig iron into steel ingots or slabs through use of an open hearth, basic oxygen, or electric arc furnace; and transforming ingots or slabs into various finished steel products. Historically, most American steel producers developed as integrated producers. The Duquesne mill was one of U.S. Steel's integrated mills that contained most of these processes.

Mini-mills, on the other hand, are much smaller operations that use electric arc furnaces (rather than open hearth or basic oxygen) and usually continuous casting technology (rather than ingot pouring and rolling) to convert scrap metal into a relatively limited number of steel products. Mini-mills are a more recent phenomenon. In 1960 there were ten to twelve mini-mills producing 3 percent of domestic steel production; by 1985 there were fifty mini-mills producing close to 24 percent of domestic production. Mini-mills have developed a considerable cost advantage over integrated producers for the range of products they make. This cost advantage is built around efficiencies in electric arc and continuous-casting technology, lower labor costs, and lower capital requirements. See U.S. Department of Commerce, *Iron and Steel Industry*; and DuBois, "Steel: Past the Crossroads."

9. U.S. Department of Commerce, *Iron and Steel Industry*.

10. Ibid.; Crandall, *U.S. Steel Industry*.

11. U.S. Department of Commerce, *Iron and Steel Industry*.

12. Jack Metzgar, "Public Policy and Steel," *Dissent* 29 (Summer 1982): 325–329.

13. Robert Kuttner, "A Troubled Union and Its New Leader," *Dissent* 32 (Spring 1985): 167–175.

14. U.S. Department of Commerce, *Iron and Steel Industry*.

15. In July 1986 U.S. Steel changed its corporate name to USX and is now a division within USX. However, since the focus of this research concerns the pre-1986 period, the title U.S. Steel will be used.

16. Crandall, *U.S. Steel Industry*, p. 142.

17. Ralph Nader and William Taylor, *The Big Boys* (New York: Pantheon Books, 1986).

18. Cynthia Deitch and Robert Erickson, "Save Dorothy: A Political Response to Structural Change in the Steel Industry," in *Redundancy, Lay-offs and Plant Closures*, ed. Raymond Lee (London: Croom Helm, 1987), pp. 241–279.

19. *Business Week*, February 2, 1985.

20. USX brochure, July 1986.

21. United States Steel Corporation, *Annual Report*, 1985.

22. Deitch and Erickson, "Save Dorothy."

23. Cynthia Deitch, "Collective Action and Unemployment: Responses to Job Loss

by Workers and Community Groups," *International Journal of Mental Health* 13 (1984): 139–153.

24. United States Steel Corporation, "Response to the Locker/Abrecht Duquesne Works Feasibility Report," 1985, pp. 29–30.

25. See Shelby Stewman and Joel Tarr, "Four Decades of Public-Private Partnerships in Pittsburgh," in *Public-Private Partnerships in American Cities: Seven Case Studies,* ed. R. Scott Fosler and Renee Berger (Lexington, Mass.: D.C. Heath and Company, 1982), pp. 59–128; Morton Coleman, "Interest Intermediation and Local Urban Development," Ph.D. dissertation, University of Pittsburgh, 1983; Brian Berry et al., "The Nation's Most Livable City: Pittsburgh's Transformation," in *The Future of Winter Cities,* ed. Gary Gappert (Beverly Hills, Calif.: Sage Publications, 1987), pp. 173–195.

26. Allegheny Conference on Community Development, *Annual Report* (Pittsburgh, 1983), p. 5.

27. Allegheny County Conference on Community Development, *A Strategy for Growth: An Economic Development Program for the Pittsburgh Region, Vol. I* (Pittsburgh, 1984), p. 9.

28. Deitch and Erickson, "Save Dorothy."

29. Locker/Abrecht Associates, "Feasibility Study of the Duquesne Works' Blast and Basic Oxygen Furnaces," 1985, p. 2.

30. *McKeesport Daily News,* January 7, 1985.

31. Nader and Taylor, *Big Boys,* p. 58.

32. United States Steel Corporation, "Response to the Feasibility Report."

33. R. Torres Tumazos, "Study on the Demand and Supply of Semifinished Steel Products in the United States: Prepared in Conjunction with the Feasibility Study to Reactivate the Duquesne Works," prepared for Lazard Freres and Company (New York, 1985).

34. Lazard Freres and Company, "Dorothy 6: Financial Feasibility of Reopening the Duquesne Works" (New York, 1986), p. 1.

35. The Duquesne mill closing and the formation of the Steel Valley Authority have been the subject of several articles by proponents and academic observers: Deitch and Erickson, "Save Dorothy"; Mimi Baron and Charles Martoni, "Steel Valley Authority: Revitalizing the Industry," *Pennsylvanian* (May 1985): 8–11; Robert Erickson and Charles Martoni, "The Steel Valley Authority: A Labor/Government Partnership," Unpublished paper, 1987; Mike Stout, "Eminent Domain and Boycotts: The Tri-State Strategy in Pittsburgh," *Labor Research Review* 1 (1983): 7–22; Mike Stout, "Reindustrialization from Below: The Steel Valley Authority," *Labor Research Review* 5 (1986): 19–35; Joseph Hornack and Staughton Lynd, "The Steel Valley Authority," Unpublished paper, 1986; Judith Leff, "United States Steel and the Steel Valley Authority," Harvard Business School, Boston, 1986.

36. U.S. Congress, House Subcommittee on Economic Development, Committee on Public Works and Transportation, *Hearings on the Economic Health of the Steel Industry and the Relationship of Steel to Other Sectors of the Economy,* 97th Congress, 1st Session, 1981, p. 61.

37. *Pittsburgh Press,* January 19, 1985.

38. *Pittsburgh Tribune-Review,* November 23, 1985.

39. Pennsylvania Municipality Authorities Act.

40. U.S. District Court for the Western District of Pennsylvania, 1986. "Amended Complaint," Steel Valley Authority v. Union Switch and Signal Division, et al.

41. Philadelphia Area Cooperatives Association, "Business Retention Study," (Pittsburgh, 1986), p. 40.

42. Ibid., p. 73.

43. The Steel Valley Authority, preferring state over federal courts, filed the case in state courts and listed as defendants two Pennsylvania employees of the American Standard Corporation as well as Radice-East Hills, Inc., a Pennsylvania subsidary of Radice Corporation. American Standard and Radice charged that these defendants should not be listed in the complaint and that diversity jurisdiction existed, thereby moving the case to federal courts. The state court agreed, and the federal judge affirmed this ruling in April 1986.

44. U.S. District Court for the Western District of Pennsylvania, "Memorandum," *Steel Valley Authority v. Union Switch and Signal Division, et al.,* 1986, p. 6.

45. Ibid., p. 4.

46. The quotation in this paragraph is from Jim Cunningham and Paula Martz, eds., *Steel People* (Pittsburgh: University of Pittsburgh School of Social Work, 1986), p. 87; the employment figures are from U.S. Department of Commerce, *County Business Patterns,* 1980, 1985.

47. Allegheny County, *Overall Economic Development Program, 1986–1988.*

48. David Levdansky et al., *Plant Closings in Southwestern Pennsylvania: An Inventory and Survey* (Pittsburgh: University of Pittsburgh Center for Social and Urban Research, 1984).

49. Allegheny County, *Overall Economic Development Program, 1986–1988.*

50. Allegheny Conference on Community Development, *A Strategy for Growth: An Economic Development Program for the Pittsburgh Region, Vol. I* (Pittsburgh, 1984), p. 13.

51. Allegheny County, Department of Planning, "Municipal Profiles" (Pittsburgh, 1984).

52. Allegheny County, *Overall Economic Development Program, 1986–1988.*

53. Ibid.

54. Jim Cunningham and Paula Martz, eds. *Trouble in Electric Valley* (Pittsburgh: University of Pittsburgh School of Social Work, 1986).

55. *Pittsburgh Press,* July 25, 1985.

56. Cunningham and Martz, *Steel People,* p. 6. See also Carnegie-Mellon University, *Milltowns in the Pittsburgh Region: Conditions and Prospects* (Pittsburgh: School of Urban and Public Affairs, 1983), and Carnegie-Mellon University, *Milltowns Revisited* (Pittsburgh: School of Urban and Public Affairs, 1987).

57. Interviews; Robert Strauss and Beverly Bunch, *The Fiscal Position of Municipalities in the Steel Valley Council of Governments* (Pittsburgh: Carnegie-Mellon University School of Urban and Public Affairs, 1987).

58. Jack Metzgar, "The Humbling of the Steelworkers," *Socialist Review* 75/76 (1983): 41–71; Jim Balanoff and Betty Balanoff, "Democracy and Bureaucracy in the USWA," *Labor Research Review* 1, 3 (Summer 1983): 57–70.

59. See Lynd, *The Fight against Shutdowns*; and Rothstein, *Plant Closings.*

60. Tri-State Conference on Steel, Newsletter, March 1981.

61. Tri-State Conference on Steel, Newsletter, February 20, 1986.

62. David Corn, "Dreams Gone to Rust" *Harpers* 273 (September 1986): 56–64.

63. David Morse, "The Campaign to Save Dorothy 6," *The Nation* 241 (September 1985): 176.

64. Lynd, *The Fight against Shutdowns*; Stout, "Eminent Domain and Boycotts."

65. Tri-State Conference on Steel, "Steel Valley Authority," p. 4.

66. Cunningham and Martz, *Trouble in Electric Valley.*

67. Allegheny County, *Overall Economic Development Program, 1986–1988.*

68. Carnegie-Mellon University, *Milltowns.*

69. Interviews; Allegheny County, *Overall Economic Development Program,*

1986–1988; U.S. Congress, House Subcommittee on Economic Development, *Hearings on the Economic Health of the Steel Industry and the Relationship of Steel to Other Sectors of the Economy*, 97th Congress, 1st Session, 1981.

70. The use of eminent domain in a plant-closing situation faces several critical tests: necessary state statutes must be in place, a public purpose must be established, and fair market compensation must be determined and provided for. While meeting these tests is not a simple process, a number of court decisions have recognized a very broad interpretation of public purpose in similar cases, and the determination of fair market value has recently been interpreted to include social values. In addition, adequate legislation allowing the use of eminent domain in a plant-closing situation was in place in Pennsylvania. See Hornack and Lynd, "The Steel Valley Authority"; Keith Smith, "Eminent Domain as a Tool to Set Up Employee-Owned Business in the Face of Shutdowns," *Antioch Law Journal* 4 (Summer 1986): 271–286; Robert Weinberg, "The Use of Eminent Domain to Prevent an Industrial Plant Shutdown: The Next Step in an Expanding Power," *Albany Law Review* 49 (1984): 95–130; and Gregory Buckley, "Eminent Domain: The Ability of a Community to Retain an Industry in the Face of an Attempted Shut Down or Relocation," *Ohio Northern University Law Review* 12 (1985): 231–249.

71. Tri-State Conference on Steel, Newsletter, March 1981, pp. 3–4.

72. *McKeesport Daily News*, August 21, 1982.

73. *Pittsburgh Post-Gazette*, August 28, 1982.

74. Deitch, "Collective Action and Unemployment"; Stout, "Eminent Domain and Boycotts."

75. Save Nabisco Action Coalition, Synopsis of the study packet presented to the Urban Redevelopment Authority on December 16, 1982.

76. *McKeesport Daily News*, April 13, 1983.

77. Tri-State Conference on Steel, "Steel Valley Authority."

78. Stout, "Eminent Domain and Boycotts," p. 22.

79. Allegheny County, *Overall Economic Development Program, 1986–1988*; Stewman and Tarr, "Four Decades of Public-Private Partnerships."

80. Coleman, *Interest Intermediation*, p. 162.

81. Allegheny Conference on Community Development, *A Strategy for Growth*, p. 8.

82. Richard Caliguiri et al., "Strategy 21: Pittsburgh/Allegheny County Economic Development Strategy (Pittsburgh, 1985), p. 1.

83. U.S. Congress, House Subcommittee on Economic Development, *Hearings on the Economic Health of the Steel Industry and the Relationship of Steel to Other Sectors of the Economy*, 97th Congress, 1st Session, 1981, p. 20.

84. However, it should be noted that Mayor Caliguiri of Pittsburgh did finally support formation of the Steel Valley Authority, but only after it was clear that the Authority would be formed. While the motivation is unclear, general comments from interviewees indicated an interest on the part of the city to be a part of any regional groups that might play a future role in economic development. In a sense Pittsburgh assumed a "big brother" role to the Mon Valley. In any regard Caliguiri did not play a leadership role in the effort to form the Authority.

85. Hornack and Lynd, "Steel Valley Authority," p. 9.

86. *Pittsburgh Press*, February 31, 1985.

87. *McKeesport Daily News*, March 28, 1985.

88. *Pittsburgh Post-Gazette*, October 17, 1985.

89. See Ralph Widner, "Physical Renewal of the Industrial City," *Annals* 488 (November 1986): 47–58.

90. As an aside, the difference between those municipalities that joined the Authority and those that declined did not seem to reflect political party affiliations. Among both joiners and nonjoiners the Democratic party dominated local politics. Voter registration statistics in all of the boroughs and cities heavily favored the Democratic party. For example, among municipalities that did not join the Authority, the Democrat-to-Republican ratios were 17:1 in West Homestead, 5:1 in Wilmerding, and 7:1 in Duquesne. In Munhall, the first municipality to approve the Authority, the party ratio was similar at 6:1. The "least" Democratic of all the municipalities that joined was Swissvale with a Democratic ratio of 2:1.

91. Kuttner, "A Troubled Union."

92. United Steel Workers of America, Newsletter, January 29, 1986.

93. For example, Tri-State's main organizer in Duquesne was a member of the local union but was seen by many as a Red because of his previous political affiliations. By several accounts this created problems in organizing workers as well as winning support from municipal officials for the Steel Valley Authority.

94. See Michael Margolis and Robert Burtt, "Assessing the Blame for Economic Decline: the Denominational Ministry Strategy, the Mass Media, and the Powers That Be," University of Pittsburgh, Paper presented at Annual Meeting of Midwest Political Science Association, Chicago, Ill., April 9-12, 1987; Patrick Kiger, "Radicals," *Pittsburgh* (March 1984): 45-51; Sid Plotkin and Bill Scheuerman, "Lessons of the Pastor Roth Affair," *The Nation* 240 (February 1985).

95. *Pittsburgh Post-Gazette*, January 30, 1985.

96. Ibid.

97. *Pittsburgh Press*, May 27, 1984.

98. Margolis and Burtt, "Assessing the Blame," p. 25.

99. While the DMS and the Network received much of the publicity, there were other groups in the Mon Valley that also raised the level of community awareness as to economic conditions in the region. The Mon Valley Unemployed Committee, for example, was formed in 1980-81 by unemployed workers from three steel mills in the valley. By 1984 the committee had 1,700 dues-paying members ($1 dollar and up) from a variety of industries. The committee supported an array of services — food banks, shelter, counseling, retraining information — as well as lobbying and demonstrations to change laws and policies relating to such concerns as mortgage foreclosures and utility cutoffs. These tactics won support in the community and helped the committee obtain funding from private foundations and government social service agencies. Like Tri-State, the committee distanced itself from the DMS and the Network. However, also like Tri-State, it added to the critique of corporate disinvestment patterns.

100. *Pittsburgh Press*, April 2, 1985.

101. Baron and Martoni, "Steel Valley Authority," p. 11.

102. A qualifier is in order. The term *populism* has been attached to such diverse political phenomena that clarity often gives way to confusion and misunderstanding. For example, Margaret Canovan in *Populism* (New York: Harcourt Brace Jovanovich, 1981), p. 13, identifies two broad categories of populism and various subgroups within each: agrarian populisms comprising farmers' radicalism, peasant movements, and intellectual agrarian socialism; and political populisms, comprising populist dictatorship, populist democracy, reactionary populism, and politicians' populism. In the American context these categories include such diverse examples as the U.S. People's party in the nineteenth century (farmers' radicalism), George Wallace (reactionary populism), and popular referendums and recalls (populist democracy). *Populism* as used in this study is most closely akin to Canovan's populist democracy.

In contemporary discussions of populism a qualifier is often attached in an effort to achieve greater specificity. *New populism*, for example, is a term used by Mark Kann to identify a movement that first developed in the 1970s around grassroots organizing. Martin Carnoy and his collaborators use the term *left/liberal populist movement* to describe the support network for what they term *economic democracy*. In another example, Harry Boyte contrasts the *right wing populism* of Ronald Reagan and his antigovernment rhetoric to the *progressive populism* of citizen action groups that favor participatory government. While a modifier could be used in this study, my preference is to avoid qualifiers and define the term in the course of the analysis. See Mark Kann, *The American Left: Failures and Fortunes* (New York: Praeger Publishers, 1982), and *Middle Class Radicals in Santa Monica* (Philadelphia: Temple University Press, 1986); Martin Carnoy and Derek Shearer, *Economic Democracy: The Challenge of the 1980s* (New York: M. E. Sharpe, 1980), and Carnoy et al., *A New Social Contract* (New York: Harper & Row, 1983); Harry Boyte et al., *Citizen Action and the New American Populism* (Philadelphia: Temple University Press, 1986).

103. Newfield and Greenfield, *A Populist Manifesto*, p. 6.

104. Lawrence Goodwyn, *The Populist Moment* (New York: Oxford University Press, 1978).

105. Carnoy and Shearer, *Economic Democracy*, p. 402.

106. Kann, *The American Left*, p. 131.

107. Boyte et al., *Citizen Action*, p. 43.

108. Kann, *Middle Class Radicals*, p. 18.

109. Kann, *The American Left*, p. 133.

110. Ibid.

111. For a general discussion, see Harvey Mansfield, "The Forms of Liberty," in *Democratic Capitalism?* ed. Fred Baumann (Charlottesville: University Press of Virginia, 1986), pp. 1–21; and R. Jeffrey Lustig, "Freedom, Corporations, and the New Whiggery," also in *Democratic Capitalism?* pp. 127–158.

112. Lynd, *The Fight against Shutdowns*.

113. Alfred and Friedland, *Powers of Theory*, p. 439.

114. See Adam Przeworski, "Social Democracy as a Historical Phenomenon," *New Left Review* (July–August 1980): 27–58.

115. Lustig, "Freedom, Corporations, and the New Whiggery," p. 153.

116. Allegheny County Department of Development, *Overall Economic Development Program, 1987–1989* (Pittsburgh, 1987).

117. *New York Times*, January 19, 1987, and January 22, 1987.

118. Ibid., May 4, 1987; *USX 1987 Annual Report*.

119. *In Pittsburgh*, February 3, 1988.

120. *Pittsburgh Press*, December 21, 1986.

121. Tri-State Conference on Steel and the Steel Valley Authority, "A View from the Valley" (Pittsburgh, 1987), p. 2.

122. In part "A View from the Valley" was a response to development proposals by Allegheny County (*Overall Economic Development Program, 1987–1989*) and a county-created task force called the Mon Valley Commission (*Report to the Allegheny County Board of Commissioners . . .* , 1987). Both organizations emphasized the need for the Mon Valley to diversify and develop outside the traditional steel-manufacturing base. Although Tri-State and the Steel Valley Authority recognized the need to diversify, they were more optimistic with regard to the revival of selective manufacturing facilities and argued for a more active community role in the process of economic change.

123. *In Pittsburgh*, February 3, 1988.

124. Tri-State Conference on Steel, Newsletters, December 1987, February 1988, April 1988.

125. Hornack and Lynd, "Steel Valley Authority," p. 2.

CHAPTER 6. COMPARING POLICY RESPONSES IN
LOUISVILLE, WATERLOO, AND THE MON VALLEY

1. Shefter, *Political Crisis/Fiscal Crisis;* Fainstein and Fainstein, *Restructuring the City.*

2. Swanstrom, *Crisis of Growth Politics*, p. 22.

3. See Boulay, *Twilight Cities.*

4. R. Jeffrey Lustig, "The Politics of Shutdown: Community, Property, Corporatism," *Journal of Economic Issues* 19 (March 1985), p. 136.

5. See John Kingdon, *Agendas, Alternatives, and Public Policies* (Boston: Little, Brown and Company, 1984) and Roger Cobb and Charles Elder, *Participation in American Politics: The Dynamics of Agenda-Building*, 2d ed. (Baltimore: Johns Hopkins University Press, 1983).

6. Lindblom, "The Market as a Prison," p. 327.

7. See Clarence Stone, "Systemic Power in Community Decision Making: A Restatement of Stratification Theory," *American Political Science Review* 74 (1980): 978–990; Elkin, *City and Regime*; and Alford and Friedland, *Powers of Theory.*

8. Lindblom, "The Market as a Prison."

9. Robert Alford and Roger Friedland, "Political Participation and Public Policy," in *Annual Review of Sociology, Volume 1*, ed. A. Inkeles et al. (Palo Alto, Calif.: Annual Reviews, 1975), pp. 429–479. See also Friedland, *Power and Crisis in the City.*

10. See Rothstein, *Plant Closings* and Solo, *The Positive State.*

11. Jeffrey R. Henig, "Collective Responses to the Urban Crisis: Ideology and Mobilization," in *Cities in Stress*, ed. M. Gottdiener (Beverly Hills, Calif.: Sage Publications, 1986), p. 243.

CHAPTER 7. RESPONSES TO PLANT CLOSINGS:
THE CHALLENGE FOR LOCAL GOVERNMENTS

1. See Archie Carroll, "Management's Social Responsibilities," in *Deindustrialization and Plant Closure*, ed. Paul Staudohar and Holly Brown (Lexington, Mass.: Lexington Books, 1987); Berenbeim, *Company Programs to Ease the Impact of Shutdowns*; National Association of Manufacturers, "When a Plant Closes."

2. Calvin Sims, "Indiana Town Loses 985 I.B.M. Jobs," *New York Times*, November 12, 1986; Andrew Malcolm, "Indiana City Grapples with Loss of I.B.M. Plant," *New York Times*, November 18, 1986; N. R. Kleinfield, "Reinventing a Company Town," *New York Times*, March 27, 1988.

3. David Bensman and Roberta Lynch, *Rusted Dreams: Hard Times in a Steel Community* (New York: McGraw-Hill Company, 1987), and Mazza, *Shutdown.*

4. Anne Lawrence, "Union Responses to Plant Closure," in *Deindustrialization and Plant Closure*, ed. Staudohar and Brown, pp. 201–216.

5. U.S. General Accounting Office, *Plant Closings: Information on Advance Notice and Assistance to Dislocated Workers*, GAO/HRD-87-86BR (Washington D.C.: Government Printing Office, 1987).

6. U.S. Department of Labor, "Developments in Industrial Relations: Ford-UAW Contract Bolsters Job Security," *Monthly Labor Review* 110 (November 1987), and "Developments in Industrial Relations: GM/UAW Settlement," *Monthly Labor Review* 110 (December 1987).

7. Wayne Wendling, *The Plant Closure Policy Dilemma* (Kalamazoo, Mich.: W. E. Upjohn Institute for Employment Research, 1984).

8. See Greg Hooks et al., "Small Towns and Factory Closings: Impacts and Alternatives," *Small Town* (January-February 1982): 7-13; U.S. Department of Labor, *Plant Closing Checklist.*

9. Hooks et al., "Small Towns," p. 11.

10. See Berenbeim, *Company Programs to Ease the Impact of Shutdowns.*

11. See Gary Hansen and Frank Adams, "Saving Jobs and Putting Democracy to Work: Labor-Management Cooperation at Seymour Specialty Wire," *Labor-Management Cooperation Brief* 11 (September 1987); Jeremy Brecher, "If All the People Banded Together: The Naugatuck Valley Project," *Labor Research Review* 9 (Fall 1986): 1-19.

12. Lustig, "The Politics of Shutdown," p. 132.

13. See Mazza, *Shutdown*; Kris Balderston, "Plant Closings, Layoffs, and Worker Readjustment: The States' Response to Economic Change," Washington, D.C.: National Governors' Association, 1986; Ruth Fedrau, "Responses to Plant Closures and Major Reductions in Force."

14. See California Employment Development Department, *Planning Guidebook for Communities Facing a Plant Closure or Mass Layoff* (Sacramento, Calif., 1983).

15. Balderston, "Plant Closings, Layoffs, and Worker Readjustment."

16. See William Batt, "Canada's Good Example with Displaced Workers," *Harvard Business Review* 61 (July-August 1983): 6-11; U.S. Department of Labor, *Plant Closing Checklist.*

17. Jeffrey Salzman, "The Canadian-American Plant Closing Demonstration Project," *Compensation and Benefits Management* 3,4 (Summer 1987): 233-239.

18. Working Group on Economic Dislocation, *Alternatives to Economic Dislocation: A Feasibility Study* (Minneapolis: AFL-CIO, 1985).

19. Ibid., p. 59.

20. *Milwaukee Journal*, January 28, 1986.

21. See John Blair and Barton Wechsler, "A Tale of Two Cities: A Case Study of Urban Competition for Jobs," in *Urban Economic Development*, ed. by Richard Bingham and John Blair (Beverly Hills, Calif.: Sage Publications, 1984); Mark Crouch, "Job Wars at Fort Wayne," *Labor Research Review* 9 (Fall 1986): 47-66.

22. See Gary Hansen, "Ford and the UAW Have a Better Idea: A Joint Labor-Management Approach to Plant Closings and Worker Retraining," *Annals* 475 (September 1984): 158-174; Berenbeim, *Company Programs to Ease the Impact of Shutdowns*; Dale Yoder and Paul Staudohar, "Management and Public Policy," in *Deindustrialization and Plant Closures*, ed. by Staudohar and Brown, pp. 183-200.

23. Hansen, "Ford and the UAW," p. 164.

24. Berenbeim, *Company Programs to Ease the Impact of Shutdowns*, p. 52.

25. See U.S. Department of Labor, *Plant Closing Checklist.*

26. See Philip Langerman et al., *Plant Closings and Layoffs.*

27. William Stevens, "Economic Swat Team Saves Jobs in Pennsylvania," *New York Times*, March 28, 1988.

28. Bryan Jones and Lynn Bachelor, "Local Policy Discretion and the Corporate Surplus," in *Urban Economic Development*, ed. Bingham and Blair, pp. 245-269.

29. Crouch, "Job Wars at Fort Wayne."

30. Terry Buss and F. Stevens Redburn, "The Politics of Revitalization: Public Subsidies and Private Interests," in *The Future of Winter Cities*, ed. Gary Gappert (Beverly Hills, Calif.: Sage Publications, 1987), p. 291.

31. Terry Buss and F. Stevens Redburn, "Plant Closings: Impacts and Responses," *Economic Development Quarterly* 1,2 (1987), p. 175.

32. Massachusetts Governor's Commission on the Future of Mature Industries, "Final Report" (Boston, 1984).

33. See U.S. Office of Technology Assessment, *Plant Closing: Advance Notice and Rapid Response* (Washington, D.C.: Government Printing Office, 1986).

34. James Barron, "New York Pact to Help Displaced Workers," *New York Times*, December 11, 1986; Richard Nelson, "State Labor Laws: Changes during 1987," *Monthly Labor Review* 111 (January 1988): 38–61.

35. Industrial States Policy Center, *Phase I Report: Review and Assessment of Existing Early Warning Programs* (Cleveland, 1985).

36. Greg LeRoy et al., *Early Warning Manual against Plant Closings* (Chicago: Midwest Center for Labor Research, 1986); and SRI International, *Managing the Renewal of Mature Industries: Beyond Smokestacks and Sunsets* (Menlo Park, Calif., 1984).

37. Balderston, "Plant Closings."

38. Elaine Charpentier, "Early Warnings in Chicago," *Labor Research Review* 9 (Fall 1986): 91–98.

39. See Steve Early, "A Model in Massachusetts?" *Labor Research Review* 10 (Spring 1987): 110–111.

40. See U.S. Office of Technology Assessment, *Plant Closing*; Antone Aboud and Sanford Schram, "An Overview of Plant Closing Legislation and Issues," in *Plant Closing Legislation*, ed. Antone Aboud (Ithaca, N.Y.: ILR Press, 1984).

41. Richard McKenzie, ed., *Plant Closings: Public or Private Choices?* (Washington, D.C.: Cato Institute, 1982), and *Fugitive Industry: The Economics and Politics of Deindustrialization* (Cambridge, Mass.: Ballinger Publishing Co., 1984).

42. See Nancy Folbre et al., "Plant Closings and Their Regulation in Maine: 1971–1982," *Industrial and Labor Relations Review* 37, 2 (January 1984): 185–196; John Addison and Pedro Portugal, "The Effect of Advance Notification of Plant Closings on Unemployment," *Industrial and Labor Relations Review* 47, 1 (October 1987): 3–16.

43. See U.S. Office of Technology Assessment, *Plant Closing*; Haas, *Plant Closures*.

44. Joann Guinan, "Notice Requirements: Federal Preemption of State and Local Plant Closing Statutes," *Fordham Urban Law Journal* 13 (1985): 333–372; *Pittsburgh Press* clippings.

45. U.S. Office of Technology Assessment, *Plant Closing*.

46. *Fort Halifax Packing Company, Inc. v. P. Daniel Coyne, Director, Bureau of Labor Standards of Maine, et al.* No. 86-341. Decided June 1, 1987. For an argument that state and local plant closing laws should be deemed unconstitutional under the preemption doctrine, see Guinan, "Notice Requirements."

47. Nelson, "State Labor Laws."

48. See U.S. Office of Technology Assessment, *Plant Closing*; Rothstein, *Plant Closings*; McKenzie, *Fugitive Industry*.

49. *New York Times*, May 25, 1988.

50. Actually, one of the first examples of using eminent domain in this manner involved a sports franchise rather than an industrial plant. In 1980 the city of Oakland, California, initiated eminent domain proceedings to prevent the Oakland Raiders from moving to Los Angeles. A lengthy legal process followed in which the possible merits of this type of action received recognition, but the courts ruled against the city. Cen-

tral to the court's reasoning was that the city's action obstructed the free movement of commerce. See Eisinger, *The Rise of the Entrepreneurial State.*

51. Barbara Dougherty, *The Struggle to Save Morse Cutting Tool* (North Dartmouth, Mass.: Southeastern Massachusetts University, n.d.); Midwest Center for Labor Research, *Labor Research Review* 1, 1 (Fall 1982).

52. While this reasoning is characteristic of the cases cited in this section, it was not the argument used by the Steel Valley Authority in Pittsburgh. In trying to prevent removal of equipment from the Swissvale plant, the Steel Valley Authority relied on its authority to preserve "industrial development projects." Under Pennsylvania law the Authority could seek an injunction to prevent the dismantling or wasting of a facility designated an industrial development project.

53. Joseph White, "Workers' Revenge: Factory Towns Start to Fight Back Angrily When Firms Pull Out," *Wall Street Journal*, March 8, 1988; and Jim Benn, "Governor Arch Moore and Eminent Domain in West Virginia," Newsletter (Tri-State Conference on Steel), February 1988, pp. 4-5.

54. Midwest Center for Labor Research, "Partial Shutdown of Diamond Tool and Horseshoe Company: Analysis, Outlook and Options for Public Intervention" (Chicago, 1987); Pat Price, "Duluth to Fight Triangle Tool Firm," *Minneapolis Star-Tribune*, February 5, 1988; Redding Finney, ed., "Duluth, Minn., and Tool & Die Company at Odds Over $10 Million IDB-Backed Loan," *Report on Development Financing* (Washington, D.C.: Development Publications, February 15, 1988), p. 5.

55. *People ex rel. Harold Washington and City of Chicago v. Playskool, Inc. et al.*, Stipulation, No. 84 CHI0806, Circuit Court of Cook County, January 31, 1985. See also David Lapakko, "Fighting Back — A Special Report." *Union Advocate*, September 15, 1986.

56. *City of Yonkers and Yonkers Community Development Agency v. Otis Elevator and United Technologies Corporation*, Case No. 87-7092, United States Court of Appeals for the Second Circuit, Reply Brief of Plaintiffs and Reply Brief of Defendants, March 30, 1987. See also Lawrence Tell, "Plant Shutdowns: The Cities Fight Back," *New York Times*, May 15, 1983.

57. *City of Norwood, Ohio v. General Motors Corporation et al.* Court of Common Pleas, Hamilton County, Ohio, Case No. A8705920, August 7, 1987. There are several other court cases that could be cited. See Eisinger, *Rise of the Entrepreneurial State*, for a discussion of a U.S. Steel case in Illinois (injunction sought by state authorities to prevent the dismantling of a steel mill) and the Colonial Provision Company in Boston, Massachusetts (eminent domain discussed by city officials to prevent a closing). Eisinger's study also includes additional details on several of the examples discussed in this section.

58. The Mon Valley is not the only site for a possible populist response to economic change. For example, in early 1988 the Tri-State Conference on Steel met with like-minded labor, community, and church-based organizations to form the Federation for Industrial Retention and Renewal. In addition to Tri-State, other members of the new Federation include the Calumet Project for Industrial Jobs (Ind.), Cleveland Coalition against Plant Closings (Ohio), Interreligious Economic Crisis Organizing Network (N.Y.), Minnesota Working Group on Economic Dislocation (Minn.), Oakland Plant Closures Project (Calif.), Seattle Workers Center (Wash.), Midwest Center for Labor Research (Ill.), Southerners for Economic Justice (N.C.), Hometowns against Shutdowns (N.J.), and the Naugatuck Project (Conn.). Major policy issues identified by the Federation include passage of a national plant-closing law, creation of regional jobs authorities, and establishment of an industrial development bank. See Tri-State Conference on Steel, Newsletter, April 1988; Federation for Industrial

Retention and Renewal, *NEWS* (Chicago: Midwest Center for Labor Research, January 1989).

59. An interesting case that captured both the problems and possibilities in a corporate player response was the government aid program to Chrysler Corporation. When Chrysler was nearing bankruptcy in 1979, the federal government assembled a loan package to help revive the company. As part of this package, a government Loan Guarantee Board was created to protect the government's interests and help Chrysler become a viable enterprise. The Loan Guarantee Board had the authority to appoint a member to Chrysler's governing body, approve Chrysler's contracts over $10 million, require Chrysler management to report to the board, and suggest alterations in Chrysler's operations. Although Chrysler accepted federal aid, it resisted government actions, such as suggestions on a new product line, that involved "intrusions" into traditional business domains. Still, as Robert Reich and John Donahue note, the government became an "active participant" in the reorganization. "Consider that for three years one of America's largest firms had to check every move with a team of bureaucrats" (*New Deals: The Chrysler Revival and the American System* [New York: Time Books, 1985], p. 286). Under the Reagan administration, however, the government role declined, the board was disbanded, and the government auctioned Chrysler warrants held as collateral for earlier loan guarantees.

60. Wisconsin Legislative Audit Bureau, *An Evaluation of Wisconsin's Plant Closing Law* (Madison, Wis.: Legislative Audit Bureau, 1988).

61. Julia Leighton, "Plant Closings in Maine: Law and Reality," in *Plant Closing Legislation*, ed. Aboud, pp. 1–12; Folbre et al., "Plant Closings and Their Regulation in Maine."

62. City of Boston Law Department, "Opinion of the Corporation Counsel—Re: Colonial Provisions Co.—Eminent Domain," 1986.

63. See Smith, "Eminent Domain"; Weinberg, "Use of Eminent Domain"; Buckley, "Eminent Domain."

INTERVIEWS

Louisville

Bill Balanger—assistant director of Louisville Community Development Department
David Banks—member of Louisville board of alderman
Hunter Beazley—staff member and later director of employee relations at Brown & Williamson
Bob Daughtery—worker at Brown & Williamson and officer in local tobacco workers' union
Henry Dosker—staff member in County/City Office of Economic Development
Charles Herd—executive vice president at Louisville Chamber of Commerce
Charles Horton—commissioner in Jefferson County
David Huber—executive assistant to county judge/executive Mitch McConnell
Tom Kiel—professor at University of Louisville
Alice Klein—staff member of Louisville Chamber of Commerce
Ted Koebel—professor at University of Louisville
Molly Leonard—worker at Brown & Williamson, union officer, and county employee
Pat Maloney—worker at Brown & Williamson and officer in machinists' union
Joe Masterson—international representative for tobacco workers' union
Margaret Mulvihill—member of Louisville board of alderman

Pam Oliver—professor at University of Louisville
Gina Smith—executive assistant in County/City Office of Economic Development
Carroll Teague—director of labor relations at Brown & Williamson
Sylvia Watson—commissioner in Jefferson County

Waterloo

Delman Bowers—member of Waterloo City Council and former Rath worker
Don Chaplain—staff member of Waterloo Industrial Development Authority
Hugh Copeland—executive director of Iowa Northland Regional Council of Governments
Marc Crudo—staff member at JTPA Dislocated Worker Center
Lynn Cutler—county supervisor in Black Hawk County
Frank Dowie—member of Waterloo City Council
Dan Dundon—editor at *Waterloo Courier*
Bonnie Feldpouch—worker at Deere and staff member at JTPA Dislocated Worker Center
Harold Getty—member of Waterloo City Council
Eddie Harold—worker at Rath and member of Employees Reorganization Committee
Paul Larsen—field representative for AFL-CIO
Jim Lawrence—manager at Waterloo Chamber of Commerce
Jim Lindsay—staff member of Waterloo city government
Dave Mazur—director in area JTPA office
Emmet McGuire—chief executive officer at Rath
Dale Mercer—administrator of Waterloo Community Development Board
Chuck Mueller—worker at Rath and officer in local union
Dave Neil—worker at Deere and officer in the union
Gene Redmon—worker at Rath and officer in local union
Leo Rooff—mayor of Waterloo
Jack Seeber—worker at Deere, official in local union, and member of Waterloo City Council
John Stevens—director of employee relations and corporate secretary at Rath
Lyle Taylor—worker at Rath, president of local union, and later management executive at Rath
Gordon Tjelmeland—manager for community relations at Deere
Don Wade—staff member of county Economic Development Committee and Iowa Northland Regional Council of Governments
Russ Woodrick—officer in machinist union
Henry Wulff—member of U.S. Representative (now U.S. Senator) Charles Grassley's staff

Mon Valley

Mel Achtzen—member of Duquesne City Council
Roger Ahlbrandt—professor at University of Pittsburgh
Rick Armstrong—director of economic development at Allegheny County Department of Development
Jim Benn—member of Tri-State Conference on Steel and steel worker at Duquesne mill
Mike Bilcsik—president of USWA local at Duquesne mill
Bob Callen—director of Steel Valley Council of Governments

Ray Christman—deputy director of Pittsburgh Urban Redevelopment Authority and board member of Steel Valley Authority

John Dindak—mayor of West Homestead

Mike Eichler—staff member of Local Initiatives Support Corporation

Bob Erickson—member of Tri-State Conference on Steel and professor at Carlow College

Geraldine Homitz—mayor of Wilmerding

Jay Hornack—member of Tri-State and solicitor for Steel Valley Authority

Joe Hohman—director of Allegheny County Department of Development

Joe Kuzma—member of Munhall Borough Council

Joe Little—president of Homestead City Council and steel worker at Homestead mill

Charles Martoni—member of Tri-State and mayor of Swissvale

Chuck McCollester—member of Tri-State, employee at Switch & Signal, and board member of Steel Valley Authority

Bob McTiernan—private attorney and solicitor for Swissvale

Ray Myers—USWA representative in District 15

Frank O'Brien—member of Tri-State, chairman of the board of directors of Steel Valley Authority, and former steel worker and state legislator

Barney Oursler—founder of Mon Valley Unemployed Committee

Tony Palamone—director of McKeesport Development Corporation

Delores Patrick—board member of Steel Valley Authority and steel worker

Dennis Pittman—community development consultant for McKeesport

Dave Poljak—finance manager for Duquesne

William Rhodes—director of USX Duquesne Job Search Assistance Center

Mike Stout—member of Tri-State, board member of Steel Valley Authority, and steel worker at Homestead mill

Karen Supansic—first executive director of Steel Valley Authority

Louis Washowich—mayor of McKeesport

Ron Watkins—member of Munhall Borough Council and steel worker

Leo Zabelsky—mayor of Duquesne

Selected Bibliography

Aboud, Antone, ed. 1984. *Plant Closing Legislation.* Ithaca, N.Y.: ILR Press.

Addison, John, and Pedro Portugal. 1987. "The Effect of Advance Notification of Plant Closings on Unemployment." *Industrial and Labor Relations Review* 47, 1 (October): 3–16.

Alford, Robert. 1969. *Bureaucracy and Participation.* Chicago: Rand McNally & Company.

Alford, Robert, and Roger Friedland. 1975. "Political Participation and Public Policy." In *Annual Review of Sociology, Vol. I,* edited by A. Inkeles et al., 429–479. Palo Alto, Calif.: Annual Reviews.

———. 1985. *Powers of Theory.* New York: Cambridge University Press.

Anderson, Charles. 1978. "The Logic of Public Problems: Evaluation in Comparative Policy Research." In *Comparing Public Policies: New Concepts and Methods,* edited by Douglas Ashford, 19–42. Beverly Hills, Calif.: Sage Publications.

Ashford, Douglas. 1977. "Political Science and Policy Studies: Toward a Structural Framework." *Policy Studies Journal* 6: 570–583.

Bachrach, Peter, and Morton Baratz. 1970. *Power and Poverty: Theory and Practice.* New York: Oxford University Press.

Balderston, Kris. 1986. "Plant Closings, Layoffs, and Worker Readjustment: The States' Response to Economic Change." Washington, D.C.: National Governors' Association.

Batt, William. 1983. "Canada's Good Example with Displaced Workers." *Harvard Business Review* 61 (July–August): 6–11.

Baumann, Fred, ed. 1986. *Democratic Capitalism?* Charlottesville: University Press of Virginia.

Bensman, David, and Roberta Lynch. 1987. *Rusted Dreams: Hard Times in a Steel Community.* New York: McGraw-Hill Company.

Berenbeim, Ronald. 1986. *Company Programs to Ease the Impact of Shutdowns.* New York: The Conference Board.

Blair, John, and Barton Wechsler. 1984. "A Tale of Two Cities: A Case Study of Urban Competition for Jobs." In *Urban Economic Development,* edited by Richard Bingham and John Blair, 269–282. Beverly Hills, Calif.: Sage Publications.

Bluestone, Barry, and Bennett Harrison. 1982. *The Deindustrialization of America.* New York: Basic Books.

———. 1986. "The Great American Job Machine: The Proliferation of Low Wage

Employment in the U.S. Economy." Prepared for U.S. Congress, Joint Economic Committee.

Boulay, Harvey. 1983. *The Twilight Cities: Political Conflict, Development, and Decay in Five Communities*. Port Washington, N.Y.: Associated Faculty Press.

Bowles, Samuel, and Herbert Gintis. 1986. *Democracy and Capitalism*. New York: Basic Books.

Bowles, Samuel, et al. 1984. *Beyond the Waste Land*. Garden City, N.Y.: Anchor Books.

Boyle, M. Ross. 1982. "Plant Closings: Options for Economic Adjustment." *Economic Development Commentary* (Fall): 17–23.

Boyte, Harry, et al. 1986. *Citizen Action and the New American Populism*. Philadelphia: Temple University Press.

Branan, Karen. 1985. "Save Our Jobs: Lessons from a Plant-Closing Fightback." Minneapolis: Working Group on Economic Dislocation.

Brecher, Jeremy. 1986. "If All the People Banded Together: The Naugatuck Valley Project." *Labor Research Review* 9 (Fall): 1–19.

Brown, Sharon. 1987. "How Often Do Workers Receive Advance Notice of Layoffs?" *Monthly Labor Review* 110 (June): 13–17.

Buckley, Gregory. 1985. "Eminent Domain: The Ability of a Community to Retain an Industry in the Face of an Attempted Shut Down or Relocation." *Ohio Northern University Law Review* 12 (1985): 231–249.

Burns, Tom, et al. 1985. *Man, Decisions, Society*. New York: Gordon and Breach Science Publishers.

Business Roundtable. 1983. *Plant Closings: A Position Paper*. New York.

Buss, Terry, and F. Stevens Redburn. 1983. *Shutdown at Youngstown*. Albany: State University of New York Press.

———. 1987. "Plant Closings: Impacts and Responses." *Economic Development Quarterly* 1, 2 (1987): 170–177.

California Department of Commerce. 1986. *Responding to Plant Closures*. Sacramento.

California Employment Development Department. 1983. *Planning Guidebook for Communities Facing a Plant Closure or Mass Layoff*. Sacramento.

Canovan, Margaret. 1981. *Populism*. New York: Harcourt Brace Jovanovich.

Carnoy, Martin, and Derek Shearer. 1980. *Economic Democracy: The Challenge of the 1980s*. New York: M. E. Sharpe.

Carnoy, Martin, et al. 1983. *A New Social Contract*. New York: Harper & Row, Publishers.

Charpentier, Elaine. 1986. "Labor-Community Alliances in Chicago." *Changing Work* (Spring): 19–21.

———. 1986. "Early Warnings in Chicago." *Labor Research Review* 9 (Fall): 91–98.

Cobb, Roger, and Charles Elder. 1983. *Participation in American Politics: The Dynamics of Agenda-Building*. 2d edition. Baltimore, Md.: Johns Hopkins University Press.

Coleman, Morton. 1983. "Interest Intermediation and Local Urban Development." Ph.D. dissertation. University of Pittsburgh.

Crenson, Matthew. 1971. *The Un-Politics of Air Pollution*. Baltimore, Md.: Johns Hopkins University Press.

Crouch, Mark. 1986. "Job Wars at Fort Wayne." *Labor Research Review* 9 (Fall): 47–66.

Deitch, Cynthia. 1984. "Collective Action and Unemployment: Responses to Job Loss by Workers and Community Groups." *International Journal of Mental Health* 13: 139–153.

Dery, David. 1984. *Problem Definition in Policy Analysis*. Lawrence: University Press of Kansas.

Dougherty, Barbara. No date. *The Struggle to Save Morse Cutting Tool*. North Dartmouth: Southeastern Massachusetts University.

Early, Steve. 1987. "A Model in Massachusetts?" *Labor Research Review* 10 (Spring): 110–111.

Eisinger, Peter. 1988. *The Rise of the Entrepreneurial State*. Madison: University of Wisconsin Press.

Elkin, Stephen. 1985. "Pluralism in Its Place: State and Regime in Liberal Democracy." In *The Democratic State*, edited by Roger Benjamin and Stephen Elkin, 179–212. Lawrence: University Press of Kansas.

———. 1987. *City and Regime in the American Republic*. Chicago: University of Chicago Press.

Fainstein, Norman, and Susan Fainstein. 1982. *Urban Policy under Capitalism*. Beverly Hills, Calif.: Sage Publications.

———. 1983. *Restructuring the City: The Political Economy of Urban Redevelopment*. New York: Longman Publishers.

———. 1985. "Economic Restructuring and the Rise of Urban Social Movements." *Urban Affairs Quarterly* 21, 2 (December): 187–206.

Folbre, Nancy, et al. 1984. "Plant Closings and Their Regulation in Maine: 1971–1982." *Industrial and Labor Relations Review* 37, 2 (January): 185–196.

Fosler, R. Scott, and Renee Berger. 1982. *Public-Private Partnerships in American Cities: Seven Case Studies*. Lexington, Mass.: D. C. Heath and Company.

Friedland, Roger. 1983. *Power and Crisis in the City*. New York: Schocken Books.

Friedman, Milton, and Rose Friedman. 1979. *Free to Choose*. New York: Avon Books.

Gappert, Gary, ed. 1987. *The Future of Winter Cities*. Beverly Hills, Calif.: Sage Publications.

Goodwyn, Lawrence. 1978. *The Populist Moment*. New York: Oxford University Press.

Gordus, J., et al. 1981. *Plant Closings and Economic Dislocations*. Kalamazoo, Mich.: Upjohn Institute for Employment Research.

Gottdiener, M. 1987. *The Decline of Urban Politics*. Beverly Hills, Calif.: Sage Publications.

———, ed. 1986. *Cities in Stress*. Beverly Hills, Calif.: Sage Publications.

Guinan, Joann. 1985. "Notice Requirements: Federal Preemption of State and Local Plant Closing Statutes." *Fordham Urban Law Journal* 13: 333–372.

Gunn, Christopher. 1984. *Workers' Self-Management in the United States*. Ithaca, N.Y.: Cornell University Press.

Gusfield, Joseph. 1981. *The Culture of Public Problems: Drinking, Driving and the Symbolic Order*. Chicago: University of Chicago Press.

Haas, Gilda. 1985. *Plant Closures: Myths, Realities and Responses*. Boston: South End Press.

Hansen, Gary. 1984. "Cooperative Approaches for Dealing with Plant Closings: A Resource Guide for Employers and Communities." Utah State University.

Hansen, Gary, and Frank Adams. 1987. "Saving Jobs and Putting Democracy to Work: Labor-Management Cooperation at Seymour Specialty Wire." *Labor-Management Cooperation Brief* 11 (September). Washington, D.C.: U.S. Department of Labor.

Industrial States Policy Center. 1985. *Phase I Report: Review and Assessment of Existing Early Warning Programs*. Cleveland.

Jones, Bryan. 1983. *Governing Urban America*. Boston: Little, Brown and Company.

Jones, Bryan, and Lynn Bachelor. 1984. "Local Policy Discretion and the Corporate Surplus." In *Urban Economic Development*, edited by Richard Bingham and John Blair, 245–268. Beverly Hills, Calif.: Sage Publications.

————. 1986. *The Sustaining Hand: Community Leadership and Corporate Power.* Lawrence: University Press of Kansas.

Jones, Charles. 1977. *An Introduction to the Study of Public Policy.* Boston: Duxbury Press.

Judd, Dennis. 1984. *The Politics of American Cities: Private Power and Public Policy.* Boston: Little, Brown and Company.

Kann, Mark. 1982. *The American Left: Failures and Fortunes.* New York: Praeger Publishers.

————. 1986. *Middle Class Radicals in Santa Monica.* Philadelphia: Temple University Press.

Kantor, Paul. 1988. *The Dependent City.* Glenview, Ill.: Scott, Foresman and Company.

Katznelson, Ira. 1981. *City Trenches.* New York: Pantheon Books.

Keat, Russell, and John Urry. 1982. *Social Theory as Science.* Boston: Routledge & Kegan Paul.

Kingdon, John. 1984. *Agendas, Alternatives, and Public Policies.* Boston: Little, Brown and Company.

Koerner, Kirk. 1985. *Liberalism and Its Critics.* London: Croom Helm.

Kutscher, Ronald, and Valerie Personick. 1986. "Deindustrialization and the Shift to Services." *Monthly Labor Review* 109 (June): 3–13.

Lakoff, Sanford, ed. 1973. *Private Government.* Glenview, Ill.: Scott, Foresman and Company.

Langerman, Philip, et al. 1982. *Plant Closings and Layoffs: Problems Facing Urban and Rural Communities.* Des Moines, Iowa: Drake University.

Lee, Raymond. 1987. *Redundancy, Lay-offs and Plant Closures.* London: Croom Helm.

LeRoy, Greg, et al. 1986. *Early Warning Manual against Plant Closings.* Chicago: Midwest Center for Labor Research.

Levine, Andrew. 1981. *Liberal Democracy: A Critique of Its Theory.* New York: Columbia University Press.

Levitt, Rachelle. 1987. *Cities Reborn.* Washington, D.C.: Urban Land Institute.

Lewis, Eugene. 1980. *Public Entrepreneurship: Toward a Theory of Bureaucratic Political Power.* Bloomington: Indiana University Press.

Lindblom, Charles. 1977. *Politics and Markets.* New York: Basic Books.

————. 1982. "The Market as a Prison." *Journal of Politics* 44, 2 (May): 324–336.

Lustig, R. Jeffrey. 1985. "The Politics of Shutdown: Community, Property, Corporatism." *Journal of Economic Issues* 19 (March): 123–152.

Lynd, Staughton. 1982. *The Fight against Shutdowns: Youngstown's Steel Mill Closings.* San Pedro, Calif.: Singlejack Books.

McConnell, Grant. 1967. *Private Power and American Democracy.* New York: Alfred A. Knopf.

McKenzie, Richard, ed. 1982. *Plant Closings: Public or Private Choices?* Washington, D.C.: Cato Institute.

————. 1984. *Fugitive Industry: The Economics and Politics of Deindustrialization.* Cambridge, Mass.: Ballinger Publishing Company.

Massachusetts Governor's Commission on the Future of Mature Industries. 1984. "Final Report." Boston.

Massachusetts Legislative Research Commission. 1983. "Report Relative to Plant Closings." Boston.

Mazza, Jacqueline. 1982. *Shutdown: A Guide for Communities Facing Plant Closings.* Washington, D.C.: Northeast-Midwest Institute.

Mollenkopf, John. 1981. "Community and Accumulation." In *Urbanization and Ur-*

ban Planning in Capitalist Society, edited by Michael Dear and Allen Scott, 319–337. New York: Meuthuen.

———. 1983. The Contested City. Princeton, N.J.: Princeton University Press.

———. 1989. "Who (or What) Runs Cities, and How?" Sociological Forum 4: 119–137.

Molotch, H. 1976. "The City as a Growth Machine." American Journal of Sociology 82 (September): 309–330.

Morris, David. 1982. The New City-States. Washington, D.C.: Institute for Local Self-Reliance.

Nadel, Mark. 1975. "The Hidden Dimension in Public Policy: Private Governments and the Policy-Making Process." Journal of Politics 37: 2–34.

———. 1976. Corporations and Political Accountability. Lexington, Mass.: D.C. Heath and Company.

National Alliance of Business. 1983. "Worker Adjustment to Plant Shutdowns and Mass Layoffs: An Analysis of Program Experience and Policy Options." Washington, D.C.

National Association of Manufacturers. 1983. "When a Plant Closes: A Guide for Employers." Washington, D.C.

Nelson, Richard. 1988. "State Labor Laws: Changes during 1987." Monthly Labor Review 111 (January): 38–61.

Newfield, Jack, and Jeff Greenfield. 1972. A Populist Manifesto. New York: Praeger Publishers.

Offe, Claus. 1985. "Two Logics of Collective Action." In Disorganized Capitalism, edited by Claus Offe, 170–220. Cambridge, Mass.: MIT Press.

Peterson, Paul. 1981. City Limits. Chicago: University of Chicago Press.

Portz, John. 1989. "Plant Closings: New Roles for Policymakers." Economic Development Quarterly 3 (February): 70–80.

Przeworski, Adam. 1980. "Social Democracy as a Historical Phenomenon." New Left Review, no. 122 (July–August): 27–58.

Raines, John, et al. 1982. Community and Capital in Conflict: Plant Closings and Job Loss. Philadelphia: Temple University Press.

Reich, Robert, and John Donahue. 1985. New Deals: The Chrysler Revival and the American System. New York: Time Books.

Rothstein, Lawrence. 1986. Plant Closings: Power, Politics, and Workers. Dover, Mass.: Auburn House Publishing Company.

Salzman, Jeffrey. 1987. "The Canadian-American Plant Closing Demonstration Project." Compensation and Benefits Management 3, 4 (Summer): 233–239.

Schumpeter, Joseph. 1947. Capitalism, Socialism, and Democracy. New York: Harper & Row.

Selznick, Philip. 1969. Law, Society and Industrial Justice. New York: Russell Sage Foundation.

Shefter, Martin. 1985. Political Crisis/Fiscal Crisis: The Collapse and Revival of New York City. New York: Basic Books.

Shonfield, Andrew. 1965. Modern Capitalism. New York: Oxford University Press.

Smith, Keith. 1986. "Eminent Domain as a Tool to Set Up Employee-Owned Business in the Face of Shutdowns." Antioch Law Journal 4 (Summer): 271–286.

Solo, Robert. 1974. The Political Authority and the Market System. Cincinnati: South-Western Publishing Company.

———. 1975. "The Economist and the Economic Roles of the Political Authority in Advanced Industrial Societies." In Stress and Contradiction in Modern Capitalism, edited by L. Lindberg et al., 99–114. Lexington, Mass.: Lexington Books.

————. 1982. *The Positive State*. Cincinnati: South-Western Publishing Company.

SRI International. 1984. *Managing the Renewal of Mature Industries: Beyond Smokestacks and Sunsets*. Menlo Park, Calif.

Staudohar, Paul, and Holly Brown, eds. 1987. *Deindustrialization and Plant Closure*. Lexington, Mass.: Lexington Books.

Stern, Robert, et al. 1979. *Employee Ownership in Plant Shutdowns*. Kalamazoo, Mich.: Upjohn Institute for Employment Research.

Stone, Clarence. 1980. "Systemic Power in Community Decision Making: A Restatement of Stratification Theory." *American Political Science Review* 74: 978–990.

————. 1984. "City Politics and Economic Development: Political Economy Perspectives." *Journal of Politics* 46: 286–299.

Stone, Clarence, and Heywood Sanders, eds. 1987. *The Politics of Urban Development*. Lawrence: University Press of Kansas.

Summers, Gene, ed. 1984. *Deindustrialization: Restructuring the Economy*. Annals 475. Beverly Hills, Calif.: Sage Publications.

Swanstrom, Todd. 1985. *The Crisis of Growth Politics: Cleveland, Kucinich, and the Challenge of Urban Populism*. Philadelphia: Temple University Press.

U.S. Congress. 1980. Senate Committee on Labor and Human Resources. *Hearings on Workers and the Evolving Economy of the Eighties*. 96th Congress, 2d Session.

U.S. Department of Commerce. No date. *Coping with the Loss of a Major Employer: A How-to Manual*. Washington, D.C.: Economic Development Administration.

————. 1985. *Plant Closing Checklist: A Guide to Best Practice*. Washington, D.C.: Bureau of Labor-Management Relations and Cooperative Programs.

————. 1986. "Economic Adjustment and Worker Dislocation in a Competitive Society." Report of the Secretary of Labor's Task Force on Economic Adjustment and Worker Dislocation. Washington, D.C.

U.S. General Accounting Office. 1986. *Dislocated Workers: Extent of Business Closures, Layoffs, and the Public and Private Response*. GAO/HRD-86-116BR. Washington, D.C.: Government Printing Office.

————. 1987. *Plant Closings: Information on Advance Notice and Assistance to Dislocated Workers*. GAO/HRD-87-86BR. Washington, D.C.: Government Printing Office.

U.S. Office of Technology Assessment. 1986. *Plant Closing: Advance Notice and Rapid Response*. Washington, D.C.: Government Printing Office.

United Way/AFL-CIO. 1979. *Assistance to Communities Experiencing Sudden Economic Disruption*. Washington, D.C.

Warner, Sam Bass. 1968. *The Private City*. Philadelphia: University of Philadelphia Press.

Waste, Robert, ed. 1986. *Community Power*. Beverly Hills, Calif.: Sage Publications.

Way, Harold, and Carla Weiss. 1988. *Plant Closings: A Selected Bibliography of Materials Published through 1985*. Ithaca, N.Y.: ILR Press.

Weinberg, Robert. 1984. "The Use of Eminent Domain to Prevent an Industrial Plant Shutdown: The Next Step in an Expanding Power." *Albany Law Review* 49 (1984): 95–130.

Wendling, Wayne. 1984. *The Plant Closure Policy Dilemma*. Kalamazoo, Mich.: Upjohn Institute for Employment Research.

Whyte, William, et al. 1983. *Worker Participation and Ownership: Cooperative Strategies for Strengthening Local Economies*. Ithaca, N.Y.: ILR Press.

Widner, Ralph, and Marvin Wolfgang. 1986. *Revitalizing the Industrial City*. Annals 488. Beverly Hills, Calif.: Sage Publications.

Wisconsin Legislative Audit Bureau. 1988. *An Evaluation of Wisconsin's Plant Closing Law*. Madison, Wis.

Woodworth, Warner, et al. 1985. *Industrial Democracy: Strategies for Community Revitalization*. Beverly Hills, Calif.: Sage Publications.

Wright, Erik Olin. 1979. *Class, Crisis, and the State*. London: Verso Editions.

Zysman, John. 1977. *Political Strategies for Industrial Order: State, Market, and Industry in France*. Berkeley: University of California Press.

———. 1983. *Governments, Markets, and Growth*. Ithaca, N.Y.: Cornell University Press.

Index